Montana Epiphany

By

Loring Walawander

Author's Note

There are shorter stories, there are better stories, but this is my story, a story that dwells deep within me, ripening and maturing for over fifty years. I called upon my own memory of these events to write this book, and any factual errors are the mistake of the author. There are no composite characters or events. I have, however, changed the names of most, but not all, of the people and some of the locations in this book.

Written in memory of...

Joseph Paul Walawander… my father, a man born to the life of iron and steel

Mary Jane Walawander… my mother, a woman of boundless love and beauty

Mary Ann Walawander… my grandmother, whose kindness was not a weakness

Gail Marie H… my first love

I dream of snowcapped mountains I need to climb
They are in Montana, and I'm in my prime
I want to stand tall and kiss the Big Sky
My soul needs to do this, or I may die

…Loring Walawander
University of Tennessee Memorial Hospital
May 1973

Table of Contents

Prologue

Three hundred feet. The length of a football field. That was the distance I had to hike, scramble, or claw in some places, to reach the summit of Ajax Peak from the south ridge. The July sun was at its zenith. Despite the high elevation snow, today was going to be hot. Patches of "watermelon" snow, pink from the algae that grows in subzero temperatures, would last the summer. There was not a cloud in the sky or a cooling breeze. Beads of sweat rolled down my face and stung my eyes. I felt like a fire hydrant without a shutoff valve.

Looking down at the clear, turquoise water of Ajax Lake, my orange-and-blue tent and camping partners were mere specks some fifteen-hundred feet below. This was the Montana Dream I'd been dreaming from the first time I laid eyes on it in a *Boys' Life* magazine article twelve years previously. I sucked in every bit of the exhilarating mountain air on Ajax as an incentive to keep my dream fresh. Inhale deeper, it feels so-o-o good, I kept repeating.

Make sure that rock is secure, I reminded myself before stepping up on it. Another handhold, and I picked my way cautiously between the scree, closing the gap to two hundred feet. Turning directly to my right, I made for a direct ascent to the summit. Go for it, my spirit screamed. My body, hardened by trail construction work with the Forest Service, was not challenged as I reached for the top.

I didn't want to do a "Bocephus," referring to Hank Williams Jr.'s near-fatal slide on pink snow on this mountain two years previously. I grabbed a rock outcrop and shinnied the five feet to the summit.

Oh man, check this out. Finally, I'm HERE! I now stood on the summit of Ajax Peak, my spirit energized, and the heels of my boots coming to a rest on the ancient, weathered rock while I pumped my right fist in triumph. Now I could record "Ajax: first summit" in my climbing journal.

I almost tripped head over heels when my right boot tip caught the top of the US Geologic Survey pin, engraved with the longitude 113.7388, and the latitude 45.3306. Elevation: 10,028 feet. Ajax would be my first summit of dozens of Montana peaks that were over ten thousand feet.

The summit formed a long ridgeline, with a rock cairn and a summit register to sign. The views along the Continental Divide were ethereal in their splendor. A red-tailed hawk soared below me, slowly turning circles on his broad, rounded wings and letting out a call that sounded like *Kee-eeeee-ar* that echoed off the mountain wall.

There were breathtaking views of Copperhead Peak and Homer Youngs Peak, which I wanted to log in my journal after Ajax.

I was young and had no fear of failing to climb higher mountains. Teetering on top of Ajax was a sharp contrast to receiving last rites of the church three years previously. I basked in the glorious and comforting feeling of being in Montana, the place that my soaring spirit wanted to be.

Montana was where my heart had been since I was twelve years old. It was an instant love affair after seeing the movie *How the West Was Won*. The opening montage of snowcapped peaks left me feeling that I was drifting along with the clouds encircling the mountains, free to forge my own destiny. There were no clouds that day over Ajax, but I still felt that I was drifting high above the Continental Divide.

Ajax Peak was the first chapter of my creation story, a story about how I wanted to start a new generation out west. At that moment, I wished I would never have to leave the summit. I was on top of the world and full of life. Working and breathing in the great outdoors, shooting across the rapids of wild and scenic rivers, starting a family, climbing mountains, leaving behind all my discontent with cramped spaces, a small sky, and generations of family men who chose to follow their fathers and mine coal or work in a steel mill.

There were no ties strong enough to hold me at home in the East and keep me from journeying to "God's Country."

My journey to Montana was a circuitous path that started in coal towns of Pennsylvania, and first detoured to the South, along a flat, carefree highway to Tennessee. It was there that I had rich college experiences. But in 1973, this highway had become steep and painful as I had lost my first true love to a heart ailment and, at the same time, become deathly ill myself with a heart ailment.

Standing atop Ajax Peak and looking to the sky with my fist pumped, I realized that I had been like Michael, the angel in Tolstoy's short story "What Men Live By." One of my college favorites, this story dealt with the angel, Michael, who was banished from heaven until he learned that people dwell best when in love, and that sometimes they did not know what was in their best interest, or they focused too much on themselves. These were truths that Michael had to learn.

Although different from Michael's, I had learned my truths as a result of my illness, an illness that had been the medical case of the year in a Pittsburgh hospital. Deathly ill with bacterial endocarditis, a staph infection in the heart that had eaten away my aortic valve, I was given odds of three to five percent of survival, but survive I did, after months in the hospital, open heart surgery, and the implantation of a prosthetic heart valve.

Standing tall, lean, and muscled on the summit, I knew that I had learned my first truth: *Never, ever, tell yourself—or let anyone else tell you—the degrees or limits from which the human body can heal itself. Never, ever give up hope.*

It's so beautiful up here, I told myself. *I'm a lucky man.* Ajax Mountain's beauty had lasted eons, but my mind wandered back to a recent memory of a young woman whose beauty on this Earth had been short-lived. I met Gail, a "something different" kind of woman, early in college. She was my first true love, and we envisioned being married one day. *Inhale, remember this moment.*

Here I was, sipping warm water from my canteen, and living my Montana Dream, thinking of a distant past and the different stages of reality that had happened along the way. My young life had been filled with participation in scouting, church activities, and Little League baseball. I had experienced the love of a good family, crazy college adventures, and being near death. I was only twenty-four and I was living my dream, but I had also lived through my first Montana winter of minus thirty degree temperatures and wages that left me with a hungry belly. That hadn't been part of my dream.

The landscape of Ajax Peak was almost lunar in appearance. My fist pump on top of the mountain was for my parents, who had encouraged me to live the biggest life possible; and the second was for the doctors, nurses, and clergy who had put me back together after such devastation. I slowly realized that I had learned my second truth: *The heart is a large muscle, but it can be broken. A broken heart is not a country song. Never, ever forget the healing and mending power of the broken heart, whether it needs surgical, emotional, or spiritual repair.*

Twelve years had passed since I craved to climb a Montana mountain, and I was in no hurry to leave. Baking under the sun's intensity, I sat on the hot rocks, with my left leg dangling in Idaho and my right leg in Montana. Ajax Peak was the first peak I saw when I arrived in Wisdom to work for the Forest Service. Anxious, ready, and rock hard by the middle of my first Montana summer, I felt the mountain was calling me, challenging me, tempting me like a seductive mistress. "Come a little bit closer. Climb me... Climb me. You wanted to climb a towering mountain, higher than hawks and eagles fly. Trust your heart. See you at the top."

Sitting on a pile of worn, craggy rocks, I listened to my deeper breathing of the thinner air. *Inhale. Exhale. Inhale. Listen to your clicking heart valve beating slower.* Sitting on the rocks started to hurt after some time, and I slowly began to rise. I arched my back as far as possible, my face aching to kiss the sky. I cleaned sweat and grime off my sunglasses with a red bandana that I wore around my neck, then bent and retied a loose boot lace. The sun was now level with my face, and I turned my Steelers ball cap around to shade my eyes as I reluctantly began my descent.

Wait a minute; think about what just happened this afternoon.

My third and final truth came to me as clear as the water in Ajax Lake: *You will only grow as big as your dreams. Dream small and you will achieve small things. You are what you dream, so dream big. Never be afraid to dream big and to have that dream fulfilled.*

4

Taking one last breath of the high mountain air, I promised myself that this climb was only the beginning of conquering Montana summits.

Part 1

The Northern Red Oak (Quercus rubra)

This oak is one of the handsomest and most majestic trees in Pennsylvania. It is fast growing with a rounded crown, and it is very adaptable and hardy in urban settings. This tree provides flaming fall color and is easy to transplant.

Chapter 1

A bird's eye view of Heidelberg, Pennsylvania, in 1960 would show a small, hilly borough fifteen miles southwest of Pittsburgh. Chartiers Creek, once surveyed by George Washington, bordered one end. There were seven bars, no churches, and one nationally famous, half-mile, high-banked, oval dirt track for stock cars that threw up clouds of red dust on race days.

The deafening roar of stock-car racing, the crack of a wooden bat against a baseball, the wind in my hair as I rode my bicycle up and down hilly streets, ice skating on frozen ponds, the acrid smell of burning coal, the itch of summertime poison ivy... all were emblems of my youth in my little town. My world was colorful, but I dreamed of a different land of mountains, rivers, and a big sky.

At age eleven, I was an altar boy, and felt special in my vestments of a red cassock and white surplice that identified me as a knight of the altar. This was also a time in my life when different tics started to manifest within my body. My eyes blinked in rapid-fire succession, or I shook my head violently from side to side, or grunted and made goofy facial grimaces. My parents had me examined for these uncontrollable tics, and I rode on a carousel of revolving doctor examinations. All the doctors and chiropractors had dismissed them as harmless, childhood tics that would go away in time. They never reached a consensus, and my mother went as far as consulting with a Hindu yogi to find more definitive answers.

At my church, I had discovered a source of spiritual strength to help me thwart the social embarrassment of these tics. During Mass when our priest went to the lectern to deliver the sermon, altar boys

7

were to face the congregation and lay sideways on the altar steps, supported by their elbow. Over the course of many Sundays, I had noticed that the early morning sun would shine more brightly through the stained-glass window marking the Twelfth Station of the Cross, one of a series of images depicting Jesus's path on the day of his crucifixion. Although the Twelfth Station is where Jesus died on the cross, I felt a spiritual message of strength coming to me from God through that light. The sun's rays entered the window, breaking into tiny prisms of light beams, bathing the parishioners in splendor.

I'm strong and invincible within this light, I told myself. *Nothing can harm me. The light is my armor. The church is my castle.* Wounding words and snickering sneers would melt in the heat of the light. I would never face darkness.

I knew I was different, but I never hid from it.

The first challenge in dealing with my tics was in sixth grade when a student teacher, Melvin Stroble, took over our class for the spring, relieving my beloved, blue-haired teacher, Mrs. Baylor. Mr. Stroble was all business and had come down pretty hard on a well-behaved class. He was an angular guy, from his perfectly trimmed flattop to his face that tapered down to a sharp chin, complemented by a pair of sharp-pointed, wing-tipped shoes. But I had never figured out one of his obtuse angles that dealt with classroom behavior.

One day has stood out in my mind, and it is why I always remembered Melvin Stroble's name. It was quiet reading time, and I was totally riveted by a paperback book about a true war story, *The Raft,* by Robert Trumbull. Completely immersed in the story, I was not aware that I was making squeaky vocalizations. These had become so common that I did not realize how they might have affected others, and Mrs. Baylor never had commented on them.

"Who's squeaking in this room?" Mr. Stroble called out, while he stared down each student's face, hoping to identify the culprit he thought was trying to be funny.

"I'm sorry, but I have something stuck in my throat," I told him when his stare locked on me.

8

"Well, then, go get a drink of water, and remember to mind your manners and not disrupt my classroom."

Mrs. Baylor must have understood the human condition and never made comments about my tics. I had never been called out for bad manners or classroom behavior. I was a straight-A student, was selected to be the captain of the school crossing guards, and raised and lowered the school flag daily. The scout oath was imprinted in my life, and I had done my best to practice the twelve points of the scout law. Telling Mr. Stroble that I had something stuck in my throat provided my first act of disguising my tics.

By fibbing, I felt that I was no longer trustworthy, breaking the first law.

Chapter 2

On a sweltering, June, dog-day afternoon in my fourteenth summer, I was anxious to catch up on reading two past issues of *Boys' Life* magazine. In the shade of my grandmother's porch, I thumbed through the first few pages of the April edition. Then, there it was, right in front of me: the images that were to capture my imagination for the rest of my life. Boy Scouts wading across a clear mountain stream in Montana's Bob Marshall Wilderness, snowcapped peaks in the background. The article instantly refreshed me, and I was chilled to the bone.

The story told of scouts leading pack-laden horses in the pouring, cold rain through thick forests. A photo showed a scout holding up a large native trout that he had caught. Dick Price's article "Exploring a Mountain Wilderness" had words that flowed like poetry: "unpolluted streams," "grizzly bear country," "cutthroat trout," and "Chinese Wall." It might as well have been the language of another planet. Most of the streams in my hometown were so polluted from mine wastes that no aquatic life or vegetation was able to survive in them, and the only fish I ever caught were catfish from a pond.

But here I had read of how Troop 7 of Missoula, Montana, spent ten days hiking the length of the Bob Marshall Wilderness, enduring twisted, tortuous trails, ankle-deep mud, and cold rain. A hired outfitter named "Smoke" Elser packed the supplies in on horseback, including tents, fifty pounds of bacon, seventy pounds of pancake flour, and fifteen dozen eggs for the twenty-five Scouts who had signed on. Elser, a former Eagle Scout and smokejumper himself, was described as a jolly man with an enormous smile. His guidance, experience, and storytelling gave the members of Troop 7 a trip to remember for the rest of their lives.

Scouting experiences like twenty-mile hikes, a mile swim, and summer camps satisfied my zest for the outdoors, but Pennsylvania was a state that never let my soul sing or spirit soar.

Carefully cutting the article out of the magazine, I placed it behind a photo frame for safekeeping. I longed for a bigger life, one filled with clear streams swimming with wild trout, high, snowcapped mountains, wild geese paddling on the water, and buffalo roaming the plains. All that was to come true, and even better, one day I hoped to meet Smoke Elser himself, too.

Later in that summer of 1966, my family left our Norman Rockwellesque town of Heidelberg and moved to our new country home in Bridgeville. My parents had bought three acres of wooded farmland on County Line Road in early 1955, and by scrimping, saving, and living with my grandmother, they had saved enough for a new, tri-level home in the country. Although the move was less than fifteen miles away, it meant changing school districts and leaving lifelong friends. Prior to moving, my grades were always above average, and I kept a busy life away from school.

The move left me feeling disconnected from community and from the things I loved most. At my new school, Hill Top High, my grades dropped from As and Bs to Bs and Cs. Playing baseball was once a passion, but not at Hill Top. Auditioning for school plays or running for student government no longer appealed to me. Hill Top felt like prison. All that interested me was working out, reading, caddying at Valley Brook Country Club, and dreaming about moving on to bigger things away from Hill Top.

Concerned about my downward academic spiral, my dad had done some investigating on his own. One day he asked me to sit with him at the supper table before dinner.

"I have asked around and think that a private school might be better suited for you, son. Hill Top is not working; I know that. In today's mail, I received information on Valley Forge Military Academy. Take a look through it, and we can talk about it later."

Barely standing five feet six inches on tiptoes, my father never displayed any resentment over his height… or mine at an inch over six feet. His physical stature was offset by his dignity and hardened

11

resolve to propel his three children to greater heights. So it had come as no surprise that he explored education alternatives when he saw how I was struggling.

The cover of the brochure centered on a Revolutionary War cannon and stacked cannon balls in front of the old brick and white porticos of the administration buildings of the academy. Flipping to the first page, I read how the school helped cadets reach their academic potential in the classroom and beyond. There were leadership classes, a rifle club, and an equestrian program. Valley Forge Military Academy promised to teach students leadership and responsibility.

Here was a chance for me to attend a school steeped in tradition where leaders were made, but it meant uprooting again to move across the state at age fifteen. Though physically strong, I was in an emotional depression after changing schools, and I became more sensitive about my tics that were manifesting facially and likely exacerbated by the move. It was shortsighted on my part, but I explained to my father that I was not ready to relocate and move clear across the state to Valley Forge. As a result, I continued to live my life in the shadows of others instead of working to access my own personal powers.

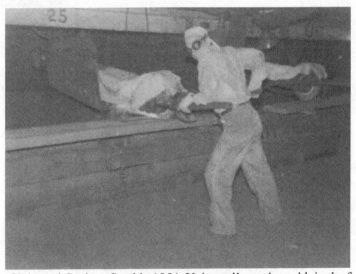

Dad at Universal Cyclops Steel in 1954. Universal's steel would, in the future, be used as heat shields on the Apollo Rockets.

My father constantly commented that I was not to follow his footsteps into the steel mill or those of our ancestors into the coal mines, but I was to go to college and "make something of yourself."

One Friday afternoon, I was getting clothes from the dryer that I wanted to wear on a date that night, when my father arrived home from work and tossed his dirty work clothes from the week into the washer. Holding a pair of clean, navy blue, casual slacks in my hands, I gawked at his soiled dungarees. My nose twitched at the smell of sweat, coal, and steel factory fumes. The red oxide dust that came from grinding new steel billets and tiny particles of chromium ore glittered against traces of black coal dust.

"Look at my work pants son, and look at yours," he told me in a steely voice. "Do you know how hard I have to work to get clothes this dirty? Do you think NASA is going to call me and say good job, Joe, on those heat shields my department made for the Apollo flights?"

His biggest source of pride from his work at the mill was creating the steel that would be used as heat shields for the Apollo spacecraft upon reentering the Earth's atmosphere. He moved his armload of clothes closer to my face. I stepped back. Never before had I seen his work clothes, as he always arrived home showered, shaved, and in casual dress. His filthy clothes shocked me, and that moment forever sealed the notion that a steel mill was not in my future, but I was damn proud of him. NASA should have been, too.

"You have a good brain, son, so use that instead of your back, and shoveling chromium ore or breathing grinding dust like me."

This was his prime directive, and he was persistent in delivering that message.

As a senior in high school in 1970, I scored a thousand and some change on the SAT and 136 on an IQ test, but I knew I was not Harvard bound.

Away from my studies, I devoured books that were not required reading. I had a deep craving for books about the military and famous battles fought in World War II. *Guadalcanal Diary* by Richard Tregaskis and *Reach for the Sky* by Paul Brickhill were favorites as the pages had acquired a deep musty smell that only book lovers could describe. At fourteen, I also read Robin Moore's *The Story of the Green Berets in Vietnam*, a book that was not pro-war but pro-soldier. The book was not enough to satisfy me, and I bought Staff Sgt. Barry Sadler's album, *The Ballad of the Green Berets*, and listened countless times about "fighting soldiers from the sky." The song, number one in 1966, out-sold albums by the Beatles and Rolling Stones that year. The songs and story reminded me of my Uncle Jim, a paratrooper with the 82nd Airborne.

My military reading contrasted deeply with other reads about the environment, like *Silent Spring* by Rachel Carson or the philosophical account of Henry David Thoreau's *Walden*. Thoreau stated, "If one advances confidently in the direction of his dreams, and endeavors to live the life to which he has imagined, he will meet with success in uncommon hours." This statement, along with continually dreaming in the direction of Montana, strongly reinforced my Montana Dream. It was my dream that I kept private in my younger years because I thought it was so bold and daring and that no one could relate. Montana was a state that was not in most people's consciousness.

For Christmas during my freshman year, my parents gave me the collected works of O. Henry, Rudyard Kipling, and Bret Harte. I devoured the golden nuggets of Harte's stories of mining camps and the American West, and I found that his words and prose constantly reinforced my desire to live in the West. *Let the buffalo chips fall where they may.* I needed to fulfill what I thought was my destiny.

Despite the urgency of my ambition, I felt directionless on how to move forward.

Moving had also doomed my chances to finish my work to become an Eagle Scout, an achievement I longed for. I would no longer be able to walk the three miles to Scout meetings when my father was at work. Completion of my Eagle requirements was so close—I needed only my community service project and a few merit badges. The connection to community and nature that the Boy Scouts provided me was over. *Perhaps I was only meant to achieve the rank of Life Scout,* I thought to myself in later years. The badge for a Life Scout is a red heart, and red hearts played a series of dramatic events in my life.

There was some solace hunting with my new Remington 870 shotgun that I was able to buy from a year's wages of delivering the morning *Pittsburgh Post Gazette* when I lived in Heidelberg. "Pow!" the sixteen gauge roared with No. 6 shot as I hunted for pheasants in the cornfields and rabbits in the wooded brush piles near my new country home. Fall hunting for small game in Pennsylvania was a weak catharsis, a substitute for my real dream of stalking a large bull elk in snow-covered western forests or reeling a rainbow trout in on an Eagle Claw fly rod from a pristine Montana lake. I envisioned myself as a scout from Troop 7, standing knee deep in frigid lake water in the Bob Marshall, yelling out to Smoke, "Fish on," as my dry fly was snatched by a native cutthroat just as it broke the shimmering surface of the water.

"Keep that rod tip up now that he's hooked. Get that slack tight," Smoke would yell from the campfire near shore. "Use your net now. That's a nice looking fish."

Chapter 3

Our new home had eight rooms and two-and-a-half baths. There was no more showering from a spigot in a concrete wall, as we had done at my grandmother's. My younger brother, Marke, and I would have more privacy, no longer sharing our bedroom with my grandmother, and my much younger sister Katie would have her own room, and not share a room with my parents. We were not used to modern conveniences such as a centralized vacuum, an indoor garage, or a doorbell.

It wasn't long before I started to miss the old comforts of my grandmother's house, but the pecan-paneled den with its woodsy appeal immediately became my reading, study, and call center. The den had built-in bookshelves where two sets of the *Encyclopedia Britannica* were lined up, giving the room an academic ambience. Reclining in sage-green leather chair, I spent many hours reading, choosing to pass up homework of translating the first act of Moliere's *The Imaginary Invalid* or factoring algebraic polynomial expressions. It surprised me when I read the back of my report cards where codes were listed for classroom behavior. Although my grades had slipped, I received the highest marks for showing classroom leadership and participation, yet that never prompted a discussion with my teachers.

By Christmas of my senior year, I was struggling to gain a vision for my future. Some vocational choices were already on my "no" list, like steel mills, coal mines, or anything to do with farming and picking vegetables. While I functioned at higher levels when acting independently, I floundered working in classroom group projects because I always had a larger vision of the project involved and was able to see the end product before it was finished. There was too much talk and not enough action for me. I bonded like contact cement with older men, like my scoutmaster or my Little League coach, as I found their wisdom came from the school of hard knocks, and I wanted to know what they knew.

In my early preteen years, my mother thought I would choose to go to seminary because I had been very connected to my church as an altar boy, with youth group activities that included Polish school on Wednesday nights to learn my ancestral language, and actively leading my Sunday school class discussions. Though drawn to the church, I realized that being a priest was not where my heart was… even though priests in my church were allowed to marry. I always envisioned a lovely wife and three children, two boys and a girl, just like my family.

Working outdoors was the best place for me, as I never envisioned working in an office or a cubicle with no windows, but I had no idea how to make that happen.

High school bored me with its small vision and its cliquishness, but I was not bored with academia itself. My high school friends were cool, but those I hung with didn't talk of bigger dreams and adventures, so I tended to drift as a follower. The social dynamics of high school conflicted with my vision of myself as a rugged loner like Linus Rawlings, the fur trapper portrayed by Jimmy Stewart in *How the West Was Won*. I dated a few girls, and could have dated more, but I spent too much fruitless time playing cat and mouse with Abbie for four years.

Finally, I thought I had captured her heart when it was time for our senior prom. It had been my desire for a long time to take Abbie, with her long brown hair and sparkly blue eyes, to the prom. I did not want to wait as word was out that several guys had thought about asking her. The right moment arrived.

"Well, Abbie, how about it? Would you like to go to the prom with me?" I asked her after English class one day.

She smiled. She always smiled at me, her blue eyes saying yes, and her mouth saying nothing. I had set this moment up for weeks, always walking her to her next class. *Of course she had to say yes.*

"Is that a yes?"

"Call me tonight."

Abbie agreed to go, and she was a total knockout when I picked her up. She was Catholic, so I gifted her with a necklace with a cross to wear that night, hoping to score more points. She was the prettiest girl at the prom without a doubt. But Abbie found it easier to chit-chat the night away with her girlfriends. *Why was she more comfortable gabbing than dancing or talking with me?* She and her friends left all the guys sitting at one table while we twiddled our thumbs. The guys were confused as I was, and there was little talk amongst us. One slow dance. No kiss from Abbie. My senior prom had been the perfect, sour-lemon frosting on my graduation cake that had baked the three years I was at Hill Top. *Why did I ever think there could be more?*

Goodbye, Abbie. I eagerly awaited college and a chance to meet women who saw life as an adventure, were exciting to be with, and loved the outdoors.

None of the other girls I had dated would or could envision a world outside of their hometown. Other high school love interests died on the vine as they were based on the necessity of finding a date for dances or concerts.

Most of my high school friends had chosen small, state teacher colleges or the larger regional universities—Pennsylvania State University or nearby West Virginia University. There was a fear within me that college would be like high school, when one teacher made silly examples of students caught chewing gum by having them stuff their mouth with as many pieces of Double Bubble as they could. I did not want to go where everyone else was going. My view of college was that it should be primarily adventure-based, with academics second, leaving me unenthused about any state schools and causing me to broaden my search.

While I had been proud of my immigrant ancestors taking work in the mines and mills, a book my father had given me for Christmas, *Profiles in Courage* by John F. Kennedy, had helped me understand the courage needed to find adventure someplace besides Pennsylvania.

The book was a challenging read, and after the first chapter, I wanted to put it down, but my dad told me to keep reading. "It is important that you understand this book," he said.

My dad, a staunch Kennedy man, exposed me to reading challenges that he himself would not tackle. What I learned from this book was that many senators in America's history had to make unpopular decisions, but they had the courage to stand up for their actions. The keynote I remember is that they all had to pay a price for their actions. There was a chapter on Sam Houston, who refused to take the oath of allegiance to the Confederacy and was thrown out of office as governor of Texas in 1861. While the book was about courage in politics, about men who voted their conscience and paid a price for doing so, I saw it as a parallel for my own plans.

I knew I could pay a high price of being disconnected from my family when I moved to Montana. But, suddenly, I realized a more personal equivalency than any character from the book. My Uncle Jim! He had moved away from a large family when he chose a military career and traveled the world, but he came home for Christmas when possible. He loved everybody, and everyone loved him. *What price would I pay? Could I pay it? Would I still be loved after leaving?*

One evening, my father let his feelings about Montana be known while I was sitting in the den and reading about Montana's state history in the encyclopedia.

"What are you reading, son? I see you have the M volume. More Montana?"

"Yeah, more Montana. Did you know Montana didn't become a state until 1889? That was the same year our ancestors left Poland and came to America at Ellis Island."

There was a pause as my father squinted his eyes and shook his head while he tried hard to digest information that had no previous relevance to him.

"No, I didn't know that, but let me get to my point. Your mother and I have heard a lot about this move to Montana someday. The way your mother and I feel is that we would rather you be happy in the middle of Montana than be back here and making us unhappy. *Czy Pan rozumie?*"

"*Tak, rozumiem.*"

On select occasions, my father used Polish idioms for effect. Yes, I understood the duality of his message. He had given me his blessing to venture forward with my Montana Dream, but the Polish twist was a gentle reminder to always remember where I was from. *How could I not?* I was the firstborn son of a man whose life was forged by iron and steel.

Chapter 4

One January morning in homeroom, I received an appointment card to meet with my guidance counselor, Verna Hopper, during my study hall that day. Mrs. Hopper had scheduled a career counseling sessions for seniors.

Feeling uncomfortable as usual at Hill Top, I took my seat in her office. It took a minute for Mrs. Hopper to adjust her reading glasses, making sure she was talking to the right student. She had once counseled a student with another student's test scores, and I thought she should have retired.

"Here are your SAT and IQ test scores, Loring. They seem out of balance with your scholastic achievements here at Hill Top High School," she stated rather quizzically, while looking over the top of her reading glasses.

Maybe because I don't like it here.

"You have scored very high in verbal skills," she said and nodded her head in approval, "but your math scores will not be able to get you into engineering school." She shook her head as if in quiet despair for my future. "And I see you are taking geography and opted out of Latin. Not a wise choice in the academic curriculum."

I read a lot, my math teachers sucked, and I love geography. Carpe diem, Mrs. Hopper.

"I'm not interested in engineering school, Mrs. Hopper," I replied, putting my hands on her desk for effect. "Do you have other career alternatives to explore?" I asked. "Maybe professions that are related to the outdoors."

There were new careers developing in forestry and ecology, and I hoped for information on these.

21

"No, I don't believe I have heard of anything like that. Is that like being a game warden?" she asked while she fidgeted with her glasses, apparently blindsided by my question.

Mrs. Hopper's counseling model was a one-size-fits-all program. If engineering or technology-related careers for the space program that was really taking off didn't interest a student, her only other recommendation was a career in education.

"We will always need teachers," was her cop-out answer to me.

I felt lost. I lacked a mentor, someone who could understand my dreams. Engineering was nothing I aspired to, and I wished Mrs. Hopper would have been able to counsel me in new and alternative careers.

That April, America celebrated its first Earth Day. My college-fresh geography teacher, Ms. Holly, had inspired me with her commitment to bring this event to our young minds. During this time, I had been reading an excerpt from the soon-to-be-published book, *The Greening of America*, by Charles A. Reich. The author's discussion about a new generation's revolution lit a fire in me, an intense fire that burned away all fears, doubts, and uncertainties about leaving Pennsylvania and moving to the West.

That was me, the new generation. Just like a true pioneer, I wanted a family, especially a son born under the wild Montana skies. *This was not to be a revolution of violence, nor could it be successfully resisted by violence.* The book argued that a change of consciousness was needed in today's world, a new way of living— almost a new man.

Coupling Earth Day and *The Greening of America*, my path away from high school had started to take a clearer, more energized—but still uncertain—route, until one day I read an outdoor magazine article that talked about clear-cutting old growth timber in the Tongass National Forest in Alaska. This enraged me.

How was it that the Forest Service had continued clear-cutting in Tongass National Forest? Tongass was one of the planet's only five remaining temperate rain forests.

There had to be a better solution than cutting these ancient trees for lumber and pulpwood, and I didn't have the background or education to react other than emotionally. I became more interested in the field of forestry, a nontraditional course and one that seemed destined for dreamers at that time. Forestry was one career in which I could combine my love of nature and trees and also be an agent of change in caring for and managing the natural resources in America that were being destroyed, depleted, and squandered.

These feelings intensified when Ms. Holly came to me one morning after geography class. Oh boy, was I was enamored with Ms. Holly… She was so young and so vibrant, and she talked of downhill skiing at Seven Springs and loving the mountains. Ms. Holly had Native American genetic markers with light bronze skin and dark eyes. Her jet-black hair was cut in a hip hairdo, which made her very easy to look at, and I looked a lot. She made geography relevant to the times, and her class offered a respite from the unbearable sense of ennui that I felt with most of my senior classes.

"I was thinking you might be interested in a special assignment, Loring. You are one of my best students and are deeply concerned about our environment. I would like to grant you a personal day away from school. Take my Kodak Instamatic camera to document all the forms of pollution you can capture on film. I would then like to mount them in the room for the class to see what is happening literally in their backyards."

"I hope you are giving me more than one roll of film, Ms. Holly," I replied with delight as she took the camera from her desk drawer and then added an extra roll of film while she smiled and nodded her approval.

Beginning on the banks of the Monongahela River in Pittsburgh, my photo journal started with belching smokestacks of the Jones & Laughlin steel mill. Included in my first photos was a decomposing fish floating near shore. Later, I stopped in Heidelberg and took some photos of contaminated water from an old, abandoned coal mine, and then I took a picture where people dumped trash along a country road.

Who would ever clean up all this crap? I focused the camera on a belly-up discarded refrigerator, damaged coils exposed, having released their Freon into the ozone long ago.

We had just covered smog in class, learning how it caused depletion of the Earth's ozone layer. Ms. Holly deserved a ton of thanks for enlightening me and furthering my passion for protecting the environment.

During one of my World Culture classes, Jim Whitehurst, a student who sat behind me, showed me a college catalog for Tennessee Technological University in Cookeville, Tennessee.

"How'd you hear about this place, Jim?"

"I got their catalog in the mail along with all the schools with good engineering programs," he told me. "Here, take it home and check it out."

Tech had an outstanding engineering school, and the prices for out-of-state student tuition were cheaper than going to Penn State as an in-state student. Aside from engineering, the school also had a pre-forestry program that offered the core classes needed to fulfill a BS degree. After two years in the pre-forestry program, I would have to transfer to a school that offered the final two years of course work for a BS.

Thinking that Tennessee could real-l-l-l-y be different, I pitched the idea to my parents.

"Look at this school, Mom and Dad," I said as I presented this option to my parents one evening, laying out the purple-and-gold-covered catalog, "Tennessee Tech: Fall 1970," in front of them. A picture of a golden eagle was emblazoned below the text. They both were bewildered at first.

"What kind of school is this?" my father asked, casually perusing the catalog, not reading the cover. "Jiminy jumped up Almighty, son, this college is in Tennessee!"

"Cool, huh?"

My mother shook her head in disbelief. "Tennessee, Loring? Seriously?"

My parents quickly acquiesced and agreed to let me chart my own college course, even to Tennessee.

Tennessee Tech admitted me. The University of Montana and its forestry school were on my mind, but I couldn't explain the inner force that drove me to the South first. There was so much left to know, and I eagerly looked forward to new discoveries and freedoms, and to see if the world was really round. A hundred colleges were within three hours of home—and I was interested in Tennessee and moving to Montana.

This dialogue had been hard for my parents, as neither had attended college. My father, an only child, had enlisted in the Navy before his senior year in high school, only to be discharged within six months when the war came to a close. He had resumed classes in high school and graduated on time with his class. He was an accordion virtuoso, and that enabled him to form a polka band upon graduation. I had seen his high school physics and algebra books, so I had always thought he could have gone to college. Though not a great reader of books, he did read the entire newspaper daily and watched the evening news on television, always keeping abreast of world events. My father took pride in his vocabulary, once telling me to not be "so *vociferous*."

My mother, the youngest of twelve siblings, was born into her own special light. Her mother had died shortly after she was born, and she worked the family farm with her older sister Kate, while her older brothers went off to war. She had grown up poor, eating lard sandwiches because the homemade butter was sold for income. Her brother Pete had given her his shoes from the Navy when he had come home on leave. Her father was cruel, and many attempts by social workers to remove her and Kate from the home had been met with a loaded shotgun. At seventeen, she and a friend slipped into the Shangri-la Bar in Hendersonville, where she met her soul mate, the leader of the polka band, who played a green Italian accordion.

I often wonder who had been her role model for parenting, how she became such a great mother when she married at seventeen. Or how she stays so beautiful after such a hard childhood.

We had been discussing her childhood one day when she grabbed my fingers and had me run them over her right shin.

"Feel my right shin here," she said with a hard edge of remembrance in her voice.

"Mom, there is a big divot where the bone was."

"That's from where my father swung a sickle at me and hit my shin and took a piece of bone out."

She had every reason to be angry and bitter about her childhood, but if she was, she never said so. Love was an action verb for my

25

mother, and her Elizabeth Taylor-ish looks made her all the more beautiful.

Though she had an eighth-grade education, she was a passionate reader of books on spiritual enlightenment, religion, and nutrition. She was in cahoots with my father in making sure that her boys kept busy and always had jobs.

One time, she told me that after all of us were through with college, she wanted to get her high school diploma.

But she had shown us her intelligence before that happened. We were extremely proud when she applied for a three-year position with North American Rockwell when they opened a plant in Bridgeville to build software circuitry for nuclear submarines. Competing with college graduates in interpreting and following the schematics of the blueprints for the electronic circuitry came easy to her, and she was the first one hired. In a short time, she became her boss's liaison with other employees. Her success with North American Rockwell increased her intention to complete her education.

Chapter 5

S ummer... I thought of Smoke, getting ready for another pack trip into the Bob, but I found a job with Clad Metals, not punching mules, but punching out skillets and soup pots. Clad Metals was in its infancy and planned to be a global giant of cookware with its revolutionary design of stainless steel and aluminum clad together. The distance from the factory to my home was exactly far enough for "Lola," the hit song by the Kinks, to play from start to finish.

All young guys preferred to work the day shift, giving them their evenings free to go out with their girlfriends or hang with the guys and drown a few chillers along pitch-black country roads where fireflies flashed to attract their mates.

The gas ovens were heated to over a thousand degrees to get the roughened steel sheet sticky enough to bond with the aluminum sheet after being rolled. The sheet, now "clad together," was dipped in an acid bath to remove oxidation, and later punched into skillets and pots.

There was never enough cool water to quench my thirst. It was over ninety degrees outside the plant and well over a hundred inside. Sweat poured off me in a steady stream that left the edge of my lips with a salt crust. My fingers were always hot, even inside asbestos gloves.

Clad Metals provided a steady income during summers and breaks from college. I learned not only the bonding of metals, but also the bonding between men who worked together in the arena of sweat, metal dust, and burned fingers. Men who resorted to mill mentality, a low-brow sense of humor that had no sacred boundaries

27

and helped make the grueling days tolerable. Everyone's shortcomings or habits were exposed. The only way I found to deal with these attempts at humor about my tics was to fire back when fired upon. A worker who displayed no fight was only targeted more.

In July, my family piled into our four-door Chevy Caprice and drove the laborious ten hours to Cookeville for my Freshman Orientation. Katie, who was ten, sat squashed between her two older brothers. The back seat was a little crowded, and our car did not have air-conditioning.

When we arrived at the Holiday Inn in Cookeville, our family for the first time stayed in a motel instead of homes of relatives. The weather was unbearably hot, and Marke splashed Katie with the water from the outdoor fountain. Katie pleaded with my mother for Marke to stop, but my mother was too busy splashing cool water on herself.

Later, in the cool of the evening, we all visited the campus, three miles from Cookeville, which sat on the Cumberland Plateau.

I was hoping to be awed and impressed, but instead the campus seemed eerie, not because of the architecture but because of the absence of students. There was nobody around except for two guys tossing a fluorescent green Frisbee in the courtyard. It seemed the college had been evacuated, and the summer quiet was disappointing.

The dorms were older but well maintained. The Student Union was new, and I found out that the football stadium had been the first in the country to install artificial turf.

The next morning I met with my faculty advisor, Dr. Harold Funk. Dr. Funk was a trim man in his forties who wore his hair in a meticulous crew cut. We met in his office, "eyeball to eyeball," as he had requested over the phone.

"Well, how do y'all like Tech so far? I saw you with your family walking the campus earlier. Loring, eh? I never met anyone with that name."

Should I comment on his name? Funk. What a cool, college name.

"Good morning Dr. Funk. I can't wait to start classes."

"You come see me about anything?" Dr. Funk emphatically asked, tapping his pen in a staccato beat on his desk. "I'm not just your advisor in academic concerns, but I'm also available to help you adjust to college life. You are scheduled in my horticulture class. This is an important first course that introduces the cultivating of plants and trees. Horticulture will give you the necessary foundation to build on to every other class in forestry you will take. I need to add that you will be required to take ROTC during your freshman and sophomore year at Tech."

ROTC? A requirement? Most colleges had done away with this requirement. I had always been a student of famous battles and thought that studying military science could provide differing perspectives.

My father was anxious to get back to where grits were not served for breakfast, and we left Cookeville fairly early in the cool of the morning.

By mid-September I began to focus on packing and buying new clothes. My mom was excited to shop for me, splurging and buying me a fringed, suede coat, identical to the one that Jon Voight wore in *Midnight Cowboy*. Despite its popularity, I knew she hadn't seen the movie, because if she had, there would have been little chance of her buying the coat. When I opened the Kaufman's box, I was blown away.

"This coat is so cool, Mom. I really dig it. Makes me feel like Davey Crockett. He's from Tennessee, you know."

"I think it looks good on you. It's a coat that looks outdoorsy."

The week before leaving I got a haircut—and that one lasted me a few years.

My plane reservations for Nashville were on Allegheny Airlines, often referred to as Agony Airlines, which was how Pittsburghers pronounced Allegheny. Once at Nashville, I would have to take a cab to the bus station to grab a bus for Cookeville. Loaded in one large, gray American Tourister suitcase were my shoes, clothes, toiletries, and a tightly rolled Easy Rider poster for my dorm room.

Katie sat on the suitcase to help get it latched, but there was no room for the coat. I had to carry it, slung across my shoulder.

On my departure day, I kissed my gram goodbye and followed my parents into the Caprice. Gram tried to be strong, but her wave was weak, and tears rolled down her cheeks as she blew me kisses. Her lips slowly formed the Polish words *"niech Bog bedzie z toba."* ("May God be with you.")

"A takze z wami, Gram."

No one in my family had ever flown before, so this was a momentous occasion, standing inside the terminal, looking at the jet that was going to fly me away to new adventures. The call to board had been given, and my parents gave me my final instructions.

"Good luck, son, and no tipping the stewardesses," my father had needled me with a wink.

"I'll make sure to call home every week, Mom."

"You better, and remember to call collect," she had warned. "Sundays are the cheapest times, but call anytime you are running low on vitamins."

The Allegheny jet sat on the tarmac at Greater Pittsburgh Airport. A new smell of high-octane jet fuel filled the air. After boarding, I found the aircraft empty, as though it was a private charter just for me. The safety talk about seat belts was given directly to me, and I wondered why flotation devices were needed for flying over land.

The two jet engines roared to life; we taxied, gained speed, and I suddenly was airborne for the first time in my life. The Boeing 737 soared south through the low-hanging Pennsylvania clouds, leaving Pittsburgh and my childhood far below.

Part 2

The Eastern Redbud (Cercis Canadensis)

The redbud tree, prolific throughout the Smoky Mountains, produces a magnificent display of dark pink or white blossoms every April. The foliage is deciduous, with deep green heart-shaped leaves. The tree, seldom growing to more than fifty feet tall, is not long lived and is highly susceptible to heart rot as it ages.

Chapter 6

Because the ginger ale that I spilled during the flight had not dried, I felt all eyes were focused on the wet spot that was in an embarrassing location on my khaki slacks. There was no jet way, and I deplaned on the tarmac, cradling my prized coat. The Music City was under sunny skies, oppressive heat radiated off the tarmac, and the humidity was high on the misery index. With my bulging suitcase in hand, I hailed the lead Yellow Cab in line. The cabbie spoke in a foreign tongue.

"All you Yankee boys coming here to school, I reckon? Sho' is hotter than a four-peckered billy goat, I tell ya. Wheere ye headed, young'un? Vanderbilt?"

"No, bus station," I replied with a newfound sense of independence but a little apprehension about the billy goat.

This was my first ride in a taxi cab. The driver was an overweight, older man whose worn khaki uniform had seen better days... and drier armpits. His jaw was full of Red Man chewing tobacco, and he spit once as he loaded my suitcase into the trunk.

The bus station was across the street from the Ryman Auditorium, a historically cool venue ever since it had opened in 1892. I stood in wonder, then walked, suitcase in hand, to the open entrance of the Grand Ol' Opry.

Posters of Johnny Cash, George Jones, and Tammy Wynette had been plastered everywhere on the outside of the building. On the street corner sat an old, black, frosty-haired blind man. He was finger-picking a guitar and crying the blues, with a tin cup at his feet. His song seemed to be the story of his life, and all the cheating women in it:

"Oh-h sweet mama you loved me so fine
I flew further than paradise
But now I can't pay your price."
He howled like a hound dog on a moonlit night.

"Man, you got your mojo working overtime on that song," I told him, flipping a quarter into his tin cup.

He slowly nodded his head upon hearing the coin land. If there weren't a bus to catch, I would have stayed for another quarter's worth of blues.

Then, another strange encounter happened! An effeminate-looking man dressed in a powder-blue seersucker suit put his arm on my shoulder. Was I on *Candid Camera*?

"Sure is a hot one today, fella. Would you like to join me for a coo-ool drink in my apartment?" he smoothly asked in a voice as feminine as his demeanor.

"No way," I told him while I twisted my shoulder away, raising my right hand up to emphasize my point. It was my first encounter with a homosexual, and I kept my distance because of my naiveté.

In two hours I had had my first jet ride and had been welcomed by extreme heat and humidity, a foreign language, a blind bluesman, and a "queer," as gay individuals were referred to at that time. And then there were the four-peckered billy goats, and I still had an eighty-mile bus ride.

The bus ride—with no air-conditioning—was a wheeled sauna. My Jockey briefs were damp and uncomfortable. This part of the interstate should have been familiar to me because I had traveled it two months previously. But this bus ride was not direct to Cookeville. It took a meandering state route and stopped at every podunk town along the way. The bus arrived in Cookeville three hours later; I took a university shuttle to the campus and was let off at Malcomb Hall, my dorm for the next year.

Dan, the resident assistant, checked me in and handed me my keys. An older, married grad student, Dan smoked a Meerschaum pipe. I had never known any young men to smoke a pipe, at least not one filled with Prince Albert from a can.

"Cookevul's in Putnam County, and Putnam's a dry county," Dan drawled as I started to leave for my room.

"What's a dry county?"

"No alcohol sales. If y'all need something to drink, let me know 'cause I go to Nashvul every weekend. I can get quarts of 'shine sometimes if you boys wanna try it."

"Yeah, well, gee thanks, Dan."

Wooooooo, white lightning. Corn likker. I am not in Bridgeville anymore.

My roommate had already arrived and introduced himself in a syrupy drawl. "Hi, I'm Phil Hallstead." Phil pronounced his first name with two syllables: "Phi-ill." He was a red-headed, pure country boy from Sparta, Tennessee, just a hoot and a holler down the road, he said.

His Yankee alarm must have sounded in his head when he saw me—he glared at my coat before I even spoke. As we struggled to make small talk, there was a knock on the door, and two other students burst in. Both of these upperclassmen were from Lynchburg, the home of Mr. Jack Daniels. John Horner, whom we later referred to as "Big Daddy," was a man of large weight but no discrimination. His bass voice was coupled with a gentlemanly demeanor, and that conflicted with his mild dislike for Yankees. Stan Giles, his Howdy Doody-looking roommate, was all smiles, and more demonstrative than John.

Big Daddy rang my ears, "Yank, you're welcome to go to Nashvul with us and check out some hot clubs near Vandy."

"Thanks John, but I just came from Nashville," I told him.

"It don't matter, Yank, you can go again. We'll be back after midnight. I strongly recommend you come."

So this is Southern hospitality? Strongly recommend? A part of me wanted to say no, but I thought I should accept this olive branch. Being called Yank told me the Civil War was not yet over for a lot of Southern boys, so I would tread cautiously at first.

"I'm starving, John. I need something to eat first."

"Get some snacks from the vending machine downstairs," John told me. "We gotta go, Yank."

Vanderbilt, an elite private university in the center of Nashville, was near some great bars, all with live music. There was a lot of music and guitar pickers everywhere, but Big Daddy and his entourage were not serious about exploring the music scene or dancing when we entered a honky-tonk that had lots of action on the dance floor and plenty of girls standing around.

"Holy smokes, check out those hot chicks chatting in the corner," I said. "I bet they wanna dance."

"Naw, Yank," John drawled. "We just come to eyeball 'em."

What's wrong with these guys? Everyone seems hung up on eyeballs.

"Well, I'm going to ask that blonde to dance, the one with those tanned legs that are shouting out. Listen, John, they're calling my name."

"Go for it, Yank," John belly laughed. "Be ni-i-ice to her, and she may give ya some sugar. Heh-heh-heh. You Yanks crack my fat ass up. No wonder y'all lost the war."

It was after midnight when I climbed into my unmade bed without brushing my teeth and pulled a cover over my exhausted body. Phil kept his light on and sat on the edge of his bed and did arm curls with a green bowling ball. What the hell he was doing? There were better ways to pump up your biceps, and I stared for a moment in disbelief.

I pulled the covers higher and drifted off to sleep, feeling homesick and out of place. That day, I had traveled five hundred miles by air, eighty miles by bus, one hundred and sixty by car, ten by taxi, and had one hot dance, the distance across a bar room floor, but my internal travel was immeasurable. *Would I be facing such a culture clash if I had first gone to Montana?*

My Sony alarm was unplugged, but I still managed to awaken before Phil and hit the communal shower. A red towel was wrapped my waist when I found Big Daddy, Stan, Phil, and a yet-to-be introduced student holding a summit of Southern minds outside my door. Some distance down the hall, another student, red-skinned with a head full of black hair, and wearing a T-shirt that had Paulsboro Wrestling emblazoned across the front, stood alone, arms crossed in blatant defiance of the particular brand of law and order that was taking place in the hall. The meeting had one purpose, and that was that Phil was *not* going to room with a Yankee, and the other student was *not* going to room with a "Yankee Eskimo." John acted as judge and jury and quickly bellowed out his verdict.

"Phil, get your stuff and move next door to me, and the Eskimo can move into your old room with the new Yank."

The Eskimo was immediately given the moniker "Tonto," and I was referred to as "Wally," as no one could pronounce my name.

If I had to take a chance, I would take the red Eskimo before rooming with a redneck, I groused, and hoped there would not be a war between the states.

The Eskimo and I introduced ourselves and formed an immediate bond of friendship. Craig Tahamont was not Eskimo at all, but a very proud Native American, belonging to the Iroquois Confederacy. *Would we be friends for life?*

When Craig was called "Tonto," my stomach sank, bringing back remembrances of my youth when blacks were jigaboos, Italians were dagos, and Jews were kikes. I had heard enough Polish jokes that I became desensitized to them and shrugged them off. "How many Pollocks does it take to change a light bulb? Three, one to hold the bulb and two to turn the chair."

Wally was not to my liking, or Yank, but I tried to go with the flow. Loring was a special name my mother had chosen for me, a name meaning "crowned with laurels," or from Teutonic legend, "famous in battle." I liked the latter.

Craig did not let the Southern students' ethnic labels and nicknames bother him that much either. Many years later, he told me, "If I had gotten confrontational, it would have only cemented the wild Indian stereotype. I wanted my actions—not someone else's label—to speak for who I am."

Directly across the hall from us were two Hoosiers, Ray and Bo. These two country bumpkins went to the same high school in Indiana and now were together again at Tech. Behind closed doors the four of us got together and agreed that we could not understand what these Tennessee people were saying. We did not know that you had to "open the hooood to check the earl level." The "tar" pressure also needed to be tested. And don't forget to pick up the student "newspiper." The one piece of survival lingo we had learned was that any town or city in Tennessee that ended in "ville" needed to be pronounced "vul." Like "Nashvul" or "Cookevul" or "Knoxvul."

Craig and the others had a different meal plan than me. My meal plan was offered by several restaurants near campus, and I had been eating alone.

"Why aren't you eating with us?" Craig had asked.

Feeling bummed, I told him, "That was the plan that some upperclassmen told me to pick when I was at orientation."

"That's too bad, bro, because I got to tell you about this outrageous, smokin' hot girl I met at the dining hall at breakfast," he said, while blowing on the tips of his fingers. "Her name's Gail. She's mighty fine, but how would you know, bro? If you were smart, maybe you should go with me one morning and see if she is there. I told her all about you. You need to check her out. If she's not taken, it won't be long before some yokel starts hitting on her trying to jump her bones."

"Then why aren't you making a move on her, my man? That's pretty damn chivalrous of you, kemo sabe."

"Well, I got a girl back in Jersey, so she can be all-l-l-l yours, brother. See how I take care of you. She told me that after lunch she was going to the student art exhibit on the quad today. Go for it. You'll know her when you see her, she is 'something different.'"

I had come to think that Craig was something different, too.

Chapter 7

There was no mistaking Gail at the art exhibit as I watched her looking at watercolor prints of Tennessee wildflowers. She had well-bred looks that were easily recognized; the way she walked from print to print and held her hands in a positive, confident manner told me this woman was no slouch. And then there was the incredible intensity of her blue eyes. I had never seen such powerful blue eyes in my life! The Walawanders and the Ambroses from my mother's side of the family were all blue eyed. My Uncle Tony had blue eyes that cut like an acetylene torch, and the eyes of everyone else in the family were compared to his. In high school, a girl once told me that I had "Joe Namath eyes," so being complimented on this family trait was very common. But Gail's eyes were hard to compare. Glacial blue was too cold, and they were certainly not cold. Baby blue was not strong enough. I settled for electric, sapphire blue.

Standing in her tooled-leather wedge sandals, with her lips raised and mine lowered, created a very kissable lip-lock zone that I looked forward to possibly exploring. Her mid-waist brown hair hung off her shoulders, giving way to large, gentle waves at the bottom. My hormone levels stabilized. At that moment, I relaxed enough to introduce myself.

"Hi Gail, I'm Loring, Craig's roommate. He said I might find you here today."

"Hi Loring," she said while covering her mouth to stop from laughing her head off. "I'm sorry, but Craig told me that you were short and toothless."

"How come you don't have a Tennessee accent?" I asked her, aghast that I opened our introduction with that statement, but I needed to say something to move past Craig's tomfoolery.

She chuckled, with a smile that stretched ear to ear. "I was born in Detroit and moved to Tennessee in 1966. My father is a teacher, and he decided the Detroit-area schools were not a place for his four girls. So we moved to west Tennessee," she said.

"So you're from Dee-troit, the Motor City? The home of the Tempting Temps. I love Motown tunes," I said, just a little amped up and ready to bust a move and start crooning *My Girl* to her.

"No, no," she pleaded. "I'm from De*troit*, not Dee-troit," she corrected me with a large laugh. I noticed a slight flicker of her eyelashes. *I hope she's flirting with me.* We chatted for a few more minutes and parted as classes were about to start, but the coolest part was that we agreed to meet later that evening.

The rest of the day I was on cloud nine but tried hard not to let my imagination run away with me. How could I have been so darn lucky? *Was it possible that she was feeling the same?* Craig had been right. She *was* "something different." And then there were her eyes. Oh how they seemed to be always dancing.

The visiting restrictions in the "Bible Belt" South were harsh. The men's dorms had resident assistants, while the women's dorms had dorm mothers. A female student had to sign out of her dorm, sign back in, and declare whom she was going to be with. There was a campus security guard who made his appointed rounds observing the women's dorms. All the windows had steel, grid work welded on them to guard the girls from intruders. The university, with all their protective and restrictive measures, failed to realize that almost any intelligent student could easily find loopholes in their system. It did not take long before I did.

I anxiously waited for Gail in the lobby of Murphy Hall, tussling my hair a little to look more at ease, just as she walked through the door.

"Would you like to take a walk around the Oval? The birds are really pretty this time of day. I remember that from when I was here two years ago for a high school convention. There is a bench under a large redbud tree, about halfway around where we can sit," she told me.

"Sounds great to me."

Truthfully, I would have answered in the affirmative to anything she suggested. The Tennessee humidity was gone for the day, and the evening was warm, with a breeze just strong enough to ruffle her hair and cast a wisp of White Shoulders my way. We found that bench in the unoccupied courtyard and delved into our lives before college.

"So what made you come way down here to Tennessee Tech of all places?" she asked, tilting her head to the side, maybe to see if mine was level.

It was hard for me not to say, "You." It would have seemed corny at the time, but years later I have come to believe that we were destined to meet, and so there was some truth to that answer that lingered on the edge of my lips.

For the next several weeks, we continued meeting, often in the evening, until the eleven o'clock chimes rang from Derryberry Hall, the signal for Gail to be back in her dorm. Her upbringing near the University of Michigan had left her with a wider perspective on the world, and she resented some of the backward, myopic, closed-mindedness of a lot of Southern students. It was hard for me not to feel the same, at least about the male students. Most Southern girls never got into the "damn Yankee" frame of mind and were much kinder, treating everyone with equal respect. They appeared stronger in their personalities than girls I had known at home, but also possessed a soft femininity, lacking the prejudice of some Southern boys who were still flying the "Stars and Bars."

With a student deferment from the draft, I wasn't interested in a senior trip to Vietnam. Neither pacifist, nor hawk, my youthful dream of being in the 82nd Airborne like my Uncle Jim, and then becoming a Green Beret, started to fade in 1967 when I noticed many of the youths from my hometown were returning in boxes. My military ambitions waned but did not disappear.

Craig and I shared our thoughts on serving in the military. His father was an officer in the Navy and Craig said that going to college while others served made him feel guilty, almost like living a life of luxury. Later, my views on Vietnam crystalized when I met many returning Vietnam veterans who enrolled in college under the GI Bill. One vet, Rob, four years my senior, and three months removed from Vietnam, gave me an earful one day on the same bench that Gail and I used.

Rob was emphatic and stressed his feelings to the max. His red beard turned hot enough to ignite.

"Don't ever think about volunteering your sweet ass to go to that jungle hellhole. Let me tell you what my day was like. Little people, women and children dressed in black pajamas, would ambush us. I shot so many of those little gooks, it was like swatting flies. Now I'm home, going to college on the G.I. Bill. I always wanted to be an artist, but now I'm being harassed for being a baby killer. They all can kiss my Tennessee ass. I can't get no relief and don't wanna talk about Vietnam no more. Sorry I got started. I got a coat for you that I wore in Nam. That's as close I ever want you to get. It's yours… Ya wanna hit? It's some really good shit."

After Rob's rant, I could find no honor for a country that fought its war with women and children. Our American G.I.s were not fighting professional, trained soldiers like those of Germany in World War II. My Uncle Tony, who fought valiantly in WW II, told me frightening war stories about landing on beachheads, but he never spoke of the morality of war. He did sum up his war stories by telling me that what didn't kill him, made him stronger. It was very clear to my Uncle Tony. We were the good guys, and Germans were the bad guys. In 1966, I felt Americans supported the war. In 1970, I recognized that Vietnam was a waste of young American lives and only the military-industrial complex benefitted.

Gail had made a friend from Lansing, Michigan, named "DeeDee" Burton. She preferred DeeDee over Darla, her given name. DeeDee resembled a slightly more robust Joni Mitchell, with the accent falling on bust. DeeDee, one of the last "flower children," on campus, was deeply involved with astrology and was known to talk to rainbows. She drove an old, blue Chrysler 300, and would let anyone borrow it. Full of free love, with flowers in her long, blond hair, DeeDee, was still hanging on to the sixties and was another out-of-place student at Tennessee Tech. She always wore a long, unbuttoned black trench coat no matter the weather. One day I met her walking alone, and she asked me what my sign was.

"Pisces, why do you ask?"

"Well your sweetie is a Sagittarius. Fire and water, baby. Those are two hot love signs. You may have a very long love life together. You two still groovin?"

"Yep, DeeDee. Still groovin. Always will, and hey, my chemistry grades are doing great, by the way."

The Yanks would often borrow DeeDee's car and head to Cummins Falls, just a few miles from campus. The falls were located on the beautiful Blackburn Fork State Scenic River. Several people had referred to it as "the best *dern* swimmin' hole in Tennessee." We never experienced the summer warmth of the water because we took our first dips in late fall. Craig and I skipped the swim trunks when we visited the falls.

It was a warm Saturday, and the thought of diving into the water of Cummins Falls sounded exhilarating.

"You want Schlitz or Stroh's at the falls?" I asked Craig, as I took stock of the mini fridge in our room that we told our parents was used for snacks, but we found it held exactly twenty-four bottles of beer.

"Figure it out bro. You're asking a boy from Philly if he wants Schlitz. Get your shit together, man. Schlitz is made in Philly. Gotta drink the home brew. How'd you get into college?"

My question had sent Craig into a state of hysterical hyperbole, and his red skin turned a shade redder, matching the Paulsboro wrestling tee shirt that I discovered was one of his all-time favorites.

"Okay, if that's what you want, Prince of Paulsboro. There are only three Schlitz left," I jabbed back rather smugly. "That leaves me, let me count, ah-h, twenty-one bottles of Stroh's."

We later dove into the sparkling, icy-clear water of the upper pool and came to the surface near the face of the wall.

"Man, that'll make your balls small," I yelled to Craig after surfacing.

"Mine are blue," he yelled back while he shook the water off his growing locks of black hair.

Gail and I would go to the waterfall evenings during the fall, when the area was free of people. We would talk loudly above the roar of the falls, lured into intimacy by the sound of falling water and the hypnotic, heavy sweetness of the honeysuckles. In our innocence, we talked of the simple things in life, about not needing much to make us happy. Living in the country was paramount for both of us.

Gail showed me how to remove the white blossom of the honeysuckle flower and suck out the few drops of sweet nectar from the long inner tube. We started out hot, with flames of desire that raged when we were together.

"Lay on top of me and let your hair cover my face," I asked her once in the silence of the mountains, away from the falls. "I wanna get lost in it."

The herbal scent of her hair in the outdoors was like a security blanket, letting us live in our own private world.

"Whisper you love me," she asked in her own whisper.

"I love you… I love you… I love you… forever."

Cummins Falls had been a little bit more than the best *dern* swimming hole in Tennessee for us.

Before we left for the holidays, Craig and I batted around at the Tech Café whether we were coming back after the holidays for winter quarter.

"I feel so out of place here, but meeting Gail has made all the difference," I told Craig as I dug into an order of greasy fries, disappointed that only generic, runny ketchup was served, and not Heinz.

"That's good for you, bro, but this place is a trip, a bad trip for me," he said, shaking his head in the hapless reality of our situation. "I've met Lilly, a girl of full Cherokee blood, and she told me how tough this place is for her. We are the only two Indians here that I know of. And I didn't tell you that I got a Dear John letter last week."

"Oh man. A DJ letter. That sucks. You should have told me. There is a lot to think about, bro. It would be crazy for me to change course for Montana now and leave Gail. Some flames burn a long time and some don't, but I feel ours will keep burning. I'm not leaving yet."

"Yeah, bro. You'd be crazy to leave the person who has made a difference in your life."

Tech was a suitcase college, lacking the vibrant atmosphere of activities on weekends and evenings that I'd been hoping for. It seemed that the Yankees never received the weekend evacuation notice. The food was strange, overcooked, salty, and fatty. I also had to learn to keep my buns straight. There was a large assortment of honey buns, sticky buns, and cinnamon buns to choose from. This food was a dramatic change from the whole-grain cereals I had eaten at home. Tech should have been called, "Tater Tot University," but I only made that remark while in the company of Yanks. Fresh fruit at breakfast was not part of the Tennessee diet.

The language was just as foreign sounding as Polish: "y'all this" and "y'all that" was how I was beginning to talk. Then there was the fact that a lot of the Southern guys definitely had an aversion to Yankees. Even in mild doses, this attitude eventually wore thin on all of us. The Southern honeyed, syrupy drawl was not the only initial trial of college life.

Clothing habits were strange as well. The male students were clad in lime-green leisure suits and accompanied by dates in dresses when they attended what I considered a very casual event—the Tech football games. And then there was the Homecoming Concert that featured the Allman Brothers Band, long before they were crowned the royalty of Southern rock.

Most Southern students had their consciousness raised to a higher level when Greg Allman belted out twenty two minutes of "Whipping Post", and they turned their backs on this new, muscular and bluesy rock. As the auditorium's outer walls seemed to flex and pulse with the music, it was ironic that Yankee students danced in the aisles while homegrown students bolted for the exits.

There was some comfort in knowing that we would all be together again after the Christmas holidays. Dane, a Vietnam vet who flew a medevac chopper and now lived in Nashville, gave all the Yanks a ride to the airport in his van the next day. Once inside the parking lot, he told us, "Wait one second, I got a little Christmas present to share with y'all."

Dane pulled out a torpedo shaped doobie of Maui Wowie that looked as round as my little finger. *Oh man, that's some serious laughing grass.* Dane fired the joint up, and we all smoked that reefer down to the smallest roach that we held with a surgical hemostat.

"Don't Bogart that joint you guys. Pass it back here," one of the Yanks yelled out, thinking he wouldn't get a toke.

He didn't need a toke. The van was full of dope smoke.

Chapter 8

Get it together, Loring. Stoned and slightly paranoid about meeting my parents, I thought I would blame my dilated pupils on the cigarette smoke in the rear of the cabin. That was partly true, but the joint, shared by the homeward-bound Yankees in the Nashville airport parking lot, didn't help either. It was after I landed that I took off on a high flight.

"I have been sending you a few extra dollars for haircuts," my father said, a small disappointed smile on his lips as he gave me a shoulder hug. "What happened there?"

"I contributed most of it to the Schlitz Taste Study that was being conducted on campus," I confessed, fearing that I had slurred and said the Shits Taste Study.

Always one to appreciate a cold Rolling Rock after work, my dad respected the honesty and humor in my reply and let the subject die for the moment as we all headed to baggage claim. It had been only three months, but I was not the same boy who had left that September. Not only was I taller, and my hair two inches longer, I was a little more experienced from having had religion all night long.

Upon arriving home, we all sat down to the scrumptious meal my mother had prepared.

"I hope you like this Polish ham, dear; it is smoked just right, I think," my mother said as she set out rye bread, Swiss cheese, homemade pickles, and all the condiments to build a "Welcome Home Sandwich."

"I'm really hungry, Mom, and could munch on anything you made. I sure missed your cooking."

Marke and Katie were filled in about college life, Craig, Southern food, and the language challenge. My mother finally got around to asking me the question I knew would come.

"Tell us about Gail. You speak so highly of her, and yet we don't know that much about her."

I'd been waiting for a good segue, and I was taken off guard by her direct question.

"Yeah, she's great," I told them. "I have her high school class picture in my suitcase. Wanna see it?"

By bedtime, Gail's smile had lit up our living room when my mother found a spot for her picture on an end table.

"Very pretty girl," my mother commented, and my father nodded his acceptance. I knew my parents approved of what I had told them about her, but there was a smidgeon of restraint in my father's reply.

"I'm sure happy for you, son. She does seem to be 'something different' from what you told us, but I'm concerned you may get distracted from your focus on education by such a serious relationship so quickly."

"All under control, Dad."

Despite his caution, he respected my right to make my own decisions and didn't try to micromanage me.

On one Saturday afternoon when I was a teenager, and I was cleaning the car for a date that night, my father came to me and spoke in his serious father-and-son voice, "Son, there are way too many miles on the car from last night to have just gone to the movies."

"Yeah, okay, Dad. I guess joyriding adds up."

"Don't drink *too* much joy, okay?" He stroked his lips with his thumb and forefinger and stood there with a pregnant pause, then hitched his pants up before moving on.

My joyriding was the forty-mile boogie down I-70 W to Charlie's Bar on the West Virginia line, where eighteen year olds could tank up on a bellyful of 3.2 beer. Once I knew that he knew, the rules had changed. I never drove to Charlie's again, but I did grab a ride with others.

Not one to shy away or back down from giving his opinion on major issues, or ask me to rethink a situation, he believed he had taught me the difference between right and wrong, and he trusted me to always do the right thing. Nevertheless, I found that when I was successful, I had listened to my father. When I failed, I had not listened to him enough.

My mother tried to boost my vitality after the fall diet of Southern cooking. She filled me up with some of her robust beef and barley soup; the boldness that my father testified to came from roasting the soup bones with the marrow.

There was also homemade cottage cheese, made from raw milk. Mom's bread made the most incredible "big guy" sharp cheese sandwiches. And, oh yes, the pie filled with enormous, chewy, monukka raisins was a family favorite. Her cooking was set apart by the fact that she never used sugar, always honey. She made sure I took my vitamins and saw to it that I had a pint of fresh carrot juice every day. We all loved the wonderful poppy seed and nut rolls she made for the holidays, and I made sure to eat my share at breakfast and before bed. The holidays could not pass without my grandmother making a roaster full of golubke, Polish stuffed cabbage rolls.

Good, homey smells and tastes in the kitchen, a Norway blue spruce from McPherson's Nursery in our living room, and lots of fresh white snow outside: Christmas was filled with all the sights, smells, and warmth that I remembered. *How many more Christmases would I have in Pennsylvania?* My Christmas present that year was a Sunbeam Shavemaster Shaver and Groomer. *Am I supposed to get a haircut and be a more well-groomed man?*

Chapter 9

I still surged with holiday spirit when classes resumed the second week in January. The New Year ushered in new friends, more rock and blues tunes from Craig, and a late Christmas gift from Gail that she delivered when I arrived.

"I made you two Christmas presents when I was home. You always complained about the crummy pillow in your room, so I made you one. Sweet dreams baby." I now had a navy blue pillow with my name elegantly stitched across the top and hers stitched on the back. There was a pine tree embroidered below my name. Under her name she had stitched a flower with many buds that were actually small peace signs. And then she gave me a red, white, and blue knitted scarf. "And this is something to spiff up Rob's army coat."

The crummy pillow jammed the trash chute that night.

Craig had brought back an enormous collection of great music after working during the holidays in a record factory in New Jersey.

"Check these tunes out, brother. We can open our own campus radio station," he laughed as he tuned me in to all the hit music he brought back. "Here's Bob Dylan, the new Eric Clapton, Creedence Clearwater, Steve Miller, and dig this, the new Jimi Hendrix."

The only problem was that we had more albums than the local radio station, but no stereo to play them on.

Lilly heard of our plight. She had a stereo but no albums, and being kindhearted and a kindred spirit to Craig, she loaned us her stereo for the year.

Once Craig put on *Electric Ladyland* by Jimi Hendrix, our mood was transformed; we felt we had everything we wanted and were connected to a much larger world than Tech.

That winter, it snowed only once in Cookeville, but it sure rained. Weekends were long, and there wasn't much going on, so Craig and I, along with the Hoosiers, played racquetball on Saturday mornings.

One Saturday after racquetball, we met this guy named Andy Landers from Maryville, a town just a few minutes from the UT campus. Andy was one big distillation of the state of Tennessee, a pure country boy with soup-bowl haircut and a love of the South. His imitation of Jerry Lee Lewis singing "Great Balls of Fire" while shaking like a rumba king was outrageous. He talked about nothing but "Big Orange Country" and Tennessee basketball. Andy would call a make-believe game extemporaneously with a broadcasting style that echoed John Ward, the voice of the Vols.

"The Vols, dressed in their home orange... inbound to Justus... Justus shoots... Give him two-o-o, as tempers flare under the boards," was typical Andy, recounting an exciting play from the most recent game. In the gospel according to Andy, Big Orange Country rented space in heaven, and the streets were virtually paved with gold.

Winter quarter at Tech also brought Tim Santos, a student who had transferred from Virginia Tech. Tim was a good-looking, well-mannered guy with wavy black hair. But he always seemed off center as he stood like a bobble-headed doll, staring into space. The only clothes he wore with his jeans were either an Ohio State University sweatshirt or T-shirt. If Andy Landers talked about the Volunteers of Tennessee ad nauseum, Tim talked only about the Ohio State Buckeyes. He literally wore us out on Ohio State until finally one day we christened him "OSU." He not only loved it, but he started to refer to himself in the third person: "OSU needs to go eat breakfast now." He was a mathematical engineering genius, but sometimes OSU made no sense.

In February, Craig and I decided to take the opportunity to go check out Mardi Gras in New Orleans, a six-hundred-mile trip from

Cookeville. We agreed that we might never be this close again, so we hatched a plan.

"Hey, OSU. How about you driving us all down to the Mardi Gras this weekend?" Craig asked him. "But I don't think that junker of yours will make it that far."

"You wanna bet!" OSU exuberantly replied. He had taken the bait.

The two Hoosiers wanted to go, too. This meant five good-sized guys were hoping to squeeze together and drive ten hours through Tennessee, Alabama, Mississippi, and Louisiana in a Volkswagen Beetle, with only enough room for the clothes on our backs. On Thursday, I told Gail about our plan to leave the next day.

"Have fun, Loring," she said, winking, "but remember, I don't have enough money to bail any of you guys out of jail."

"I wish you could come, but we don't have the room. I really feel lousy about leaving you behind, but don't worry about me, baby. We'll behave ourselves, and besides, I'll be with Craig."

"That makes me feel so much better, Loring," she said, lightly smacking the heel of her palm to her forehead and shaking her head. "You two together, I just don't know. And with OSU too! Ah-h-h-h."

"Oui, je suis encore parti le bayou! Laissez les bon temp rouler!"

Chapter 10

Typical Tennessee weather that time of year—lots of rain, fog, and mist—was forecast. Our Tech quintet brought a loaf of bread and a giant jar of Jiffy Peanut Butter with grape jelly swirled through it. None of us had known what to expect on this adventure as we had little money and no place to stay, but we expected to join one heck of a party.

Hunkered together with cramped legs, our little car had just fifty horsepower and took up to thirty seconds to reach interstate speed. It was a miserable ride. The windows inside the car fogged up because the little Volkswagen motor could not generate enough power to rid the interior of condensation. There was a very long stretch of highway between the Alabama and Mississippi line where dead, stinking, skunks were smashed in the middle of the road every couple of miles. Then there was a thump. We had a dead skunk wrapped around the car's suspension. It finally shook loose when we plowed through some large puddles crossing Lake Pontchartrain... and then there was a sign in Mandeville... New Orleans... 10 miles. Party time had arrived.

"We're kicking ass now," OSU cheered, rocking his torso front to back and side to side.

"OSU, what's going on?" Craig yelled out as we suddenly lost speed in the middle of heavy traffic. At the height of our excitement, the Volkswagen Bug had died. Dead. Kaput.

OSU had just enough speed to coast into a twenty-four-hour service station, which had several extremely large, red tow trucks parked in the lot. One attendant about our age, named Billy, came out as the car coasted off the highway into his parking lot.

"Let me take a look under that ho-o-o-d and run a few tests, boys," Billy said, scratching his scraggly beard. "See these *wharrs*, ain't no insulation on 'em. Yer distributor cap is cracked too. That's probably why y'all broke down. You boys need to get some sleep if y'all are goin' to party hard tomorrow. Y'all climb up into the cab of one of dem trucks and grab some shut-eye. While y'all sleeping, 'Midnight Auto Parts' is back in business."

Across the highway from the service station was a large junkyard with a fence around it. Billy knew where the Volkswagen junkers were located and he planned to climb the fence and strip the distributor cap and plug wire from the first one he came to.

Sleeping in a tow truck was a new experience, but the cab was large enough for me to stretch out completely, except the gearshift rubbed my back. I scrunched the army jacket into a makeshift pillow. There would be no partying that night.

A couple of hours later, a smiling Billy knocked on my window, while the VW idled smoothly.

"She sho is a good running piece of chit now, boys. Y'all think of Billy while y'all are partying and checkin' dat titty."

Dawn was breaking as we climbed back into the Bug while OSU gassed up. A local pulled up to the adjoining pump to refuel his old, rusted Ford pickup. He asked us where we were from, and we told him.

"Sorry, boys, Mardi Gras was last week," he replied with a straight face and a glare. "You boys might as well turn that Bug around and head on home. You drove all this way for nothing because there's no party here."

"I know this guy is jerking us around," I told the guys in a hushed voice. "I was an altar boy, and I know that Mardi Gras is over this coming Tuesday. I'm pretty familiar with the liturgical calendar, so don't listen to him."

OSU stared at me. "What the heck is a liturgical calendar?"

Tired of peanut butter, we decided to get a bite to eat and check out the city. However, OSU accidentally got onto another causeway going east, and we came upon a sign that read, "Welcome to Mississippi."

"I think OSU screwed up," OSU blurted out in his third person persona.

"C'mon OSU, get it together," Craig shouted out, getting a little tired of OSU being OSU.

Stomachs growled, and we all groaned about being back in Mississippi. We came up to a café near the town of Pass Christian just as its shutters and doors were swinging open.

Prying ourselves out of the car, with backs bent, we all headed into the empty diner and took a seat at the bar, where a wizened ex-Navy cook with a stained apron—and a large anchor tattooed on his left forearm—took one look at us and shook his head pitifully. "You boys look in rough shape." Our heads nodded in agreement. "I just fixed a batch of the right stuff to get y'all squared away," he said, wiping down the bar with a ratty dish towel.

He perfectly poured five drafts of cold beer into frosted beer glasses, with no foam spilling over. *Beer for breakfast?* The glasses looked like fish bowls on stems, with "Dixie" etched in green on the side. I didn't say a word, but let the beer foam lining my lips do all the talking.

We all had the same foamy smiles when we dug into steaming bowls of seafood gumbo the nautical wheeler put down for each of us. The gumbo was thick with chunks of catfish, crawfish, shrimp, and okra floating in a chocolate-brown, roux-based broth that was ladled on top of a scoop of hot rice. After he served our brew and gumbo, he caught our eyes and slid a shaker of earthy filé gumbo powder and a bottle of Crystal Hot Sauce down the bar. Every ache in our bodies vanished, and our drowsiness was replaced with newfound stamina and a lifelong love for seafood gumbo.

The upper eight blocks of Bourbon Street that ran towards toward Canal Street were full of bars, strip clubs, and restaurants; this area was the epicenter of partying during Mardi Gras... and our destination. Beer and wine were pouring openly and freely along Canal Street. Combat tactics were required to stay standing in the crowd. The most popular drink was Boone's Farm Apple Wine, and most everyone had a bottle of it except us. We decided not to take a sip from an unknown bottle because Boone's Farm didn't make people that goofy.

On Canal Street, a parade passed by, and Krewe float riders tossed strings of colorful beads and doubloons, and aluminum or wooden dollar-sized coins impressed with the Krewe logo. Mass hysteria ensued as people got on their knees, begging and pleading for "doubloons, doubloons!" to be thrown their way. Bourbon Street ladies flashed their bare breasts to entice the float riders to toss a coin to them, and it worked to perfection.

In the ensuing chaos, I became separated from the other guys. A necklace flew my way, and I grabbed it out of the air. And then another. My first doubloon landed short, and I lunged for it. Grabbing it came with the price of a spiked heel coming down hard on my hand.

Owwwww!

Down on my knees, I looked up to see the wearer of the shoe: a Catholic nun, dressed in full habit, but sporting a day-old beard. *Was this person dressed in costume—or was she truly a holy sister?* In doubt, I surrendered the doubloon.

Together again, we all staggered into a club and got a good glimpse of the action inside. Bare-breasted women with foil stars pasted on their nipples, wearing masks, body paint, and scanty costumes, danced on the bar in dizzying spins and twirls under the flashing kaleidoscope of strobe lights, while tinny speakers blasted out distorted rock tunes.

In the morning after a full night of revelry, we found we had just enough money to make it back to Cookeville, with a few extra bucks for food. Our impressive cache of doubloons carried no cash value but would be worth a lot more in memories.

Our first stop of the morning was at a diner where we were refused service because of our "Yankeeness."

"I really feel bad for y'all, I really do," one waitress told us as our breakfast never found its way to our table. "You boys take these doubloons that I got at yesterday's parade," she said, while trying to make amends for the owner's bias. "You can't eat them, but at least y'all will leave with a good memory."

Back at Tech, I sensed I had traveled back from another dimension of time and space. In eighteen hours, I had gone from seeing topless, young Cajun queens dancing in a feverish frenzy and shaking their boobs in my face, to requesting permission to see my girlfriend. All that glittered in New Orleans was not gold, and Mardi

Gras made me realize what a special woman Gail was, and how I wanted to honor that relationship in the future. Tech had left me and others feeling trapped in a place we had outgrown.

Chapter 11

I'*m sorry, Dave. I'm afraid I can't do that.*"
One Friday night, Gail and I went to see the movie *2001: A Space Odyssey*. Walking back to campus in the fresh, floral-scented spring air, I started talking like HAL, the computer. Gail howled, and I started to laugh so hard my face hurt. We walked on and I let go of HAL. However, in a moment the mood changed from one of hilarity to one of significance.

"So, have you decided what you're going to do about the ROTC scholarship you were offered?" she asked, while she tucked her long locks behind her ears, revealing the gold hoop earrings that hid beneath.

Before my Mardi Gras trip, my ROTC instructor, Captain James Maxwell, a two-tour Vietnam vet, had called me into his office and offered me a full scholarship for my undergraduate degree in exchange for six years of active duty as a commissioned officer upon graduation.

"Yeah, I thought about it a lot. The captain told me, 'I'm not just here to teach military science, I'm also looking to recruit leaders and I see leadership qualities in you.'"

"And then what did you say?" Gail asked almost breathless with excitement.

"I was speechless. No one else I know had a talk like that. Guys usually decide if they want that career, but I was selected by Captain Maxwell. The captain told me that he liked my command presence, my classroom savvy about tactics, and he reminded me that, with rank comes privilege. I told him I needed some time to think about it, and I had once thought of trying to be a Green Beret. After I heard his speech, I thought about the military once more in a different light."

Gail wanted to delve deeper, though, stopping our walk and putting her hands on my shoulder. It seemed to me that she had spent some time preparing to ask me her next question, but it still caught me completely off guard. She looked straight into my eyes, blue locking on blue.

"Loring, I know you really well, but do you know what causes those facial tics and body jerks? It doesn't matter to me at all, but do you know what causes them? Can I help you? I want to help you if I can. Is that why you're having trouble deciding on that scholarship?"

Taking a deep breath and collecting my thoughts, I wanted to tell her what I knew about these tics... and about some of the nightmares that went with them. Yes, there were facial tics, sometimes vocalizations, or a combination of these two, along with some body spasms as I got older. However, I found that while I could not completely control the facial tics, I could redirect my focus to my stomach, for example. Twitching my stomach was not as noticeable, but I could only sustain this redirection for not much longer than a class period. The tic had to surface somewhere. I was never diagnosed with anything besides tics and was not that sensitive about my involuntary movements. I never talked with my family about it, nor did they talk to me. Maybe my parents were still optimistic about me outgrowing them as some doctors claimed. Something about Gail's total acceptance gave me courage to finally open up.

"Well, I was an altar boy at age ten or so, and my parents got to see me from a distance as they sat in the pews of the church. They noticed my facial tics at home, but in the stillness of the church, when they saw me for twenty minutes uninterrupted, it raised their awareness to a higher level. They were concerned enough to take me in for a medical exam. There was a consensus among the doctors and even chiropractors that these were just childhood tics that I would outgrow. But I never did... yet."

"So there is nothing we can do about them, to help you?" she asked, moving her hands to cradle my face, soothing the spot of the now-vanished tic.

"Not that I know of. My mother feels an enormous amount of guilt over my tics. She thought she was doing everything to promote strong, healthy children—she raised us on organic foods, vitamins, and daily doses of fresh carrot juice—but now she wonders if that healthy lifestyle caused the tics and grunts."

"But your brother and sister don't have these tics," she questioned. "Or do they?"

"No, I don't think so, at least not yet," was my doubtful but hopeful reply. "By age ten or eleven, I knew something was different about me. I could not go more than ten seconds without making some form of movement or sound. At night before going to sleep, I would play an imaginary game in which I was captured by German soldiers and bound to a chair. If I made any sound or movement, I would be shot. Every night I tried to live a little longer, but the game always ended the same way. Whatever is causing this is still unknown."

"Oh, my God, Loring!"

"Gail, look, I think my personality disguises my issues. No doctors can help, and I am tired of listening to their wild-ass guesses. It's something I gotta live with. I guess we all are born with a box of rocks, and I don't want my box to weigh me down. So I've tried to rise above the narrow minded and just keep on truckin'. I know how people talk. Some days I wonder if my body will still twitch after I die," I said, appealing for some comic relief.

"Oh, Loring, stop that," she cried out, drawing me closer, burying my head in her hair.

Safe. Loved. Just as I was. She kissed me softly many times, and I believed her that tics would never be a problem between us.

"I never want to forget this moment and how you made me feel. I don't feel alone against the world."

Sometimes, I noticed my tics pushed some people away, but they brought us together.

Deep in my heart I knew Gail was the woman with whom I wanted to spend the rest of my life.

There could not be any further denial of my condition. Captain Maxwell deserved an answer. He did not know how I could cover up my involuntary tics for short times while in uniform, and he needed to know that I would never pass the army physical.

"Yes, Loring. You said you wanted to see me. Take a seat," Captain Maxwell offered, as the afternoon sun that streamed through the window reflected brightly off his two parallel, silver "captain bars."

"Yes sir. I wanted to tell you that I considered your scholarship offer, and although I appreciate this opportunity and your confidence in me, I have decided to decline."

Then faking a cough, I covered my mouth to hide a tic.

"I hope you are not letting Vietnam be the basis for your decision."

"No, sir."

"Vietnam is an ugly mess; I've been there. I know how this shit is messing with your generation, and you don't understand why we are involved. This war will not last forever, but the fact is that you could be called into a future conflict. I stand by my judgment in thinking that you would make a fine officer."

I was caught in a trap of my own setting. A few months earlier, Rob, a grunt G.I., had strongly advised me against ever setting foot in Vietnam. Captain Maxwell had just told me that Vietnam would not last forever, and I would make a fine officer. It didn't matter, as I had failed to tell Captain Maxwell the true reason for my declination. Once more I had waivered, just like I did with Mr. Stroble. I tried to disguise my tics, so I could be normal in other's eyes.

What were they? What caused them? What a mystery. There had been a time when I thought that military service and my Montana Dream could both be accomplished. Now, I had come to grips with the fact that I had not outgrown these tics, and they took away any chance of following in my Uncle Jim's footsteps. The path to my Montana Dream had just been cleared.

Chapter 12

Waves of students headed to the Carolina or Daytona white sand beaches for spring break. The sand in my shorts was the red, grinding dust from Clad Metals. Those two weeks with hardened, blue-collar steelworkers and millwrights who did the same job every day without complaining, with the same limited view of rollers, presses, and furnaces, kept me connected to my heritage. However, while I respected those men for their hard work, I knew I wanted a broader life.

Millwork motivated me to do well in college. It was the only way to make it to Montana one day, and to fulfill my dream of climbing towering peaks, hearing elk bugling, and feeling the hit of a trout on a dry fly. Feeling like a son of the pioneers. I still craved to live in a remote, new land, with new challenges and freedoms, and an opportunity to start a new generation of Walawanders in the West.

Spring. Such a wondrous season in Tennessee, when the flowering dogwoods lined the paved walkways. Forsythias busted forth in their yellow blooms. The taller redbud trees were the most attractive floral displays on campus, filled with pink-to-purplish flowers. Cardinals, robins, and bluebirds started each day with their glorious, chirping rhapsody of peeps and tweets. Mornings were cool, as the oppressive humidity of summer was absent.

However, that day during a physics lecture, I was introduced to the second law of thermodynamics. Entropy, viewed then as the law of disorder, left me believing that somewhere, at some moment in time, my life would change from order to one of disorder. It was a natural law, so it was bound to happen.

OSU started to act more and more strange, withdrawing from everyone and holing himself up in his room, never showering or changing clothes. At times he thought he was Mick Jagger of the Rolling Stones. OSU's father came and withdrew him from school, had his Bug sold for scrap, and took him back to Columbus.

We were freshmen in college and didn't understand the severity of the problems we were witnessing. How could his parents send him off to college needing help? OSU remained a mystery, as we never heard from him again.

Gail and I were done with classes by two p.m. on Tuesdays and Thursdays, and we tried to meet at our favorite bench to hang out and soak up the spring sun. One Thursday, I waited and waited for her in the courtyard, pacing around our bench, wondering where the heck she was. There was no reason to be alarmed. I assumed she might have needed some extra time with a professor after class or something like that. Finally, I returned to my dorm to get some reading done, planning to meet her after dinner.

Later that evening at the entrance to Murphy Hall, I was met outside by Catherine, one of Gail's friends, who seemed in panic.

"Loring, do you know about Gail?" she asked with a shudder.

"No, I don't. What's going on? She didn't show up this afternoon on the Oval."

"Shortly after lunch, Gail told me she felt funny, and her chest was hurting, and she wanted to go to the infirmary. The doctor called an ambulance, and she was rushed immediately to some hospital in Nashville."

"What!"

Catherine was too shaken to remember any further information, so I called Gail's parents in Detroit. Her father, Ed, answered the phone but didn't know much, except that Gail's mother, Barb, had already left for Nashville after being notified that Gail had been admitted to St. John's Hospital.

The hospital would not let me speak to her... She was sedated they told me. But right before hanging up, Barb got on the line.

"What's going on with Gail?" I asked. "How sick is she?"

"She has acute pericarditis. The doctors told me it was an inflammation of the heart lining."

"How serious is that?"

It was the memory of my red heart badge that crept back into my life. Heart trouble... at 19 years old... There was only one way for me to get to Nashville early Saturday. On Friday afternoon, I tracked DeeDee down at the Student Union having coffee with Rob.

"DeeDee, I got to get to Nashville in the morning. Gail is really sick with a heart problem."

Before I finished, DeeDee was already fumbling around in her oversized handbag, dumping the contents out, until her car keys finally appeared.

"Here you go, sweetie, and for God's sake, be careful," she said, giving me a big hug. "I hope your sick chick will be okay."

So did I.

Barb was nervously pacing the floor when I arrived. She hugged me. I held her hand. A hush fell over the nurse's station.

"Gail is heavily sedated and is in an oxygen tent. I have seen her but haven't talked with her."

"When do you think I can see her?" I asked. "Why is she heavily sedated?"

"I'm so sorry Loring, but the hospital is only allowing family members in to see her."

"No way."

I felt like I just got punched in the face. How could I have been turned down? The initial diagnosis was correct, and she was being treated for acute pericarditis with complications that involved too much fluid putting pressure on her heart and not allowing it to fill properly. Later that evening, Barb offered to pay for my room at the Andrew Johnson Hotel where she was staying.

Managing to sleep in fitful spurts and constantly interrupted by my rambling thoughts, I needed to be in motion. It was before dawn, and I could not take being motionless in bed another minute. The easiest relief from this anxiety I knew was to be alone and take a walk. Legs that were always the strongest part of my body were now rubbery, but they carried me out of the hotel and down dirty and empty Nashville back streets. *How could Johnny Cash know that*

there was something about a Sunday that makes a body feel alone?
He sang it. I felt it.

That's how it was for me, alone on an empty city sidewalk, unable to see the love of my life.

Persevering in my efforts to find peace and comfort that morning, I walked aimlessly, while my mind made me a prisoner of my own fears of the possibility of losing Gail. I kept walking until pausing in front of the first church I came to, not caring about the denomination. It was still early, but the front doors were open in preparation for services. The narthex was unlit, but votive candles near the altar flickered behind red glass holders. The wick of the votive candle, deeply embedded in the wax, refused to light... but then it burst into a blue, hot flame, seemingly helped by a divine hand. This had to be a good sign, even though my fragile faith had been shaken. I transcended to a familiar place and time of peace when I was a knight of the altar and the prisms of light were my shields. I prayed for Gail's healing and comfort, but I also prayed, maybe a little too selfishly I thought later, for my own desire for her to heal, so that she and I could be married one day. The vision that came to me was Gail dressed in white, illuminated by the morning light filtering through the stained glass of the Twelfth Station, healthy, happy, with her blue eyes lighting the world.

Back at the hotel, Gail's mother had called the hospital and was told she was in satisfactory condition, with little change overnight. I asked once more about seeing her.

Tell me the truth, Barb. Give it to me straight.

"I don't think so. The doctors are picky about letting only family in. I'll call you the minute there is a change in her condition," she promised.

We hugged, and I saw an emotional vacuum in her eyes that had to have come from the uncertainty of Gail's life.

Heading east on I-40, windows rolled down in Dee Dee's cruiser, I let the Tennessee springtime air cleanse my face and refresh my spirit. The sudden onset of Gail's sickness was not a burden but a test of spiritual strength for me. Perhaps I was naïve, but I failed to realize how sick she was. Sedated. Oxygen tent. Family only.

Back at the dorm, I flopped on to my bed and updated Craig on my emotional weekend.

"Aw, I didn't even get to see her. 'Family only' they said. I think she's sicker than what her mother told me. You know how it goes. They don't want you to worry."

"Take it easy my man, she is going to be okay. No worries," Craig replied, throwing me an extra pillow.

That was Craig at his best, always the prime minister of no worries.

Gail was released from the hospital after two weeks and returned to Michigan. Deciding to return to Michigan to teach, Ed had taken the family with him there just prior to Gail's illness. When she called one evening, she sounded wonderful but gave me some unsettling news.

"Guess what, Loring? My doctors in Detroit told me today that I have to take the summer and fall quarter off from school. I feel fine. I'm supposed to stay at home and take it easy for the next six months. Six months! I'll go stir-crazy, just reading and sewing new summer dresses. I miss you so much. I hope my doctor will allow me to walk to Elizabeth Park to watch the birds."

"We'll make it, okay. Detroit is less than three hours from my home, and I'll come all I can this summer, so just stay cool and listen to your doctor. Sew a black dress for me. I think you would look hot in a black dress."

It was now clear to me that she had been sicker than I thought. She wrote me nearly every day to stay connected. In one of my cards to her, I enclosed a dogwood flower pressed inside. She told me she cried when she received it. An everyday relationship had turned into a long-distance one almost overnight.

Craig and I spent many Friday nights talking about Gail's condition and our futures and our pasts, sometimes until the sun came up or the beer ran out. With Gail's return to college in doubt, I needed to refocus my direction.

"What do you think of Landers's idea about Big Orange Country?" Craig asked, looking at me as if I knew the answer. "UT sounds cool to me."

Andy Landers had cast a Big Orange spell over both of us. Montana was temporarily out of focus.

"I'm in bro. They have a world-class forestry school."

I needed to meet with Dr. Funk. Throughout the year, we had met several times, but it was always about course work. Dr. Funk had seen the low retention rate of Yankee boys over the years, and my meeting with him came as no surprise. It was hard not to feel a little guilty turning to him for personal counsel about transferring.

"Dr. Funk, do you think the University of Tennessee's forestry school would be a good fit for me?" I asked.

"Absolutely," Dr. Funk responded in such a way that revealed he had similar conversations before. "I happen to have the new UT catalog right here. Look through this, and we can go over the forestry curriculum sometime next week. I want you to know what to expect. The forestry program there is of high caliber, one of the best in the country."

"I only want the best Dr. Funk. Thanks."

There were some interesting facts about UT in Dr. Funk's catalog. UT was perennially ranked in the top one hundred of colleges and universities in the United States. There were over 40,000 students on the main campus in Knoxville, and they represented over one hundred countries. UT also had the distinction of being one of the oldest public universities in America, dating back to 1794. The more I read, the more I envisioned myself at UT the following year, in a leading forestry school with a huge cultural diversity of students. And, hey, their football team was not too bad either.

Craig and I agreed we had experienced a microcosm of the state at Tennessee Tech. If we went to Knoxville, there would be the Great Smoky Mountains, as well as wild and scenic rivers to float, like the Hiawassee, the French Broad, and the Nantahala. Many times I dreamed of the white-water rapids, and softly rolled the name "Nan---ta---ha---la" off my tongue. I craved more pine scent and running water in my life. And when Gail returned to Tech, we would be less than a hundred miles away from each other.

Understanding that I was seeking a bigger challenge and was handling the unknowns of Gail's condition in a mature way, my parents gave me thumbs-up on transferring. Knowing that I thrived on challenges, my dad continuously supported me in reaching for higher ground, once commenting that no moss grew under my feet. And none would, I assured him.

I packed my bags. *Easy Rider* rode into the trash can. Tater Tots were a bad gastronomic memory. However, a sweet kiss, with no gravy, awaited me in Detroit, and I planned on breaking every rule of social etiquette about public displays of affection.

Chapter 13

Bam! Bam! Bam! I was once again the Man from Clad. The press rang my ears as I punched out more soup pots and sauté pans at Clad that summer.

One Thursday, my mother came to me before I showered and asked how I was doing being back home after the freedom of college. It was evident that my thoughts were a million miles away, both in Montana and at UT, but my immediate need was to get out of town and head to Detroit. Missing Gail showed in my everyday demeanor, and my mother had easily diagnosed my heartache.

"Look dear, I know how hard it must be to be away from someone you love. You and Gail had a very tough spring. Why don't you make a plane reservation for this weekend and go see her?"

"Thank you, thank you."

Friday's round-trip flight to Detroit cost $28.00. I offered to pay half, but my father put the kibosh to that plan. He told me to keep my money as payment for all the grass I had cut. I planned to follow his instructions and have a good time.

On Saturday afternoon while walking through Elizabeth Park, Gail popped a question about a topic that we had never discussed.

"I'd like to try to go with you to church tomorrow and other Sundays you are here. I've never had a big church experience like you, and since I was sick, I would like to share attending church together. Sometimes I'm scared about what happened."

"Don't ever be scared, okay. I know faith can be confusing at times, but being sick tested yours. Just never doubt it. If in doubt, just recommit, that's the key. That was one of my first lessons from being an altar boy. I'll help you."

This was new ground for us to explore, and I wanted to make it easy for her.

"I see now why some thought you would be a priest when you were younger," she said, raising her hands up to my shoulders and looking deeper into my eyes than she had ever done before. "You sound like one now."

Hands on my shoulders. She's serious.

"Church is church to me. We all worship the same God. That's why I wear both a Christian cross and a beaded Native American prayer necklace."

"That's why I love you so much. Different doesn't describe you."

We attended a service at an Episcopalian church the next morning where the parishioners made a big fuss over us with their handshakes and hugs. I felt closer to her than ever before, and I sensed that her faith, which had been shaken, was now restored because of the joy that showed in her face. How could I have kept from singing?

Other trips that summer cooled my jets about flying. I rode my thumb once and got a ride with a kitchen appliance salesman who went a few miles out of his way and dropped me off at Gail's door.

Another trip was on a Greyhound bus. "Relax and leave the driving to us," was their motto. It was hard to relax on the four-hour ride as everyone had brought chicken dinners on board and threw the bones on the floor. At a stopover in Cleveland, I wanted to get off and thumb the last hour.

Summer ended, but there was time for one more jaunt to Detroit when Gail unveiled the black dress she had been working on all summer.

"We have to go out, and you gotta wear that dress," I pleaded.

She had sewn one groovy masterpiece, a long black dress that was splashed with different flower patterns that made it very summery.

"How about a movie and then maybe a walk by the river?" she asked me, holding the dress close to her body so I could envision it on her.

"Oh-h-h yeah."

The night ended, after we watched *Carnal Knowledge*, with a short walk by the Detroit River, but not before we came upon a rock band playing in a pavilion in a city park.

"I crave to dance," she implored, tossing back her hair and pulling my arms. "I feel good, and it'll be fun. My doctors said it was okay, so don't worry."

She wants to dance... I want something more intimate.

My summer ended with a beautiful, smiling, sweaty woman dancing in a black dress, tossing her curled locks in my face.

Chapter 14

"Can you believe this place, bro? Landers was right. I've never seen so much orange," Craig raved.

A waiter appeared at our table at Sam'n Andy's, a popular UT campus hangout. I held up my finger to Craig while I called out our order to our waiter.

"Two pitchers of Schlitz half and half, two glasses."

Craig and I chose not to be roommates, looking to experience new relationships, but we hooked up immediately after arriving at UT.

"How's your new roomie?" he asked with a cheeky smile.

"Good guy. His name's Albie. From Dover, Delaware. Not as handsome or as red as you though," I said with a straight face, trying to swell his head a little. "It's a Big Orange world here. Do you know I have to catch a bus to ride to the Ag campus where my forestry classes are? And my dorm is co-ed. Can you dig that? A hundred miles away at Tech, the girls are locked up at night. There's forty thousand students here, man."

Craig, wiping the foam from his lips after he downed his first glass of Schlitz, shook his head, his eyes now squinted in disappointment.

"Thought I broke you of ordering glasses... This place rocks. Classes tomorrow, and then a football game with Auburn on Saturday."

"Hey, you smell those hot hoagies? Ham and hot pepper cheese. You want one?"

"Cram that ham, bro. Make mine a Philly cheese steak."

Chapter 15

Well, if my finger count is correct, I count exactly one hundred students in this year's forestry class," said Dr. Barnett, our silver-haired silviculturist who was head of the Forestry Department, told us at orientation.

On that note, Dr. Barnett turned to the chalkboard and wrote the number ninety-nine and the number one. *Oh, that squeaking chalk. Turn the edge, man.*

"Now using higher math, even college students should figure this out," Dr. Barnett joked. "Ninety-nine men and one woman makes a hundred students, right?" and he wrote the number *100* and circled it several times. Then he extended a tree branch from the circle, and on one end he wrote the number ninety-seven and on the other end he wrote the number three. *Where's he going with this?* He looked at us and pointed a long finger to the number three. "This number, lady and gentlemen, is how many in this class will actually be employed as professional foresters." Then the finger went to ninety-seven. "And this is where the rest of you will be. Teachers, car salesmen, homebuilders, and auto mechanics."

He was kidding! Why admit one-hundred students? There seemed to be a big disconnect. The university took our money and would educate us in a field that had no jobs. *What new consciousness? No jobs?*

The class remained unfazed, as everyone only saw themselves in the circle of three. Dr. Barnett finished up with a brief overview of UT's rank in forestry schools in the country and wished us all luck in the future. *I need to get lucky.*

Two hours later, same location…

Dendrology 201. The study of trees. Dr. Edward Buckner. This was how the mimeographed syllabus read for my first forestry class at UT. Dendrology was the first class that kick-started my forestry education and was one that I anxiously wanted to sink my teeth into. Dendrology was taught by Dr. Buckner, who I had already met as my academic advisor. I freaked when we first met as he could have been Dr. Funk's twin brother. And like Dr. Funk, Dr. Buckner had that same avuncular quality that made my transition to a world-class program a little easier.

The class met three times a week, but one day was listed as a lab. Dr. Buckner explained that the labs were going to the Smokys each week to study one of the most ecologically diverse ecosystems in the world. College classes held in the Smoky Mountains! *Is he serious?*

"We will be looking at areas where the white oak thrives, and we'll see how hickories can flourish in moist bottomlands or drier upland sites. There will be a trip to Newfound Gap to view the 'ghost forest' of the dead and dying Fraser Fir, caused by a little bug called the balsam woolly adelgid. We will recognize the biological community and their physical environments. Class, come ready to explore, learn, and bring a big lunch."

One day a week hiking in the Smokys! How could I sit through organic chemistry when my mind thought of the mountains and rivers of my next trip to the Smokys?

Chapter 16

Public speaking was a required elective that quarter. Our class met on the top floor of the Humanities building, the tallest building on campus. It was here, after my first class, that I faced questions about my tics.

Professor Rosser, a rather tall, fiftyish woman whose once flaming-red hair had patches of gray sprouting along her temples, introduced herself and handed out the class syllabus. She wasted no time in introducing us to public speaking, one of the most important electives we would take, she emphasized. We were all to take a turn at her lectern and introduce ourselves, and then tell the class in five minutes or less a short history of our lives.

My turn came, and I was so ready to speak to the class, feeling that command presence that Captain Maxwell recognized surge within me. *I only have five minutes?* Words flowed off my tongue like the Tennessee River that was in view from the window. The class heard how I grew up in the smoldering coal mining towns of Pennsylvania, had a girlfriend in Detroit, was a forestry major, and looked forward to adventures in the Smokys, but the mountains of Montana were my ultimate destination after graduation. Getting all that out in five minutes left me speechless.

However, after class, Professor Rosser asked if she might have a moment with me.

"Loring, your extemporaneous speech captivated me with its passion and dreams, but may I ask you a personal question?" she asked with a caring concern.

I nodded that it would be fine, but I found this peculiar because I had never met Professor Rosser before that day and was startled to be asked a personal question.

"I could not help but notice that you twitched and grimaced during your presentation. At one time, you seemed gasping for air. Were you nervous giving your speech? Is this something I should be advised about?"

"No, no, it was nothing about being nervous. I've had these tics since childhood and no doctor has ever diagnosed them," I replied. "I'm sorry if I frightened you, but sometimes a tic can look scary to someone who doesn't know me. You don't have to be concerned about my well-being."

"So, you are okay with speaking in front of groups? Public speaking is public, and I wanted to clarify your condition and see if I could help if it was just nervousness."

In five years of college, Professor Rosser was the only instructor who had enough courage, or nerve, to ask what my tics were. And then I thought of my own lack of courage to tell Captain Maxwell why I declined his offer. Regret was a word I seldom used. When I didn't pursue my Eagle Scout rank was one regret. Failing to tell Captain Maxwell the facts was another.

Chapter 17

When my parents and Katie drove down for Parents Weekend at the end of October, I had fallen in love with the UT experience. I was proud to show them the campus, as my father just shook his head and whistled at the sights.

"You can get lost around here, son. Do you ride those orange and white buses?"

"Yeah," I laughed. "Every day. Let's all hop on one, and I can show you what it's like for me."

A bus pulled up just as it began to pour in buckets, as it never just drizzled in Knoxville that fall.

"Hop on, everybody."

The buses were always full, and now with the rain, there were no seats, so we had to stand, clinging to poles for support. It was an everyday event for me, but my parents wanted out at the next stop, the bookstore.

"Do they sell umbrellas there?" my mother asked, her hair dripping wet, as the rain began to ease.

She didn't know that very few students carried umbrellas. They were a pain to deal with on the buses, and walking the crowded sidewalks at class breaks, you had to watch your eyes. But Mom thought I needed one, and I wound up with the biggest orange and white umbrella in the bookstore.

Parents Weekend... Homecoming... Football... Smoky Mountains... Forestry classes... Craig. I had it all. And Gail got cleared to return to school in January. It was a large life, and I've never felt as large as I did then.

Chapter 18

Tennessee sunshine. I loved to soak it up. The last of the dogwoods had finished blooming. Students were leaving. Taxis honked. School was out for the summer. Lying on the grass outside my dorm, I waited for Gail to pick me up and drive me home. *She should be here by now.* Leaving UT for the summer and returning home to Clad was a bummer, and I thought how fast spring quarter had flown by. Summer in the Smoky Mountains or summer at Clad Metals? *Some choice.*

The spring rain and misty mountain mornings in the Smokys gave way to the peachy-orange color of the flame azaleas, and the showy white bouquets of rosebay rhododendron that bloomed along creeks were easy to fall in love with. The Smokys were an old mountain range, formed nearly 800 million years ago, and the dirt smelled just as old. My Montana Dream was still very much alive. This dream would take me to the Rocky Mountains, and they were formed 80 million years ago. I visualized the differences in my future, but fondly thought of my recent Tennessee adventures.

Gail had returned to Tech in January, and although we were only a hundred miles apart, the halcyon days we shared the year before were ancient history. With heavy course loads, we didn't have time to share each weekend. But she came back to school with a 1970 green Camaro, which made it easy for her to cruise to UT on alternating weekends.

"I know, you want to drive the Camaro," she always offered, while having me guess which hand her keys were in, only to find that she had slipped them into her purse.

I always accepted.

"Show me the Smokys," she asked on a visit during a warm Saturday in February. "You must know some cool places by now."

"Oh yeah. I'm getting to know the Park pretty good. I bought this book on hiking in the Smokys by Carson Brewer, and his knowledge of the mountain trails has really helped. We can try Greenbrier Cove today. I loved sitting on the banks of Porter's Creek and listening to the water fall over all the different-shaped boulders. It reminded me of Cummins Falls a lot, but you weren't there."

"Well, I'm here now."

We made more memories at Greenbrier Cove, which we agreed was more magical than Cummins Falls. It was during this visit that my Montana Dream butted heads with the fairy-tale adventures I experienced in the Smokys. *Would there be a clash of Titans?* Familiar, old mountains versus undiscovered new mountains. Rounded summits climbed, or craggy summits in wait. The East against the West. *Which side would Gail choose?*

She chose to arouse me out of my slumber in the grass.

"Wake up, Loring. We have ten hours on the road. Were you sleeping, or just daydreaming again?"

"I don't know. I think I was dreaming about you."

I was also good at sleeping.

Chapter 19

How was I to be a man in motion without wheels? What car could I afford? The answer was as close as my neighbor Larry's very used Volkswagen beetle, a car not much different than OSU's, right down to the faded paint and rusted body.

Larry wanted a hundred bucks for it, but my dad was reluctant to support me. Stemming from his strong union membership with the United Steel Workers of America, he had no love for a VW made in Germany. If it had been a beat up Ford Maverick, it would have been a different story.

My dad relented and offered to buy me a set of tires, one thing he never compromised on. He was right that the car wouldn't pass inspection because of a rusted hole near the fender that exceeded code, but Pennsylvania state car inspections were a rip-off for the most part. Larry bought a counterfeit sticker that would get me through the summer. I was able to cover the rust holes by pop riveting a piece of sheet metal and spreading Bondo over it, then sanding it. The finishing touch was buying two quarts of Rustoleum Candy Apple Red paint, and I brush painted the car. Presto! From fifty feet away, it looked like it just rolled out of the showroom. The good part was that round-trip to Detroit would cost four dollars for gas.

A month later...

"How are we ever going to get everyone a place to sleep here? You boys are going to have to give up your room," my mother told Marke and me in early July, as she was making plans for relatives to stay for my cousin Elaine's wedding. There would be no one staying in a hotel. Family stayed with family.

"No problem, Mom. I'm sure I can stay with Larry and Barb next door."

A Lithuanian wedding, complete with a polka band, traditional foods, and dancing, was only three weeks away, and excitement stirred the muggy air.

"Hey, Mom, do you think we can squeeze in one more person?"

"I think so, if Gail doesn't mind rooming with relatives."

My mother was way out front on the possibility of Gail attending.

"She won't mind at all. I can leave after work on the Friday, drive to Detroit and spend the night. We can be back here in the morning by eleven. The wedding's at five."

Gail was going to have to wear that black, flowered dress again. A year had passed since we danced near the Detroit River. Now I could look forward to her wearing it at a family wedding.

Never had my home buzzed with so much energy, happy people, or classic perfume. Gail fit right in and exchanged good-natured kidding with my father, who asked her to cut the grass of course, but the best one-liner came from my Aunt Helen: "Gail, would it be possible for me to borrow your hair for the day?"

My mother ready for the wedding.

My mother was simply stunning in a floor-length, tangerine-colored dress. She took a moment to put her arms around Gail and me and give us both a hug. My mother had placed a dab of Chanel No. 5, an eternal scent that embodies femininity, behind her right ear. Gail had on a delicate drop of her classic, floral-scented White Shoulders. I stood in the middle of the two sweetest smells and two biggest loves I had ever known, while my arms encircled both of them.

Take me to paradise, because I'm crazy in love here.

"You two look so happy together. I'm so glad you could make it, Gail," my mother said, as she oozed her sweetness over the both of us. Across the room, my Uncle Joe was crooning "That's Amore" in Italian, and we were going to a Lithuanian wedding, but it worked to perfection because everyone could feel it. Love was everywhere.

Later… at the wedding.

Elaine was gorgeous and smiling, standing at the altar with her new husband, David, surrounded by flowers, a priest, and two altar boys. The newlyweds turned to begin the recessional, and the church's pipe organ burst into Beethoven's "Ode to Joy." At this moment, the music moved me, but time stood still. Gail looked at me and squeezed my hand. I squeezed back. *Yes.* We shared the same wish, the same desire, and the same passion: "That will be us someday."

Later on the dance floor, my summer was about to end the same way it ended the year before. I would dance again with Gail in her black, flowered dress, not listening to a rock band along a twinkling river in Detroit, but dancing a foot-stomping polka at a small fire hall in Muse, Pennsylvania, a classic southwestern "coal patch" of a town.

Gail in her black dress.

Chapter 20

I'll be right there," I yelled from the kitchen of my off-campus house that I had rented for my junior year.

Who was knocking at my door on a Saturday afternoon? Opening the door, I was shocked to see my old roommate, Albie. The year before, Albie and I had been roommates at Morrill Hall, but both of us had moved off campus for our junior years. Albie was a good guy, but I never reached the depth of friendship with him that I had with Craig. Craig did not return to UT for his junior year and decided to work in a record factory in New Jersey.

"What's going on dude?" I asked Albie, while trying to sneak a look at what he was holding behind his back.

"Here, these are for you." Albie handed me a giant bouquet of fresh flowers, although they were a little wilted. "I picked these up from a wedding I worked this morning," he joked.

Albie was majoring in hotel administration and was working part time at the new Hyatt Regency in Knoxville.

What could bring Albie around with a bouquet of flowers after nearly a year apart?

As if he could hear my thoughts, Albie blurted out his mission, "I got a favor to ask of you."

"Whatcha need?"

"Well, you told me last year that you went to Mardi Gras with Craig in seventy one, and I wondered if you are tough, or crazy enough, to go again. My new roomie, Gary, said he would go if you were our escort. So, how about it, dude?"

It was the last week in February, only three weeks 'til finals and spring break.

"I don't know, Al. This is really a short notice. Mardi Gras is next week."

If I decided to go, it would again be in a Volkswagen Beetle—Albie's newer, blue, 1970 model. At first I was apprehensive about traveling with rookies, but I confirmed that I would meet Al on Friday, bayou-bound once again.

Albie was clueless on what to expect, but I loved travel. Adventuring had been a major component of my genetic toolkit, and it was hard to say no. I knew from experience how hard Mardi Gras on the cheap was on the body. Ten hours on the road, and it was just past dawn when I wriggled awake in the back seat and tried to work the kink out of my back.

"Let me out of here. I feel like I'm in a sardine can with no oil," I said. I never cared to be confined in tight places.

"I can't do anything until I find my glasses," a panicked Albie said.

Albie was frantic, struggling to find his wire-rim glasses that had fallen off the rearview mirror, and lay twisted on the floor. Outside, I stretched my back more, rubbed my eyes awake, and glimpsed a bakery across the street.

A cup of chicory-laced coffee brought us to attention, and a small indulgence of a fresh-baked beignet readied us for the day.

"We have to stick together along Canal Street because, once the crowds and parades start, we can get lost in a sea of altered humanity."

"No sweat," Gary said, but we became separated in the next ten minutes.

Three pretty, hip girls dressed in Tulane University sweatshirts found me alone, leaning on a Bourbon Street lamp post. They groaned at how I had gotten separated from Albie and Gary. For solace, they treated me to another Dixie beer.

One of them, Mandy, a girl of medium height and heavily dosed with patchouli oil, wore her dark hair in a long shag cut.

"Your hair looks like Jane Fonda's," I kidded.

"No protest from me," as she raised a closed fist with her left hand and hung her head. "You're funny. I think you owe me a Dixie."

Mandy offered me a jungle hammock on her outside balcony to crash for the night. Strip joints and more Dixie beer no longer interested me.

Miraculously, I found the car the next morning, but it was an hour later when my two missing comrades appeared, looking a little Dixie-worn. Albie literally hugged his car with a huge sigh of relief, his wire-rim glasses resting lopsided on his nose. He conceded that Mardi Gras had kicked his butt.

Dark, ominous clouds loomed overhead as Albie pulled into a Dixie gas station about three hours later. A cool rain started to fall when I opened a bag of barbecue potato chips while waiting for the car to fill. About two miles from the gas station, I noticed a small pup, just barely weaned, on the side of the road, with no homes in sight.

"Stop, Al," I barked. "That pup will probably get run over by some wild-ass kid in his daddy's pickup truck."

Albie pulled over, and I got out of the car and coaxed the pup to come to me. He was wet and shivering as I reached down to pick him up. There was no collar on him, but there was no denying that he was a pricy, purebred, black and gray German shorthaired pointer, a popular breed in the South used for hunting quail. Putting him inside my coat, I asked Albie to return to the Dixie station.

"Nope, nobody's asked about a dog," said the bony, old man behind the counter. "Been here all day."

Somehow, I felt responsible for that pup. *What's the right thing to do?*

"Let's go, Al. This dog's history in Mississippi. He's going to Tennessee. The way they run skunks over down here on a rainy night, I'm not sure this pup could make it to morning."

"He sure is a good-looking dog. What are you going to name him?" Gary asked, twisting around in the front seat and sounding somewhat envious of my new charge.

"Dixie, of course."

One more year in Tennessee little guy. Then you will be in Big Sky Country, and you will never miss Alabama, chiggers, ticks, or the Crimson Tide.

Chapter 21

Dixie was the first dog I ever had owned, and he adapted well to Knoxville. We walked and ran in the evenings along Northshore Boulevard and sometimes wrestled on the bed. The only problem was, I had just a little more than two weeks left in the winter quarter before I'd be going home for spring break, and I didn't know what I was going to do with him then. I was flying home, as my old Volkswagen Beetle, held together with Bondo and sheet-metal screws, was only trusty enough for campus commuting or a trek to Tech.

Two high school girls, Susan and Amy, lived next door to me. Amy, who had worn her hair in pigtails in middle school, was the youngest and liked to talk about college life when I was in my yard.

"In college, are you allowed to chew gum in class?" she asked.

"Amy, I could tell you some funny stories about gum chewing in high school, but yes, you can chew gum in college. Some guys even chew tobacco. By the way, I'm going home for spring break and don't know what to do with Dixie. Would you like to watch him for me?"

"I'll ask my dad if I can take care of him over at my house," she said. "He could play with our sheepdog, Maddy. Our yard is fenced, and he will have lots of room to run. You can just buy a big bag of Puppy Chow. I think Dad just came home from work, and I'll go ask him."

Amy came by later that evening and said her father had agreed. I went over and thanked him for taking Dixie. I got the feeling that he wasn't overly thrilled with the dog-sitting plan, but he couldn't say no to Amy.

Gail had come to Knoxville for a Cat Stevens concert that week, and I had scored amazing seats on the ground floor about twenty feet from center stage. It was a small concert, and the seats were just perfect, as they drew us close to Cat's spiritually enlightening music.

"I know he is going to play 'Peace Train'," she said, flashing a peace sign. "I can feel it." Gail believed "Peace Train" was a song with a breath of hope for all of humanity.

"Oh yeah, I'm sure you do, but I would rather be followed by a 'Moonshadow.'"

"Moonshadow?"

"Moonshadow."

We both laughed at this exchange of lyrics, and the music made us happy. However, the next morning, she left me with a mysterious air of uncertainty about when we would meet again. There was a certain aloofness within her that I had never experienced before. We had ridden the waves of her sickness through the low tides, and now I thought we were at high tide, sailing on smooth water. But maybe I wasn't sailing. Maybe I was grounded on a sandbar, bogged down by dreams that seemed important only to me.

Are we drifting apart, or is it simply her urgency to get back to Tech for morning classes?

We phoned each other often and spent a couple weekends together, but we both seemed busy in new directions. For me, there were available scuba-diving trips on Sundays to various Tennessee lakes. On Wednesdays, I tutored fourth, fifth, and sixth graders in reading at a predominantly black Baptist Church in Knoxville. On Saturday nights, I tended bar at the Foxey Lady, one of the hippest clubs on the Cumberland Strip. My forestry classes were demanding. Gail was trying to catch up on her course work, as she was still a sophomore in credit hours and I was a junior.

Gail liked the quieter, flatter Tech campus and made a circle of friends there. UT's pulse, hills, and kinetic energy were my gusto. She was always interested in hearing of my Montana Dream, but she was a pragmatist and I was a dreamer.

But... together for two and a half years, through sickness and in health, we still recalled my cousin Elaine's wedding, when we promised each other, "That will be us someday." There was one special conversation that I remember when Gail's eyes were focused on the future.

"My sister got married last summer right after she graduated from high school. I don't think we're ready to get married, but I kind of feel good that she is going to live in the country in west Tennessee with a guy she really loves. I never saw myself as a country girl until we moved from Michigan. It would be cool if we could find a place like that someday, with lots of trees and a creek."

"Well, you know me. I could be perfectly happy living in a small, country home with a couple of kids to cut the grass. But I think I would eventually plant lots of fruit trees around our home and get rid of the grass. West Tennessee doesn't have any mountains, and you know how I dream of moving to Montana."

"I think you've mentioned that once or twice."

"So, what do you say? Do you think you could live in Montana?"

"I could live just about anywhere with you once school is done, but one thing you have to know. My sister likes to ride horses way more than me. I like to hike. Deal?"

Chapter 22

During spring break, I punched the familiar time clock at Clad Metals. Jiggs, who had scheduled me for daylight shift again, welcomed me with his habit of morning histrionics. "How arrrrrrre we, Loring?"

Jiggs never changed his workday greeting for as long as I had worked at Clad Metals. He was a very short, intense Italian man who was jacked up on nicotine and caffeine and paced throughout the plant like a wild mouse. We loved him as he was not only a good boss, but our cheerleader when the ovens were hot and the flies dropped out of the air.

"Just fine, Jiggsy. I'm so happy to be here."

"I bet you arrrrrrrrre."

While other college students were at the beaches, I was back at Clad Metals, but I had had my Florida beach and scuba trip that December, and there was still sand in my ears.

A week later, I developed a sore throat, not just a normal sore throat, but one of intense fire and burning. I had never had a sore throat in my life. During lunch, it was too hard to swallow my cheese sandwich, and my throat pain intensified like someone had flicked a Bic lighter on it. After phoning our family doctor, Dr. Rittenhouse, his office assistant told me to come immediately for an exam.

Dr. Rittenhouse told me upon examination that I had a mild fever, my throat was very inflamed, and he was going to give me a shot of penicillin. He instructed me to gargle with warm salt water when I got home—and rest. I was only to go to work the next day if I wasn't feverish and my throat was better. It all seemed routine.

My mother had started a pot of chicken noodle soup for supper. I loved this soup because she used the Polish kluski noodles, wide egg noodles that did not fall apart and gave her soup an extra depth of flavor. Ah, the warm broth soothed my still burning throat at supper.

Supper finished, and upstairs in my bedroom, I sneaked a peek to make sure that my article on Smoke and Montana was still tucked behind the glass of my baby picture. Seven years had passed since I had stashed it away for safekeeping, and seeing the article once again was like taking a reality check on my slow-moving dream. Yes... it was still there, and so was my dream.

"Are you coming back home to work at Clad Metals this summer?" my mother asked while she put the dishes away.

"Did you forget? I won't be home this summer because I have my required courses to take at Ames Plantation, the UT Agriculture Experiment Station down in west Tennessee," I explained. "A forestry degree requires more credits than any other BS degree. After that, I have three straight quarters to complete to graduate next May. Cool, huh? I'm almost done with college."

"Where would you stay while you are there?" my mother questioned. "Do you have to cook, too?"

"No, no, Mom. There are sleeping quarters there and a cafeteria, too. We have one class all day for two weeks. Then we get another subject for two weeks. That's how it goes for eight weeks."

"Good gravy, son," my father interjected. "That is quite a schedule—and one way of getting out of cutting the grass around here."

Oh, yes. There was always grass to cut, and it was my father's greatest obsession to make sure one of his sons got it done. I still recall the two-stroke Lawn Boy mower as it cut the green grass... green... the color of life... the color of peace, and how I zipped along shirtless, jolted by the roar of the repulsion engine. The reward was how proud I was to have the lawn reflect the pride my father had in his home.

"Marke can handle it, Dad," I said, laughing. But underneath the laughter I felt remorse that I was always away, always on the move. I missed cousins' weddings and uncles' funerals. I missed Katie's brilliant piano recital at Heinz Hall in Pittsburgh. I missed flying opportunities with Marke, who became a licensed pilot at age eighteen. When I was home, it was heartbreaking to watch my grandmother keep her distance between us as she was so used to me being away. She feared the closer she got, the harder it would be for her when I left. "I think you should leave before the traffic picks up," was always her cue that she wanted to be alone.

I tried to square up my finances with my father and pay for some of my dive trip with my Clad Metals wages. He told me to keep my money and use it for spring expenses. His generosity hit hard. He went to work every day in a thankless job, without complaint, but was so proud to give his son every available opportunity to have a larger life than he did.

Chapter 23

There was a knock on my front door. It had to be my Dixie-sitter.

"Amy, I'll be right there," I yelled from my bedroom while I unloaded my suitcase.

Opening the door, I found Amy with a much larger Dixie. Dixie was so happy, jumping up on his hind legs to my chest to welcome me home.

"Wow, Amy, you did a good job," I told her, getting down on the floor and wrestling with Dixie.

"We had so much fun, Loring. He sure is a good dog. I think you owe my father for some extra Puppy Chow."

That was a small price for what Amy did for me.

Ahhh yeah, spring quarter once again in Tennessee; I walked to the UT Bookstore that week. *Winter's dead.* The dogwoods were in full bloom throughout the campus, and their white petals and faint scent mixed curiously with the bright pink flowers and floral fragrance of the redbud trees.

Tolstoy wrote that spring was a time of plans, and I refreshed mine. Deciding that I had fulfilled my quota of tutoring, I planned to give it up for the spring quarter. The thrill of floating some of Tennessee's and North Carolina's rivers—the French Broad, the Hiawassee, and the Nantahala—awaited. Hikes to Trillium Gap, Mount Leconte, and the Chimney Tops in the Smoky Mountains were first on my agenda. The lush flora and various fauna had mesmerized me in the past, and I looked forward to renewing that feeling. The outdoors were a good prescription for happiness and having Dixie made it great, but Gail would make it out of this world. Sometimes school got in the way of my outdoor adventures.

One evening in early April, my phone rang fairly late.

"Hello."

"Hi, Loring."

Gail's voice startled me.

"Oh, baby, it's good to hear your voice. I was ready for bed." The phone call revved up my heartbeat.

"Did I tell you that after three weeks, I finally got your hilarious postcard from Mardi Gras," she said affectionately. "When do I get to go? I think it's my turn, don't you? Aren't you tired of going with guys?"

"Always thinking of you, baby. Spent my last dime on that card. Sorry it took three weeks. You bet someday I'll take you to the Mardi Gras, but you can drive your Camaro. I'm through going in VW bugs, and with guys. And we only go with hotel reservations, no jungle hammocks for us. What's going on in Tech world these days? How you feeling?"

"Oh, school is going good, but I called because I want to see you really bad. I need to talk to you."

"Okay, I want to see you really bad, too, but can't we just talk?"

There was a slight pause, without a reply, and then I asked her again how she was feeling.

"I'm doing all right. My grades are good. I feel pretty good, really."

"Okay, how about Thursday? I have only one morning class, and then I'm done for the day. I can't make Friday because my forestry class is taking an overnight weekend field trip to get an on-site overview of several Appalachian strip mine reclamation projects."

"That will be cool," she said, sounding more upbeat that we could meet so soon.

What does she want to tell me? My Piscean psychic sixth sense alerted me that something had changed. Was the love we once knew now at an end? No woman was going to ask her boyfriend to drive a hundred miles to deliver a Dear John letter in person. Would we ever get married? Was my talk of Montana unsettling? *Cut the head noise, Loring.* Our relationship was special and maturing, and she must have had something good to tell me. When women had good

93

news, I found they always wanted to share it quickly. This thought brought temporary relief.

The east and west sections of Interstate 40 were not completed between Cookeville and Knoxville. Midway, about forty miles west of Knoxville and close to Crossville, the interstate ended, and westbound traffic was on temporary construction, elevated above the eastbound traffic. There was little traffic that day in either direction, so when I saw a green Camaro with a black vinyl roof heading east to Knoxville, I freaked. It sure looked like Gail's car.

"Oh no, it can't be her," I screamed out the window. Sticking my head farther out, I tried vainly to get one last look at the Camaro heading east. It was out of sight. Somewhere in the rushing wind that tumbled off the Cumberland Plateau, I thought I heard the sound of goodbye.

Just as I was within the city limits of Cookeville, a flashing red light appeared in my rearview mirror. A city cop had his hand out the window and signaled me to pull over. He got out of his patrol car, straightened his holster, sucked in his gut, and moseyed to my window.

"Dri-vuh's license and registration. Please get out of the car," he ordered. He looked at my license, then my face, and once more at my Pennsylvania driver's license.

"What makes you in such a gol' darn hurry this morning young'un?" he asked while hitching up his holster. "You a Tech student?'

"No, sir, I was a Tech student two years ago. Well, officer, uh, the truth is, uh, I have a woman waiting for me at Tech, and I'm hot to see her. You know what I'm saying."

"Here's what I'm sayin'. You're better off to her alive and hot, than dead and cold. Take it slow in Cookevul, ya hear? She'll keep. Trust me. They all do." And that was it.

I never got to knock on Gail's door as her roommate, Catherine, was just leaving.

"Oh my, Loring. Gail left about two hours ago to see you in Knoxvul. She didn't know you were coming here."

"I didn't know she was coming to Knoxville. I think I passed her car near Crossville. What a screwup. Is everything all right?"

"She didn't say anything wasn't. You're welcome to stay and wait for her," Catherine offered.

"Thanks, but I think I'll head back to Knoxville. I have an early field trip, and there is no telling when Gail will be back. Tell her I'll call her early next week."

It was a bummer not seeing Gail because of the miscommunication about the trip to Cookeville. *It was just a royal screw up. She'll keep.* Before I turned out the light, Dixie jumped onto my bed, and licked my face. His weren't the lips I really wanted.

Chapter 24

Sundays were always the day to call home. That morning I was achy and tired, but figured it was from a busy weekend and sleeping on the hard wooden floor of a high school gym on our field trip.

"Hey Mom, I got a ride home with Carrie, a grad student, for Easter, so I won't be flying. I want to be home for Easter, but I don't feel that swift. I hope I'm not catching a cold."

"Double up on your Vitamin C," she lectured in her mom vitamin voice.

That was my mother. She would never say, "Take some cold and flu medicine." Instead, she reminded me to double up on my Vitamin C.

Feeling sicker on Monday, I struggled to make it to class. By Tuesday, I had developed a low-grade fever and wasn't thinking clearly at times. Calling Gail was not a good idea because of my delusional state. She didn't call me either, and that was odd. Wednesday morning found me too sick to attend the last day of classes for the week or to drive to the student clinic. I called Sam, a fellow forestry major. Sam couldn't make it but said his wife, Karen, would be right over.

"You have all the classic signs of the common flu," the clinic doctor, who still looked wet behind the ears, told me. "I want you to rest, drink plenty of fluids, and use these rectal suppositories for the aches and fever."

Rectal suppositories. Groovy.

As sick as I was, I was relieved it was only the flu. Barely able to hold my head up while talking on the phone to my mother, I went straight to my bed and immediately fell into a deep slumber. Hours later, the urgent call of Amy's voice outside my door woke me.

"Come in," I moaned.

Amy found me under the covers, shaking with the chills.

"Loring, Dixie is barking his head off in his pen, and his water bowl is empty."

"Oh God!" I had forgotten about Dixie in my fevered state. "Amy, I'm really sick and supposed to stay in bed. Can you watch him for a day or two till I get better?"

"You do sound really sick. Sure, I'll watch him."

On Thursday, I thought I was getting over my flu; the fever was down and the suppositories helped with the aches, but I was still weak and spent the day in bed. Friday morning, Good Friday, the fever returned with a heated fury. There were no liquids that could quench my thirst, and I knew that I needed to see the doctor again. Unable to drive, I called Karen once more, hating to interrupt any Easter plans she may have had.

Because of the Easter holiday, the campus was deserted, and the infirmary was virtually empty. Slowly shuffling and wobbly at times, I used my right arm against the clinic wall for support. The same doctor was on duty.

"Doc, I'm so sick. I feel like I'm dying. I've been resting, but these aches and fever are getting worse," I struggled to tell him, hoping he would admit me to the hospital.

"Well, the flu can be pretty tough sometimes, even with a healthy, well-built guy like yourself. I'm still sticking with my previous diagnosis. These are textbook flu symptoms," he told me, handing me more suppositories to use for the fever and aches. "Rest," he said. "Rest."

Back at my house, I climbed back into bed, and noticed what a beautiful, warm, sunny day it was outside. But my body continued to get warmer on the inside. I drank more ice water and more juice, and climbed back into bed, chilled and shaking in the heat of the day.

For the next forty-eight hours, I was in a state of delirium. At times, I did not know where I was and could not recall if I had been to the doctor or needed to see a doctor. There were periods when I was really confused, unable to focus, and hallucinated. *What is going on?* In one fluctuating period of consciousness, I took my temperature. *Is it really 105?* Taking off all my clothes, I climbed into the cold tub in the bathroom. Lying in a tub without water was uncomfortable, but the coldness of the porcelain seemed to draw heat out of my body. My brain was a tangled mess, and I never thought of filling the tub with cold water.

Is it night or day? I have been so confused. Is that a telephone ringing? Where's that damn telephone? Where am I? I have no clothes on. Why am I so hot? Why?

Sunday morning. Easter. I lay sprawled across my bed, naked, and still burning up. The telephone was just inches from my face. *Ring, ring, ring. Ring, ring, ring.* Reaching for the phone receiver, I accidentally knocked the phone off the desk.

"Happy Easter, dear. How are you feeling?"

"Mom, I'm so sick." The receiver fell to the floor, and I lapsed once again into unconsciousness.

My mother took immediate action. Her son was sick. It was Easter morning, and she was five hundred miles away, but she found a way to save my life. Calling the University of Tennessee, she was connected to the Campus Security Office. The conversation, I later learned, went something like this:

"Good morning, UT Security, Archie Perkins speaking."

"Yes, good morning. My name is Mary Walawander, and I am calling about my son Loring. I know he is sick and needs help."

"Well, ma'am, I can probably say that he is a typical college student and got his nose wet last night and got too friendly with Jose Cuervo. I get calls like this all the time."

"No, no. His name is Loring Walawander, and he lives at 2119 Maplewood Drive. He is sick. Don't you understand? Can't you do anything to help him?"

"Look Mrs. Walawander, I'm sure he is just sleeping it off. Don't worry. Call him in an hour or two. Thank you, and Happy Easter."

My mother rose like a grizzly bear defending her cubs. She repeated the call. Same response. Relentless in her approach, and now heated with her pleas, she repeated the call for the third time.

Finally, Officer Perkins said, "You win, Mrs. Walawander. Any mother who would call three times on Easter morning has got my attention. I'll take a drive over and have your son call you."

Unconscious on my bed, I came partially awake when I heard men in my bedroom. Two men in uniform stood at the foot of my bed, the taller man shaking my leg and then propping me into a sitting position.

"Say, young fella, are you Loring Walawander?"

I had been unconscious ever since my mother had called, but now awake, I told him "Yes," in a dying voice.

"I'm Officer Perkins with UT Security. Your parents are worried about you."

"I'm sick," I answered, and fell backward onto the bed.

"Are there any drugs here in the house?" Officer Perkins asked me.

"No, no, no."

"Have you been using drugs or shooting drugs?"

"Nooooo man, I'm sick. Help me please."

"Okay, let's get you dressed. Your parents want you home, and I'm taking you to the airport."

Lying on the bed while the two officers dressed me, I had to hold on to Officer Perkin's arm as my head had violent spins. Round and round I went, like a spinning top, unable to focus.

I passed out on the way to the airport and remember Officer Perkins shaking me awake at the United entrance. Both officers supported me to the United Airlines ticket counter. Officer Perkins had let go of my arm, and I braced myself on the counter with my forearms to keep from falling over.

"I-I need a-a ticket on the-the Pittsburgh flight," I slurred to the ticket agent.

The ticket agent looked directly at Officer Perkins, "I'm sorry, but this young man is too sick to fly."

I fell to the floor—unconscious and just out of reach of Officer Perkins's extended arms.

Chapter 25

*B*eep... *beep... beep.* I heard it before I could see it. *Beep... beep.* I was so cold. My eyes wanted to open, but they seemed so heavy. I felt something coming out of my arms... tubes. Tubes were taped to my arm and wires to my chest. I shook from the cold. *Beep... beep. Where am I? What is that sound? The mattress is cold, the blanket is colder. Beep... beep.* Slowly my eyes started to open. I was in a green hospital room. I was connected to several monitors, each flashing red or green lines in wavy patterns. There was a bag dripping something into my left arm, and an oxygen tube in my nose.

My eyes, now open, wandered to the foot of the bed where I tried to focus my attention. There were about a half dozen people in the room, dressed in hooded, green surgical gowns. They all wore masks over their mouths and noses, allowing just enough room to see. *Who are those people?* I asked myself. The last two people on the right, the ones with bright blue eyes that overlooked their masks... they looked familiar. A surgical gown and mask provided a thin disguise for my father's nose and my mother's blue eyes.

My mother's hands were folded and head bowed in thankful prayer for my awakening.

"You had us worried, son," my father managed to get out between sniffing and holding back tears.

A doctor explained that I had just regained consciousness after nearly twenty-four hours. I was in isolation in a quarantined room at the University of Tennessee Memorial Research Hospital.

Dr. Allen, head of infectious diseases, spoke for the medical team, "Loring, you're a very sick boy, but I will give you a minute with your parents before we ask you some questions and run some tests. Right now, we are treating you for spinal meningitis, which is why you are quarantined. The cold mattress and cover are to bring your core body temperature down because of your high fever."

On one side of the bed, my father rubbed and stroked my hair, not caring how long it had grown. On the other side, my mother held my hand, staring with eyes full of answered prayers.

"When Officer Perkins called, we tried to make that afternoon United flight to Knoxville, but it was too late. Your mother and I loaded the car and drove through the night. Katie's with us, and she is in the waiting room."

"Thanks, Dad. I'm gonna be okay," I reassured him, unaware of the odds I was up against to survive. "They said I had the flu."

My parents were ushered out, and Dr. Allen—surrounded by interns and doctors with clipboards—started asking me questions in rapid-fire succession.

"Are you an intravenous drug user, shoot up, anything like that?" he asked.

"No way," I answered. *Why all the questions about drugs?*

"Loring, this is very important, so try to remember. Tell me about the past several weeks leading up to now. What activities were you involved in, where did you go, and what did you do? Stuff like that, okay?"

I went as far back as the trip to Mardi Gras. He again asked about drug use. Was he trying to trap me?

"Dr. Allen," I said, "I told you that I don't shoot drugs. How could I scuba dive on drugs?" Proceeding with my story, I described my sore throat and the shot of penicillin.

"Stop right there. When was that?" he asked, putting his pen to work.

"About the third week in March, I think," I said, but I was getting confused and feeling sluggish from the sedating effects of Valium.

But Dr. Allen was insistent and questioned me with urgency about my doctor visit and the penicillin shot.

Was I in a courtroom? I wasn't a doctor; what-out-of-the-ordinary circumstances was he probing for?

"I drank from a creek in the Smoky Mountains about three weeks ago."

"No, that's not relevant. Anything else?"

"I was playing with my dog, and got scratched by his paw," I remembered.

"No, that's not the cause of your illness. We are not absolutely sure about your diagnosis, but like I told your parents, we have to wait three days for the culture to grow to determine the cause of your infection. We lost a UT track-and-field athlete last week to spinal meningitis. It is important that you are quarantined to contain the disease from spreading, in case you test positive for spinal meningitis. You are showing the same symptoms. I'll order some new blood work and another chest X-ray. Hang in there, Loring," Dr. Allen said, patting my shoulder and handing his orders to an intern.

Later that afternoon when I returned from a chest X-ray, my first jolt of excruciating pain, about the intensity of an exploding grenade, blasted through my right thigh.

"Oh, Jesus-God, owwwww! Ah, ah!" I shrieked as I saw only black through my eyes.

My breaths were shallow and rapid as I screamed to high heaven, and I thought I was going to pass out from the pain. Everything was still black when I heard a nearby intern loudly order the nearest nurse, "Ten milligrams, Valium, IV, stat!" The Valium turned me into a marshmallow, but the cause of the pain had still not been diagnosed. For treatment, I was given a hot pack to hold on my thigh several times a day.

It was three days of quarantine before Dr. Allen informed my parents that I tested negative for spinal meningitis but tested positive for bacterial endocarditis, a staph infection in the bloodstream. The infection had attacked and damaged the aortic valve in my heart, and a brain scan showed some infection there, also.

Out of quarantine but still on the cooled mattress, I shivered day and night, but the fever never broke. My heart had become enlarged from the aortic insufficiency, so the powerful diuretic Lasix was prescribed to remove excess water and ease the stress on my heart. I had lost twenty pounds, and the pain in my right thigh had still not been diagnosed.

On my fourth day in the hospital, I was alone for a short time after lunch—no nurses, no doctors, and no exhausted parents. Now

I was clear and strong enough to make that overdue call to Gail and let her know I was going to be laid up for a spell. It had been two weeks since our failed meeting.

Catherine answered the phone, "Loring, Loring, I called your house all last week, but no one answered." She was almost hysterical. "Gail is sick again, and she was rushed to Nashville the day after you were in Cookeville. I've been trying to get ahold of you." It was the same conversation I had had with Catherine exactly two years earlier.

Why is Catherine always the designated harbinger of bad news?

"Is she back in St. John's Hospital?"

"Yes, she is. I'm sorry but I don't have anything else to tell you."

"All right, all right, I'll call the hospital. Try not to worry," I told Catherine, not revealing my own illness.

The hospital connected me with Gail's mother. She seemed to withdraw from any questions about Gail's condition.

"How are you doing, Loring? Ed and I have been thinking about you."

Thinking about me?

"Well, Barb, I'm in UT Hospital, fighting a serious staph infection that doctors say has damaged my heart."

"Oh no, that sounds serious," she cried. "Are your parents there?"

"Oh yeah, they have been here since Easter Sunday. I'm full of infection, and the doctors are trying to fight it and lower my fever with some special drugs they flew up from the infectious disease center in Atlanta." I paused. "When do you think I can speak with Gail, Barb?"

"Loring, Gail is very sick with her heart, too," she told me in a worried, far-off sounding voice. "She is unconscious and in an oxygen tent right now."

How could this be? Less than two weeks ago we had planned on seeing one another, only to miss our meeting as we passed each other on the road. Now, we were both in a hospital, fighting for our lives; our hearts that once beat so strongly for each other were each now beating against the odds to survive.

After the call, my afternoon nurse, Laurie, entered the room with my meds.

"Hey Laurie, what's the possibility of two twenty-one-year-olds both being in critical condition, with heart problems, at the same time?"

"Does Dr. Allen know about this?" she asked, while she plumped my pillow.

"No, I just found out."

"Well, he needs to know."

Within minutes, Dr. Allen and his legion of doctors were in my room, armed with notebooks and pens, and asked me what Nashville hospital Gail was in.

Later, Dr. Allen told my family he had contacted St. John's Hospital and spoken with Gail's doctor.

"What we have determined is that there is no correlation between Gail's illness and Loring's," he explained.

"Thanks, Dr. Allen," I told him, hoping that Gail's condition was not as dire as mine.

I closed my eyes and shook my drooping head, envisioning Gail, sedated, alone, in an oxygen tent.

Come on baby, you got to get better. Recommit. Recommit. Why am I never able to connect with Gail when she's sick? What had she wanted to tell me? What if she dies without telling me?

The doctors could not give my parents any timeline on my recovery. My life still could have gone either way, as a staph infection literally destroys the body's organs and functions. I overheard that my odds of survival were about three to five percent, but I was holding my own. The fever came down slightly, but as long as I had any fever, the staph was still present.

That weekend, I saw the sun shine outside my window. Spring was in high gear in Tennessee, and I was trying to survive it in low gear, a day at a time. That was my spring plan. Another day that passed was one day closer to getting out.

I spent more time thinking about my Montana Dream to distract me from the realities of hospital life and Gail's illness. I saw red-tailed hawks and eagles flying, and that lifted my spirits higher and higher along with it. I envisioned snowcapped peaks that fractured a big sky. I wanted to quench my fevered thirst by drinking a quart, maybe two quarts of melted glacial ice, water that was ten thousand years old. That was how strong my thirst was for surviving.

Tuesday. May first. A new month. Looking at my pillow freaked me out because my hair had started to fall out from the medication. The doctors had completed their morning rounds, and I was expecting my mother, father, and Katie to arrive soon, but they seemed to be running late that morning.

I was propped up in bed, reading, when my family, at the head of a group of solemn-looking doctors and nurses, walked to my bedside. Taking my hand, my mother clasped it between hers, her eyes moistening, then a solitary tear ran down her face. She looked into my eyes, "I'm sorry, dear. Gail passed away this morning."

"It's okay, Mom," I whispered to her, unable to find my voice or a breath.

Looking up into the blue sky outside my window, I knew our love story had ended. I collapsed back on to my pillow, breathless, my eyes squeezed shut and holding back a tear.

It's a beautiful day for her soul to fly...

I knew I was in higher hands, but maybe heaven wasn't ready for me. My prayer was simple, a prayer for life that echoed far off, on some Montana mountain.

The unexpected tragedy of Gail's death had taken the two of us to two different places in an instant. Returning to the Twelfth Station, I bathed in white light and dreamed of mountains. The white light was my armor. Nothing could hurt me; nothing could frighten me. This light had shown me the way in uncertain times.

I shed no tears that day in my hospital room. My grief was private and unique as the woman she was. My mind raced through the time I first saw her in the Tennessee sun with her eyes aglow, through our swims at Cummins Falls, and through lying side by side in the sunny outdoors as honeysuckle hung in the air. Night talks and day walks. Elaine's wedding, but not ours. Gone forever were those electric sapphire eyes. God had turned the power off. Gone was the scent of White Shoulders, now replaced with a more heavenly scent. Gone were the hikes to Greenbrier Cove and the nights dancing in Detroit with a beautiful woman in a black, flowered dress.

"Would you like for your father and me go to Detroit to attend Gail's funeral?" My mother's soothing words were barely audible later that evening, while she brushed the remaining loose strands of hair on my head.

"It's so hard for me to believe she's dead. I just talked to her. Oh God, I miss her, Mom. And it's only the first day."

"I know, dear. We don't know what God has in store for us on any day. Try to relax and always remember her as you last saw her. Time heals the biggest hurts."

As much as I would have liked to say yes to my parents attending the funeral, I also realized they were living out of a suitcase and were already stressed from being by my side throughout each day, never knowing how my condition could change.

"It's okay if you don't go Mom. Ed and Barb know what you and Dad have gone through. Can you send some flowers though? Gardenias if they have them. They were her favorite."

The days lagged on as I looked out my window, fighting back the urge to become the rock that felt no pain, or the island that never cried that Simon and Garfunkel sang about. No, I never cried, but yes, my love for Gail brought me pain. I was neither bitter nor angry about her death. My heart was enlarged from sickness, and now it had swelled even larger with heartache.

Decades have passed, and I still dream about her, more often than I would have ever thought. I savored every waking moment of remembering of what I came to call a "Gail Moment," and then rolled back to sleep in a state of bliss. The dreams came in gentle waves, except for one breaker that shook me from slumber early one morning. It was near the thirtieth anniversary of her death, and she appeared to me, her lower body in a cloud, and her long, beautiful hair how I remembered it, with the gentle wave at her shoulders. She held her hand out from a white gossamer shroud, "Come with me now, Loring."

"I can't come to you now," I told her in my dream before bolting straight up, shaking. I thought it was real life and not a dream, and I looked for her to stay with me. I didn't understand dreams, but I had a dream lover. *Are dreams supernatural communication or a means of divine intervention?* I never went on a vision quest to actively visit her spirit world, and yet she never stopped appearing. *Are dreams one-sided? Does her spirit form have a desire to visit me?* It was these dreams of Gail that reinforced my faith in a kingdom to come, and knowing that I would get the answer to why she had wanted to see me. These dream feelings were more evolved than when I was a teenager. After a dream, some men went to the local tavern and checked the dream book, searching for the three-digit number that closely paralleled their dream. The number and their bet was given to a bookie to play it for them, with hopes of parlaying their dreams to cash. Organized crime was not concerned what your dreams meant. I wanted to know.

My love for her didn't end with her death. I felt she returned to me to let me know that she was all right. I had no other way to reconcile her appearances in my dreams.

Twenty years passed before I visited Gail's family and visited her grave. Later that day I talked with Barb about Gail and us not connecting on what she wanted to talk to me about. Barb smiled, as only a mother who had lost a child could smile.

"I know why she wanted to see you," she confessed, but did not go further. "I have some pictures that I think you should have. Here is one of Gail taken just weeks after her twenty-first birthday."

I never pressed for the answer, preferring to let the conversation between mother and daughter remain private, and my wondering continued, and the pain stayed unresolved.

Chapter 26

After Gail's death, I had a tremendous amount of support from all the doctors and nurses at the hospital. Most nurses were around my age, and knowing of my loss, pampered me with longer back rubs or a late-night chats when I couldn't sleep. The nurses' gentle care helped ease my sorrow, and they instilled within me a belief in recovery.

One morning a nurse interrupted my window-gazing to ask how I was doing. I told her that most days I was doing okay, some days I felt like it was a bad dream, and then there were days I looked to my future and climbed the tallest mountain in Montana and pumped my fist to the sky in victory.

"Those are beautiful thoughts, Loring. You must remember one thing. Just because Gail died does not mean you are going to die. Got it?"

"Got it."

"Got what, dude?" came the booming voice that filled my room.

"Jimmy, how did you know I was here?"

Jimmy Segura, the six-foot-two, fighting-fit, and well-sculpted, All-American linebacker from the UT football team packed my doorway. Jimmy and a lot of other Vol football players came by the Foxey Lady on Saturday nights for chilled beers and hot coeds. There were plenty of both.

"Hey buddy, we miss you at the Foxey Lady. Please tell me tequila didn't do this to you," Jimmy said, joking. "I heard you were really sick, and you lost your girl too. Man, I'm sorry to hear that. She was really classy. The guys feel for you."

"Thanks, man. And no, it wasn't the tequila. I got sick a few weeks ago with this staph infection that ate away some of my aortic heart valve. I'm going to need surgery, but I don't know when. Gail died last week. I feel like one of your tackling dummies," I ribbed, trying to sound more solid than I felt.

"Hang in there, buddy. We'll be thinking of you. Remember, you are like me, a Vol for life, and that means a lot. You never, ever forget that."

I preferred short visits, and Jimmy sensed it was time to leave.

"I'll be looking for you on Sundays. Oh hey, would you sign my poster before you leave?"

"Sure."

In my room hung a popular, black-and-white poster of a cat hanging by his claws on a fence. "Hang in There, Baby," it said. I don't remember which nurse brought this poster to my room, but it had become a talking point in the hospital. People I didn't know would stop in and wish me well, and I would have them sign the poster.

My Aunt Virginia had driven over from Raleigh to assist my mother while my father was shuttling back and forth to Pennsylvania. Only two years previously, she had lost her young husband, Jim, quite suddenly. Jim was a career army sergeant stationed with the 82nd Airborne at Fort Bragg. It was his picture in uniform and jump gear that inspired me as a young boy. Aunt Virginia, a sturdy Catholic, had a solid faith that could handle anything that came her way. A short chat with her could turn into a long visit.

One morning Joyce Greenwood, a middle-aged nurse, brought in my morning medication. Aunt Virginia was in the hall and struck up a conversation with Joyce when she left the room. Within five minutes, Aunt Virginia reported back to us.

"Did y'all know that Joyce was from Paducah, Kentucky, and has a twin sister, Josephine, who is also a nurse, but is divorced with two children? I asked her if she was related to the Greenwoods in Fayetteville, and she was. My, my, what a small world."

This was typical Aunt Virginia, meeting strangers, engaging them in heartfelt conversation, and leaving them with a sense of a positive human bond when the surface of their souls were scratched by a stranger. I saw the power of reaching out to others, and how life could teach us priceless gems of evolvement, if we only looked, even from a hospitable bed.

Chapter 27

A month passed. The doctors had previously told me that I would probably need heart surgery at some point. My right thigh still continued to throb and ache, and warm packs were still my treatment option.

One night toward the end of May, I started to have a tickle in my throat. Then I started to cough intermittently. Then I started coughing frequently, until I was finally coughing nonstop. At first, I thought I was catching a cold, and I told my nurse about it. She didn't hesitate after hearing my cough, and called for Dr. Spiva, the intern on duty.

"What's going on?" he asked, putting his cold stethoscope to my chest. "Take a deep breath."

"Man, I can't stop coughing, and my throat is constantly tickling," I told him.

"Okay, I'm going to get you something for your cough." He examined my feet and ankles for swelling. Then, once again, he listened to my chest from the back and then from the front. He seemed overly concerned. The nurse returned with a syringe that she injected into my IV line.

"This should help your cough and allow you to get some sleep," Dr. Spiva told me in a comforting voice. "Let's get that oxygen mask back on," he said to the nurse, while he updated his notes of my condition.

I awoke to find Dr. Allen and his medical team, including a blurry-eyed Dr. Spiva, consulting with one another. Dr. Allen noticed that I was awake and asked, "How do you feel this morning?"

"I feel really good, Dr. Allen," I told him, in a mildly euphoric state.

"Well, I should hope so, Loring. We treated you with morphine last night because you were in pulmonary edema. That tickling in your throat was water that was accumulating in your lungs from your heart insufficiency. The morphine enlarged your veins, making it easier for you to breathe. I talked with your parents already. After the night you had last night, we have decided to move you to another hospital, one that specializes not only in infectious diseases, but also in heart surgery."

"Okay, when do you think that will be? In a week or two?"

"No, we hope to have you out of here before lunch."

"Before lunch?"

"I talked with your parents and we have three choices of where to send you: Birmingham, Dallas, or Pittsburgh," Dr. Allen continued.

"Pittsburgh!" I gasped. There was only one choice to consider, not three. I could be back in Pennsylvania by dinnertime. My parents could sleep in their own bed. My father would not have to eat grits. Pennsylvania, the state that I claimed had never let my spirit soar was now my only hope of recovery. Instant karma. Pittsburgh, with its holy trinity of iron, coal, and steel, also had one of the leading heart hospitals in the country—Presbyterian University, or Presby for short—and it was about to receive its most challenging medical case of the year.

The air ambulance had room for a nurse and my mother. This was my mother's first and only airplane ride. My father would have to fly to Pittsburgh on the afternoon United flight.

McGhee Tyson Airport was our destination, the same airport that a month before I had collapsed at. We wound our way over the tarmac to a red and white Beechcraft Twin Bonanza airplane, where the pilot, whose build resembled a long string bean, directed loading me to the hospital bed in the plane. My mother took a cramped seat on my left, and Laurie, the nurse selected to accompany me, was on my right, busy uncurling the oxygen tube and placing the mask on my face. Laurie was in her mid-twenties, very gifted, and had previously served a year on a hospital ship, the USS *Hope*. Laurie's

112

patient care was not only comforting but was among the best I had. The pilot completed his preflight checklist and looked back into the cabin with a reassuring smile, while he polished his aviator sunglasses. His headphones cackled with the voice from the tower.

"We're cleared for takeoff. Just a little over ninety minutes to Pittsburgh, folks," he told us.

Breathing the oxygen in slow and deep reminded me of scuba diving. My eyes closed until I heard the right prop fire to life. Then the left one fired. Now at full throttle, the cabin and gurney vibrated, the noise deafening.

"Don't worry, Mom," I said as I squeezed her hand. "You're sitting in first class you know."

She squeezed me back, and a faint smile cracked her lips but not enough to mask her fright.

Goodbye Big Orange Country. Cleared for takeoff, the Bonanza taxied down the runway, gained speed, and finally slipped the surly bonds of the red dirt of Tennessee.

Part 3

The American Chestnut (Castanea dentate)

This tree was once one of America's most valuable hardwoods, but the species has been virtually destroyed by an accidentally introduced Asian bark fungus (Cryphonectria parasitica). The chestnut blight of the early 1900s was responsible for killing over three billion chestnut trees. There is one American chestnut in Pennsylvania in the county of Columbia. It is a hardy, nut-producing tree. The wood of the chestnut is rated as very durable.

Chapter 28

I was an instant celebrity, and a swarm of a dozen doctors were buzzing around me at Presby's Emergency Entrance. There were Chinese doctors, hippie doctors with Dingo boots, and Indian doctors with turbans. Stethoscopes were put to my chest, my back, my neck, and even my right thigh. *Why's my case generating this type of response?* Orderlies relieved the drivers and—with Laurie on one side and my mother on the other—my gurney was wheeled to the elevator, the orderly pressing the button for Ward 93, the heart floor.

Exiting the elevator, I saw that my arrival had drawn even more doctors and staff. The head nurse approached Laurie to have her sign off on the exchange of the stack of medical files, reports, and X-rays. Laurie turned and lightly squeezed my left shoulder and gave one final tuck to my blanket.

"Get well, Loring," she said with a large, attractive smile of hope. "I expect a visit when you come back to UT. Promise me?"

"I'll be there, Laurie."

It was gut-wrenching to see her leave. The UT medical staff—who had kept me alive for the past five weeks—were now the stuff of memory. I was now in a world-class hospital, and my future was not only in higher hands, but also in the hands of some of the world's most gifted surgeons, doctors, and nurses. All was calm. I knew I was going to walk out of that hospital. I just knew it. I had a Montana dream to fulfill.

I had never lived in an aquarium before, but when I was moved to my new room, all that was missing was water and some tropical

115

fish. The room had four glass walls, leaving me in full view of everyone. IV lines with antibiotics—oxacillin and vancomycin—flowed again, now in different ratios. A small team of doctors came to examine me, each holding some of the medical records from UT. Leading the team was Dr. Donald Leon, chief cardiologist; he was assisted by Dr. Ralph Siewers, a surgeon; and two or three more doctors in infectious disease.

Dr. Siewers, a man in his mid-thirties, had the command presence that Captain Maxwell talked of.

"Loring, you are a sick boy, and you are going to be sicker before you get better. But you are going to *get* better, okay? Roger that."

"I'm going to walk out of here, Dr. Siewers," I answered, with invigorated hope and half a grin. "I promise you that."

"Good. Now, can you explain to us in detail, from the beginning, what your activities were from right after your Mardi Gras trip until the Easter Sunday when you were brought to UT hospital?"

"Again?"

"Yes, again. Please."

Telling the story over and over to each new doctor and nurse who treated me was monotonous, but I complied. This time, Dr. Siewers asked about my tics.

"How long have you had those facial twitches?" Dr. Siewers inquired, his pen at the ready.

"I don't know. They come and go in intensity, but they started about age eleven. Did they make me sick?"

"No, no. I don't see any correlation with tics and your infection. Do they trouble you?"

"Aw, just sometimes my jaw and neck will hurt from all the clenching and jerking, but that's about it."

My answer had just dented the surface, and it was another fib. Yes, the tics had worn me out physically and socially at times. I had just lost my biggest cheerleader, and thinking about tics, prisoner of war games, Captain Maxwell, and my feelings of exclusion seemed to be de minimus topics with which to beleaguer a renowned surgeon trying to save my life.

Dr. Siewers later returned to my room, alone, carrying a small tray with a long needle, a syringe, and some iodine swabs. "I want to have a look at that right leg."

"Am I going to lose it, doctor?"

"No, don't even think that, but you may have trouble playing basketball on it someday."

"I don't care about playing basketball, Dr. Siewers. I want to hike and climb mountains in Montana. How about that?"

It seemed that Dr. Siewers knew exactly what was going on and simply wanted to confirm his diagnosis. He swabbed my thigh with iodine, and, after putting on surgical gloves, he gave me a numbing shot, then inserted a long needle into my thigh and withdrew it, nodding his head in agreement with his own diagnosis.

"You're not going to lose your leg, Loring, but I will need an angiogram to take pictures of the extent of the damage in your thigh. The staph infection has eaten through an arterial wall, and blood is leaking into your thigh, causing what we call an aneurysm. When the clot breaks is when you go into orbit with the pain. You will need surgery to repair it, but let's wait till we get some pictures before anything else. Don't worry."

Other doctors worked through the night, delving into a medical challenge that tested the limits of their treatment skills. These doctors first rose to that challenge on my arrival by developing a new treatment plan, comprised of different dosing levels of the same antibiotics. There was one intern, Dr. Phil Phinney, who never moved from the table all night, rereading my case, line by line, as he propped his head in his hands. Dr. Phinney, with a bushel full of black, curly hair and a long moustache, bore a resemblance to Frank Zappa, the rock music innovator.

"Then call me Dr. Zap," he joked when I gave him my assessment.

The difference in care in a world-class hospital was startling. I had suffered excruciating, blackout pain in my right thigh for five weeks in a Tennessee hospital. I was given warm packs to hold against my thigh for relief, but they never helped. Dr. Siewers, in four hours after I arrived at Presby, confirmed an aneurysm requiring surgery. My initial fears soon abated when I saw these healthcare professionals in action. My doctors were pioneers in the fields of infectious disease and heart surgery, but my case had challenged the best brains.

In the morning, Dr. Leon briefed me and my parents on my status.

"After Loring arrived, we were considering immediate surgery. However, during the course of the evening and night, his vital signs stabilized. Dr. Siewers confirmed the aneurysm. There is no edema, and his temperature is now normal. There is no medical rationale to explain these events. We only adjusted the flow of his antibiotics and now would like to see him stay fever free for forty days to ensure that the infection is completely gone. Then we can look at heart surgery."

Dr. Leon could not explain my turnaround, but Dr. Leon did not know my will, or where my indomitable strength came from. I was eventually wheeled out of my fish-tank room to a semiprivate room on a Saturday morning. A nurse told me that I had two visitors.

Yeah, sure. Let them in.

My two visitors were Gail's parents, Ed and Barb, who had driven down from Detroit.

"Hey, Bub, how are you feeling?" asked Ed, showing his best game face, not letting me see any grief and heartache that he might have had.

Barb's beautiful, soulful face was etched with lines of grief, strain, and numbness that lingered a month after burying her daughter. She reached for my hand, shaking a little, but tried to smile. "How are you, Loring? We've been thinking about you."

Thinking of me?

"I think Barb and I are going to make our way to Virginia Beach," Ed said, relieving Barb for the moment. "A change of scenery will be good for us. We haven't been to the beach in years, and I always liked the soothing sound of the waves breaking. I heard that when men grow older, they yearn for the sea."

The exchange of small talk ended, and silence hung over all of us like a thick fog. We stared at one another, all wishing for that one word, that one phrase, that one miracle, that would take the pain away.

"I'm always going to miss her," I told them. "Gail was not a coincidence in my life, and I will be a better man for having loved her."

No other words could explain what the depth of her loss meant to me, and oh, how I wanted to rise above that cloud of pain into the sunshine, but it wasn't going to be that day.

"We know, Loring. You will always be in our thoughts," Barb said, leaning over to give me a hug.

The cloud finally opened up and released its burden of tears.

Chapter 29

After my leg surgery, I was finally allowed to walk on crutches or use a wheelchair on my own. I became a man in motion, wheeling down the floor creating havoc. There was a solarium at the end of the hall that provided me a welcome respite from lying in a sterile hospital room with "Hang In There, Baby" staring at me. My family found me there one morning, reading an article about the Shroud of Turin in *Argosy* magazine. *Everyone's smiling. I wonder why?*

Katie pranced forward and handed me three Polaroid pictures.

"Surprise!" she cried out with unbridled joy.

The pictures were taken in the front yard of my home, showing Katie playing with a dog.

"What?" I cried. "How can it be?"

The dog was Dixie, frolicking with Katie in the grass. Once I had left Tennessee, my father had arranged with Amy's father to send Dixie to Pittsburgh on Northwest Airlines. First, Amy got to enjoy Dixie, and now my sister took care of him. I looked forward to the day when I could enjoy Dixie, too, but I was happy beyond belief that my dog was out of Tennessee and in the caring hands of my sister. Dixie was now in Pennsylvania, and my connections to Tennessee were temporarily suspended.

"After looking at the aneurysm on the angiogram, and considering Loring's stable condition, I'm going to put him on the schedule for surgery tomorrow morning and get this fixed," Dr. Siewers stated that afternoon. "From what I see from the angiogram, there is quite a large blood clot in his thigh that we need to act on."

120

After surgery, Dr. Siewers entered the room to give his post-op report: "The surgery went very well. I removed a blood clot that was bigger than a grapefruit and repaired the artery. There is a six-inch incision and some drain tubes for now. You should be able to play basketball on that leg."

"Remember, I don't play basketball, Dr. Siewers."

"Oh, yes. Well, good enough to hike mountains someday. Where was it you wanted to move to? Wyoming?"

"No, Dr. Siewers. Montana."

Visitors poured in as news of my arrival at Presby got out. My uncles Frank, Pete, and Paul visited weekly. My uncle Tony, a more frequent visitor, remembered to bring his soap box and tell me war stories. And then there was Father Ben from our church. Father Ben had come to All Saints Polish National Catholic Church when I was fourteen and ready to retire my altar-boy cassock. A tall, ruggedly built man, and an avid outdoorsman, Father Ben was happy that I was planning to move to Montana, and he told me so on his first visit.

"Send me pictures when you get there," he requested. "I can only dream about how wonderful it must be, but you have such a beautiful dream, my son. I see a son in your life someday, Loring. He will be God's gift to you to enjoy Montana all the more."

I believed him.

Two different hospitals, nearly two months, and it was hard for me not to get a case of the Presby blues. The young nurses' sunburned faces, reddened by contrast with their starched white uniforms, reminded me of a life outside the hospital. I listened to their chatter about their mornings, or about a guy one met walking through Schenley Park the night before. Their tenderness and kindness went above and beyond, and I thought it contributed to my overall healing.

One such kindness was in a league all of its own. One morning before lunch, Head Nurse Jen came into my room.

"I'm busting you outta here," she whispered. "Slide into this wheelchair so I can fix your drip lines. Hang on!"

Jen wheeled me down the hall to the elevator and pressed the button for the ground floor. I had no idea what she had in mind, but

I was in a hospital gown, barefoot, being pushed outside by a good-looking blonde nurse in a starched white uniform and cap. *Is this legal? Is she serious?* I didn't care—and yes, she was serious.

The great escape was a success, and Jen pushed me down the sidewalk of Fifth Avenue in Oakland. The streets were filled with college students from Pitt University, doctors, businessmen, street musicians, and a few Hare Krishnas soliciting the crowd.

"I'm taking you to see my friend," Jen yelled over my shoulder.

After two months in hospitals, I found myself overstimulated by all the sounds and smells of the real world. We passed a bus stop where an idling bus was filling the morning air with noxious diesel fumes. A food cart with hot dogs and kielbasa smelled so wonderful. Horns honked. Jackhammers hammered. Police whistled, directing traffic.

Jen slowed her pace and pushed me through the door of a head shop. My nose, which had grown accustomed to the antiseptic hospital smell, came alive with the familiar, sweet smells of patchouli, sandalwood, and gardenia incense. One of my favorite rock tunes, "Layla" by Derek and the Dominos, had just finished its legendary piano exit. Peasant dresses hung from the ceiling, and glass bongs were precariously perched on a shelf. The smells and sounds reminded me of a college life that seemed a distant past from another world.

"Hey man, I'm Stew-ball. Can I play ya a tune?" a long-haired, bearded guy yelled down to me, looking past my physical condition and smiling at Jen as he stood on a short ladder stacking tie-dyed T-shirts with peace signs emblazoned on the front. "I see Jen broke you out," he said, laughing in her direction.

We shook hands, and I tried to choose a song. First, I thought about a kick-ass song, like "Street Fighting Man" by the Rolling Stones to ease those Presby blues, but then I changed my mind.

"Stew-ball, how about 'The Question' by the Moody Blues?"

"Man, that's not an everyday rocker," Stew-ball said, grinning. "That's a memory maker."

"Right on."

"The Question," slow and dreamy, was a song that Gail and I had listened to a lot, and it always made us feel spiritually connected. I allowed myself a chance to relive a precious memory as Stew-ball queued it up. This song was comprised of two parts, which I always found interesting. The first part dealt with questioning the Vietnam War with its pain, confusion, and fear. The second part was about a lost love. I often wondered if it was a foreshadowing of things to come. They sing of a land that I once lived in and a woman was waiting for me.

I was comforted by the transporting power of music because the song made me feel so good inside... remembering the tender moments with Gail.

"Thanks Stew, but we don't have time for a concert. I have to get my patient back before he's missed," Jen said, interrupting with an urgent tone in her voice, as she wheeled my chair into high gear.

Outside, raindrops had begun to fall from a darkened sky.

Chapter 30

The Fourth of July... picnics, barbecues, and cold beers. But I had none of that fun and had lost my appetite. I was tired. I grew a beard, feeling too worn out to shave or brush the remaining strands of hair on my head. These were not encouraging signs to the medical staff. Dr. Siewers came into my room and playfully tossed a wet washcloth at me. Then he chewed my butt.

"I told you that you were going to be sicker before you got better. I thought you wanted to walk out of here."

"I am."

Jen visited at the same time and encouraged me to eat more.

"Please try to eat something. I have some yogurt with strawberries. It's something new on the market that you might like to try."

"Don't worry, Jen. I'm not giving up. I'm drugged out. Is there a gym in this hospital, so I can work out?"

Dr. Siewers scratched his head and left the room.

A large number of parishioners had gathered at our church to hold a prayer vigil for me the previous evening. Father Ben came in the morning, not to talk about the great outdoors of Montana, but to administer Last Rites, also known as Extreme Unction or Anointing of the Sick. I was an altar boy, and I knew what Father Ben was doing as he prayed over me and anointed me with oil. Afterward, Father Ben held my hand, and he looked down at the boy he had once thought would become a priest. He closed his eyes, nodded his head, and squeezed a little tighter when I told him that I was going to walk out of Presby.

Wednesday, I was more tired than usual, and Dr. Leon scheduled a heart catheterization immediately.

Dr. Leon did not mince words to me or my family the following morning during rounds.

"After looking at the results from the heart catheterization, we have decided to do the heart surgery tomorrow morning."

That day would be Friday, July 13, 1973.

Stillness came to the room after Dr. Leon and the doctors exited. I had known this day would come, but now I had less than sixteen hours to think about it. I ate my lunch of liver and onions quietly, with my parents sitting at my side. At two o'clock, Dr. Leon returned, escorting a tall, sinewy, gray-haired doctor holding what appeared to be a small, clear case in his right hand.

"Loring, this is Dr. Bahnson."

Dr. Bahnson was the head of the University of Pittsburgh Medical School, and it was the heart transplant that he performed in 1968 that put Pittsburgh on the international stage.

"Loring, Henry Bahnson. I will be performing your surgery tomorrow."

I reached out, hardly believing that hands that better resembled an auto mechanic's would be making cuts into my damaged heart. Nurses later told me that when Dr. Bahnson had surgical gloves on, his hands and fingers looked longer, lithe and lean, and worked speedily in miraculous harmony.

Dr. Bahnson appeared to be a man on a mission, urgent in nature, with every minute measured. He showed me the contents of the sealed case, a Bjork-Shiley aortic valve prosthesis.

"This is what I will be suturing in to replace your damaged aortic valve."

The prosthetic valve appeared to be a circular ring with a small cage attached and a floating disc inside the cage. The cage was made of titanium.

"See the cage holding the disc?" he said, pointing one meaty finger. "It is one degree off from a perfect circle. This will allow the disc to be always rotating with every heartbeat and to be self-cleaning. Two-hundred-fifty-year half-life."

With another handshake, he pirouetted and left the room, the tails of his lab coat trying to catch up with him. This man who had scaled

Mount Everest and Mount McKinley was going to patch me up to climb Montana's mountaintops one day. Later, I discovered Dr. Siewers's life history. He had studied theology before turning to medicine and serving as a surgeon in Vietnam. Was it Karma that my two surgeons and I shared kindred spirits? It just had to be.

Later in the afternoon, Dr. Siewers visited.

"I will be assisting Dr. Bahnson in the morning. Are you nervous, Loring?"

"No, I don't think so."

The truth was that my fear lay under a thin veneer. I always had an inquiring mind, but I did not want to know the particulars of my surgery. I did not want to hear about the removal of my heart from my body while I was hooked to a heart-lung machine, or about how my chest would be sawed open, or about how bloody it would be.

"Is there anything you would like to know before the surgery?"

"Do you think I could have a cold beer with my father, Dr. Siewers?" I asked, half in jest.

"I don't see why not. One is not going to hurt you."

"Then I would like an Iron City."

Dinner was about to be served. *Will it be my last supper?* The last procedure of the day was a body shave that left me pink as a baby rabbit.

"Does the moustache have to go too?" I had asked my body barber.

"No, Dr. Siewers said you could keep it, and your eyebrows too," the head shaver told me without cracking a smile.

Back in the room, my parents and Katie clung to every minute before visiting hours were over.

Chapter 31

Wake up Loring. It's Friday, your surgery day. But first the enema," Anna called out.

Anna got my full attention when she said there would also be a second enema. After showering and shaving, I found a piece of hard candy, an Orange Twister, on the bathroom shelf.

"What is in your mouth?" Anna yelled. "Do you want to have your surgery postponed because of a penny piece of candy? Spit that out. Get in bed so I can start prepping."

"All right, stay cool."

"This one will start making you sleepy, and the second one is atropine, which will help your heart and decrease saliva during the surgery. Remember, when you wake up there will a large tube in your mouth and throat that will assist you in breathing until you are able to do so on your own. Don't freak out, okay?"

"All right, I think I got it. Don't freak out."

Orderlies rolled me onto a gurney that transported me to the operating room for the seven o'clock surgery. The OR was unnervingly quiet. The lights were low. Stainless-steel surgical instruments were laid out with practiced precision. A masked nurse approached me with an injection aimed for the port near my shoulder.

"Where is everybody?" I asked her.

"Don't worry about that. Everyone will be here shortly after scrubbing," she told me, softly and right into my ear.

Her words faded out, the room got dimmer, and I drifted away.

Near the end of the eight-hour surgery, I had an out-of-body experience. I hovered over my body and watched the interns close my incision, even though it would be nine hours before I awoke. This was my first memory after I awoke.

"Don't freak, okay?" The words echoed distantly through my head.

I tried to wake up, but my eyes were so heavy. The whooshing sound of the ventilator roused me gradually. I realized there was an exhaust pipe-size tube down my throat. I wanted to gag, I wanted to panic. I wanted it out. Sarah, the intensive care nurse, was at my side, smiling and stroking my forehead. I pointed to the tube and let her know I was in discomfort. She had a small pad of paper and a pen that she gave to me so I could scribble my questions.

When coming out? I wrote, and pointed to the tube.

"It's just past midnight and perhaps it can come out in the morning. It all depends on how you are doing."

Intensive care was chilly, and the lights were turned down low. Outside the entrance to the unit, my mother dozed in an older, wingback armchair, keeping a night vigil. Listening to the rhythmic ventilator helping my heart, I eventually fell back to sleep.

I stirred to the sounds of Dr. Bahnson, Dr. Leon, and several interns reviewing the notes from Sarah's night watch. Dr. Bahnson speed-read the notes, then put his stethoscope to his ears and bent over to listen to my heart. The look on his face relieved me.

"Would you like a listen of your new heart?"

I was scared to because, before surgery, I only had tics. Now, after surgery, I also clicked with a sound that was unsettling at first.

"Your valve sounds tremendous. There is no indication of leakage."

Waving my hand, I pointed to the tube.

"Out by noon. Just a little while longer and then you can be back on the floor by dinner time."

It felt like my stomach would be on the end of the tube when it was pulled. With the tube out and the ventilator off, I now heard my heartbeat without the aid of a stethoscope. The clicking was a new sound, and it reminded me of my own mortality.

There was no lying around after heart surgery. The expectation was to get up and move. I felt no pain, thanks to the anesthesia. The first time I got out of bed and stood, I froze in my tracks.

My chest was making grinding noises. I was coming apart.

"Your cartilage has not grown back together, yet. You are fine," my nurse said, laughing, then added, "You have six wire loops holding your chest together that will stay in you for life."

Color had returned to my face immediately after surgery. I was still on Lasix, and that kept me at least fifty pounds below my normal weight. By the second day, I needed morphine to control my pain. On Monday, Dr. "Zap" came to remove my chest tubes.

"Quick, look out the window, Loring."

With one swift move he had pulled one chest tube out, and then, with no hesitation, the other. The tubes were well up in my diaphragm, and I got squeamish when I saw how long they were.

"Oh my God, ah, ah, ah, ah."

"It doesn't hurt so badly if you don't look."

Dr. "Zap" put a stitch in each incision where the tubes had been.

"What do you think my life will be like once I'm outta here," I asked him while watching him stitch. "I mean, right now I can barely pick up the phone receiver to make a call. My chest is wired together. Will I ever be able to hold a small child or hike in the mountains?"

"My good man, you can expect to lead a normal life. This is how you feel now, but you will bounce back. You are young, and that is in your favor. I think the only limitation would be playing offensive tackle for the Pittsburgh Steelers."

By the beginning of the second week post-op, I asked Dr. Leon when he thought I could go home.

"Let's plan for Saturday."

In five days, I could be discharged. After four months in hospitals. My mother shopped for some new clothes for me to wear home because clothes from college hung like monk's robes on my skeletal frame. My waist had gone from a size 34 to a size 28.

Four days. Three days. Two days. Saturday. I looked longingly at the new clothes that hung in my room, so ready to give up the hospital gown. But my hopes were squashed when Dr. Leon came into the room.

"I'm sorry, Loring, but one of your lab reports was a little off. We are going to keep you at least another day."

Sunday morning dawned with high expectations. My new Levis and yellow-checkered shirt hung in the closet and increased my anxiety to leave. *Am I going home today or would another lab result be out of the level of tolerance?*

One more shower. One more shave. One more Presby breakfast. My parents and Katie arrived early, and we all sat in great anticipation, waiting for Dr. Leon to give us the thumbs-up when he entered the room.

"Good morning, everyone. Are you ready to go home, Loring?"

"That would be great."

"Let's get you dressed, and then I will discuss your discharge instructions and medications with you and your parents."

I remembered feeling as if I had just finished climbing the world's highest mountain. Some days were three steps up, and the next were two steps back. The Red Heart trail crossed paths of pain and many turbulent rivers on an uncertain route to the summit that was shrouded in clouds of uncertainty. At times the air was rare, and I needed oxygen. My Guide was very old, all knowing, all powerful, and ever present. While along the trail, he had never left me in a place that I could not handle. I had fought the fight of my life against great odds and was going to walk out of Presby a little thinner, a little frailer, a little scarred, but thankful for answered prayers for the gift of life, even as a vision of a snowcapped peak and a big blue sky came to mind. *I have a little hitch in my get along, Smoke, but I am coming to Montana. Trust me.*

The image that looked back at me from the bathroom mirror was that of a battle-tested, stitched-up warrior. I wore new Levis and a yellow-and-white checkered shirt—long sleeved—to hide the bruises and incisions on my arms. Gone was the gray hospital gown, which now lay rumpled on the floor. My new clothes seemed to fit well, but my pair of Jockey briefs felt uncomfortable, tight and confining, so I took them off. Only after I kicked off my slippers and slid into my comfortable, old boots was I ready for the world outside of Presby.

I took baby steps at first, leaving my room and walking with a hunched back that resembled an early form of *Homo erectus*. I took one last look at the surroundings and shivered away the memories of the past two months.

I felt like a stranger in my own skin. My mother had already removed "Hang in There, Baby" from the wall. The world outside this room frightened me. I needed to slow down.

Why is there a wheelchair waiting for me at the nurses' station? Nurses, doctors, my parents, and Katie were all smiling and cheering as I strode toward them. Gentle hugs and handshakes came from everyone, but then everything froze to a halt as I approached the wheelchair that Jen was making ready.

"Have a seat, Loring. Your chariot awaits."

I was never an argumentative man and avoided conflict if I could, but I refused to sit in that wheelchair.

"You can push that wheelchair away. I'm walking out of this hospital."

"I'm sorry, Loring, but this is a hospital rule," Jen explained, hoping I would comply without causing a scene.

"I'm sorry, too, Jen, but I'm walking out of this hospital. You can push that wheelchair behind me if you want."

I understood the hospital's view. They were responsible for me until I stepped off the curb into the family car, but I also had a personal promise that I'd made to myself, and I was not backing down.

Smiles returned as I started down the hall, my family flanking me while several nurses pushed a wheelchair behind me, making up the rear guard as we slowly made our exit.

I wished for a pair of sunglasses, not only for the sun that bore down on me like a blistering blanket, but also to hide the tear or two that broke loose in my realization that I had just walked out of Presby.

I stood on the curb while my father brought the car around. Jen pushed my Stew-ball wheelchair away. I gave my last hugs to the nurses before they helped me into the front seat of our Caprice. With Katie and my mother in the back seat, my father pulled away from

Presby and gave a one-blast horn salute, while I threw a kiss out the window.

Exultation turned to fright in the first minute as my father merged into Pittsburgh traffic.

"Slow down, Dad," I shrieked.

Although my father was a very safe driver, every oncoming car felt like a ballistic missile zeroed in to wipe us out. There were no nurses or doctors within reach if we were hit. I was no longer tethered to Presby's lifeline, and it was frightening.

"It's okay, dear," my mother said, trying to calm me from the back. "Your father is a good driver."

"I know, but I'm not doing well as a passenger."

My father took it all in stride and did his best to still my fears. He exited the parkway and took an alternate route home. The farther I got from Presby, the more scared I felt, until we finally reached a rural area outside the city. We passed Portman's Farm where fresh corn was being hauled in from the field and the smell of fresh-cut hay filled the car. I finally started to relax in the comfortable surroundings of cornfields I once hunted in. Just ahead, I saw the old, weathered barn at the top of the hill, "Chew Mail Pouch Tobacco" painted on the side, and we made our final turn onto County Line Road.

Only one more mile, only one more mile, thank God.

I saw my Gram out in the yard, restless for our arrival. Marke was with her, cutting the grass on the front lawn. Our driveway sloped down, so I waited for Marke and my father to help me out of the car.

"Lean on me, brother," Marke said before I attempted to walk.

I took four or five short steps before I was knocked off my feet by a charging Dixie, the Wonder Dog, who had jumped high onto my chest with excitement.

"Down, boy," I gasped, scared I had just taken a direct shot to my chest.

Dixie had knocked the wind out of me, and as much as I wanted to play, I knew I needed to rest. Katie settled Dixie down while Marke and my father helped me to the house.

My parents had moved my bed downstairs and set up a bedroom in the den for convenience and ease. I wanted to slow down, slow my breathing, and just rest.

Standing at the window with my arms resting on the glass, I watched Marke finish mowing while my gram returned to her lawn chair by the spruce tree. I had traveled a long, winding road from that dreadful Easter morning in Knoxville, but now I was safe in the arms of a loving family, in a home on a beautiful country road.

I stared more. Was this real? Peace had come to me. That felt weird. It was a Sunday afternoon and not many cars passed the house, but I saw the old, white Ford pickup driven by Ralph Williams speeding by Nancy's house, a stone's throw away.

My father had constantly complained, "That Williams kid always drives like his pants are on fire."

Dixie stood on the edge of the road, looking down into our yard. *Does he notice me in the window?*

In the next moment, the Williams kid flew around the turn in front of Nancy's house and headed straight for Dixie! Dixie was hit so hard that he became airborne and landed in a broken, bloodied heap a few feet away in our yard.

Katie and my father ran to his side, but there was nothing they could do.

"No, no, God no!" I screamed from inside the room. There was no peace. Williams, you are such a flaming asshole.

I could have been angered by the loss of Gail, followed by the loss of Dixie. I wasn't sure if I felt anger as I seemed to be mostly numb. *Is my anger suppressed because of a drug?* I heard the rapid clicking of my heart valve break the silence in the room. But if I chose to be consumed by anger, I could have lost hope. *Who am I supposed to be angry with? God? That wild assed son of a bitch?* I found anger to be a most uncomfortable feeling, even more so after I had received the gift of life. But in that moment, in my skeletonized frame and wired together chest, I still wanted to go down to Ralph Williams's house and kick his ass, country style. He never even stopped to apologize.

What reimbursement was due me for these losses? Could I have bought my way out of these tragedies? I found that maintaining self-control was a more powerful weapon. Anger would only promote more anger. It would be best to let it go.

The Boy Scout Oath served as an early template in how to lead my life—to keep myself physically fit, mentally awake, and morally straight. My faith said to trust in God to reveal the good in all things, but I found I had a hard time coming to terms with this. Bitterness had knocked on my healing heart, but I would not let it enter. I had suffered, but many had suffered more and wound up with less. I had a wonderful family and no restrictions on pursuing my Montana Dream. I could not answer why I had such early suffering in my life, but I resolved that my suffering would not make me bitter, but would make me better.

Anguished and tormented, I saw my father wheel Dixie in a wheelbarrow down to the bottom of our property. In the roasting July heat and humidity, he had stripped down to a sleeveless T-shirt and tied a wet, red bandana around his head to chill off before digging Dixie's grave in the cool, clay dirt under the shade of a solitary black locust tree.

My chest still physically hurt from Dixie jumping on me, but now the hurt was lodged deeper within. My family had invested love and money in bringing Dixie home for me, and I had him for only a moment. Any connections to both my Tennessee loves were now buried. *Do I ever want to go back there?*

Chapter 32

My life's rich wheeled past of traveling in Volkswagen Beetles continued with Marke's brand new model. It was orange, but not Big Orange. He was the family's transportation manager, shuttling me back and forth to Presby for biweekly checkups and blood tests.

Marke and I had never been extremely close. Some things we had in common—the desire to help people, the interest in learning new things and taking on projects we had no experience in. We both found enjoyment in carpentry, gardening, and cooking. But our dreams in life were different. I wanted to head to Montana, forge a path in a new field, plant new roots. Marke's ambitions were closer to home. He was drawn to the familiar and heeded the pull of family and consistency. I was meant to climb mountains, and Marke was born to fly over them. Still, we were brothers, and we loved each other. That brought us closer together when I needed him most.

He and Nancy took me to Baskin-Robbins every night after dinner, and I looked forward to a double scoop of the new flavor… daiquiri ice. These little jaunts slowly initiated me back into the real world outside of the hospital. One night on the way home from Baskin-Robbins, Marke pulled into Clad Metals, where he worked full time. It was lunch break, and the crew were all outside carrying on with their usual rendition of the working man's blues and how stupid the managers were. When I got out of the car, there was a lot of cheering from the guys, but in genuine blue-collar fashion, Jerry, the plant's biggest wisecracker, in between bites of his baloney sandwich, hooted, "Hey, Loring, we need someone on the skeleton crew tonight." That was really funny, and it was the hardest I had laughed in a very long time, hard enough to hurt in my chest.

A few of the nurses from Presby started phoning my home. Each asked if I would like to get out of the house some nights. First was Liz, a cool redhead who called one afternoon.

"Hey Loring, are you up for a Pirates doubleheader against the Mets tomorrow? Seaver and Koosman pitching for the Mets. I can pick you up and take you home, too."

"Yeah, that sounds great, Liz. I'd love to watch the Bucs win a twin bill."

Five days later, Robin, the nurse with the warmest hands, rang me up.

"Hi Loring, how would you like to go see the rerelease of Franco Zeffirelli's *Romeo and Juliet?* I missed it a few years ago. Would you like me to pick you up?"

Romeo and Juliet? How fitting.

"Sure, I missed it back in 1968, too. It'll be tons of fun, Robin. Can't wait to see you in street clothes."

These dates helped me adjust to life out of hospitals, but I was confused by all the attention. *I wonder if it was my dramatic story with Gail that brought out empathy and the Florence Nightingale Syndrome in nurses my age.* Regardless, I found Presby nurses to be great company.

Another friendship developed with Marlene, a young woman who lived at the end of County Line Road. Marlene had graduated high school that spring and was uncertain about college or career, but she had a lust for the outdoors and riding her Honda motorcycle. I didn't know her that well, even though we lived on the same road. Marlene stopped by the house one day to visit, as she had heard from Nancy that I had been really sick.

"Would you like to go for a bike ride?" she asked one afternoon. "I brought an extra helmet."

September had arrived, and the autumnal sunshine was not to be wasted. The invisible, crisp, fall air was exhilarating, probably more so on a motorcycle. There was a popular commercial at the time, "You meet the nicest people on a Honda," that caused a big sensation. I caused a bigger fright sensation for my mother that day when I put the helmet on and climbed on the bike with Marlene.

"I can't believe this," she said, throwing her hands up as I buckled the helmet. "After all you went through."

Marlene was fantastic company with her bubbly demeanor. I raved on how her hair had flown out from under her helmet when we were flying down the highway. And she looked darn good in tight blue jeans.

We spent some beautiful mornings and afternoons, each taking turns on driving the windy, curvy back roads of western Pennsylvania. The oaks, maples, and hickory trees were a riotous mix of splendid reds, yellows, and browns. The smells of wet, musty leaves and coal smoke swirled around the space inside my helmet.

Several times, Marlene said, "Here, you can have the bike all to yourself. I want to visit with your mom."

My favorite rides were on the back-country roads to small coal-mining villages, like Bulger and Atlasburg, each having about four hundred residents. The rides were very therapeutic as I was once again a man in motion.

There was one morning ride outside of Bulger, when my shifting and the curves in the road were in perfect harmony. Suddenly, I had to hit the brakes. A pack of dogs of many colors and breeds stood in the middle of the road. A decrepit, ancient woman wearing a babushka held a long rod or staff in her arm as she tried to herd her dogs back onto her property. Sunshine warmed my face as I flipped the visor up and noticed the shimmering water of a small pond, ringed with cattails, nestled between the trees. The cattails were releasing their seeds from their puffy heads in the morning breeze. Two mallards landed at the water's edge. I watched the old woman gather her pack of dogs off the road, and I made a mental note to bring Marlene there and explore the pond. It seemed so Thoreau-like.

Marlene provided a fun friendship for the next four months. She had the looks and exuberance to turn men's heads, but I didn't see the relationship deepening and kept my hands to myself. Many times, I thought I was much older than the three years that separated us.

"What are your plans for the future?" I asked her one day after we had been adventuring.

"I haven't thought about it much. I just graduated high school in June."

"But Marlene, high school was over four months ago. Are you planning on college? Or the military? Do you have a dream of what you would like to do?"

"No, I don't, and I don't think college is for me. Are you going back to Tennessee?" she asked, fluffing her hair after removing her helmet.

"I'm planning to go back to Knoxville in late January, work a small job probably, and then go back to college in March."

"You ever plan on moving back here after college?" she asked optimistically.

"No, I doubt it. I'm heading to Montana after graduation."

A sudden sadness swept over Marlene's face, a sadness that eye shadow and eyeliner could not cover. I knew that she had become more attached to our relationship than I had thought. Marlene was so cool, and I never wanted to hurt her. I was sorry she thought that there was more to us than riding her motorcycle or hiking in the woods. I just lived for the moment. Marlene would have been lost in my Tennessee world, and she had her own world to explore. It was a small consolation, but I still felt like crap.

One afternoon in early November the phone in the den rang.

"Hello."

"Guess who?" a cluster of high-pitched voices shouted out, but not loudly enough to hide their Tennessee accents.

"Oh, no, you sound like a wild bunch of nurses who stuck needles in me in Tennessee."

"Yeah, well we heard you had your surgery and wanted to check up on you and see if you're behaving yourself. And you're calling us wild. You sure gave us a rough time, buster. When are you coming back to UT and see us?"

I wondered what that would be like.

"I'm doing well and am looking forward to returning to UT for spring quarter. I'm still working on getting back to my fighting weight, you know, but I think it's because I'm not eating enough biscuits and redeye gravy."

"Yeah, too bad, but we can fix that. Anyway, we thought we would give you a call to let you know we didn't forget about you. Make sure you come see us first thing when you get back, okay? You take care, and remember to take your meds and be good to those nurses."

After this chirpy phone call, I wanted to go outside and take the walk that was part of my daily regimen, but I made it only to the basement stairs. Taking a seat on the steps and resting my chin on my hands, I stared into cellar space, overwhelmed by the outpouring of support that came to me. Even if I were to live a normal, healthy life, I would be forever changed, branded by the events of the past months. *Why did I live and Gail die?? Why did I go to Tennessee in the first place? To meet Gail?* Or maybe it was a litmus test—how badly did I want my Montana Dream?

I promised myself to lead a good life to pay tribute to hers. I asked myself how I could make the best choices in my second chance on life to honor the commitment of all those who helped me walk out of Presby. Nurses had just called me from Tennessee.

Others still believed in my dream, and that made me more determined to return to Tennessee, graduate, and live under the Big Sky. *I have already paid a big price for this dream and wonder if I will have to pay a still higher one.*

Right before Christmas, I called my old friend Rudy, a fellow forestry student who also minored in barroom studies, about available work at the Foxey Lady.

"Hey Rude, I'm ready to come back to UT for spring quarter. What's happening in K-town these days?"

"Ya know, Bob's looking at hiring a guy in January to bartend and take inventory during the day. No nights, but no chicks either. It'll help you get back to K-Town and find a place to live before school starts. Just give me the word, and I'll tell Bob."

After talking with Rudy, I reconnected with my old self. If I stayed away from college any longer, I could lose momentum in pursuing my goals. By Christmas, my strength and stamina were much improved, and I was ready to move on and take the job.

The old feelings of leaving home had resurfaced. *Man in motion. Head west young man. No moss grows under Loring's feet. Thanks for patching me up, Mom and Dad, but I'm leaving again. I will call. Send me a letter. Goodbye, Marke and Katie. Big brother has a date with Smoke and the Montana wilderness. I'm so sorry, Marlene; you are awesome. Love you, Gram.*

Part 4

The Loblolly Pine (Pinus taeda)

Loblolly Pine is the most important and widely cultivated timber species in the southeastern United States. It is considered to be in the group of Southern yellow pines and shares many characteristics with other species of this group (Longleaf, Shortleaf, and Slash Pine) such as: being hard, dense, and possessing an exceptional strength-to-weight ratio. It is the most hardy and versatile of all Southern pines in terms of its ability to reproduce and grow rapidly on diverse sites.

Chapter 33

Would y'all lookie here who's come to see us," Stephanie hollered from her seat at the nurses' station at UT Memorial Hospital. "My, my, aren't you a sight for sore eyes. And that hair."

My new hair had grown back in Shirley Temple-like curls, almost like I had had it permed. The reception was overpowering, but it felt very strange to be there. *Has it almost been a year already?*

"I told y'all I would be back. Y'all get to see even more of me because I have to get my blood work done here every two weeks. I get stuck every time I come here, not like I haven't given you enough blood already."

"I would know that voice anywhere." It was Laurie, my Life Flight nurse from the air ambulance, who had just left a patient's room.

"No plane ride today, Laurie. I'm grounded." I laughed as I spread my flapping arms out like wings. Laurie was different than other nurses at UT. Though she was in her mid-twenties, she was more than a pillow fluffer and temperature taker. She had the personal skills that made her invaluable to doctors and families of the sick.

Dr. Allen even swung by, and it made for a joyous reunion, but I felt I had had about enough of the memories and the smells, so I tried to wrap things up.

"So what are you doing for fun outdoors these days?" Laurie asked, as she walked me to the elevator.

"Well, I drove up to Cades Cove last weekend with my friend Rudy and did some walking, but I'm ready for more, maybe a hike to Abrams Falls."

"Gee, Loring, a hike. Maybe you shouldn't hike alone at first?"

This was no curve ball, and I saw it leave the pitcher's hand. It was a fast ball all the way, and I hit it out of the park.

"Do you like to hike?" I asked her.

"I'd love to hike with you. Maybe we could do Abrams Falls. I think that would be a good beginning hike."

Laurie was an avid hiker but still a nurse, taking my pulse after a climb of steep stretches on our first hike.

"You're doing so well, and boy, have you come a long way since last year," she said, puffing from exertion.

We spent several months hiking, enjoying the rapid approach of spring with the blooming of the trilliums, spring beauties, and azaleas in the lower elevations of the Smokys.

"I think I'm ready for the big one," I told her early one Saturday. And on short notice we climbed Mt. LeConte, the highest peak in the Great Smoky Mountains.

"I have never been with a guy who loves the mountains as you do," Laurie said one rainy Sunday morning at the trailhead to the Chimney Tops. "Are you sure you don't want to go to Gatlinburg and have a cup of coffee in front of a fireplace?"

"No, nice try. These are all just warm-up exercises, Laurie. I hope to climb bigger mountains someday. Put your rain jacket on."

Our friendship on mountain trails continued to grow until I prepared to leave for summer session at Ames. I had grown significantly stronger, and my talk of Montana, meeting Smoke, and climbing mountains caused Laurie to lose her zest for hiking on the weekends, and suddenly, I was on the trail to nowhere. My world was still one of a college student, full of dreams and far removed from the real world. I found few people could relate to Montana or point to it on a map.

It was hard to understand the stress and emotions that Laurie occasionally had after losing a patient, especially a child. She had been transferred to the cancer floor, and one day told me how draining it was to deal with people from Appalachia not getting early diagnoses.

Gail was gone, but there remained small, glowing embers deep inside that served as a reminder of our past and a barometer for my future relationships. These embers did not ignite into a rampaging fire with Laurie. I treasured all the time we had hiking, the pulse checks, and being together on mountain trails and dinners afterward, but eventually I saw that she was the nurse archetype, wearing her uniform of compassion. Both Presby nurses and UT nurses shared a Florence Nightingale commonality. A pattern had developed, and I needed to break the mold.

Our parting after my summer session at Ames was mutual and amicable, as we had out-hiked our relationship. My journey to Montana continued, free of all ties or binds from a painful past.

Chapter 34

Ames Plantation was over 18,000 acres that included 3,500 acres of loblolly pine and 2,600 acres of bottomland hardwoods that were dedicated to forest and ecological research. Ames was located forty miles east of Memphis and three miles north of the Mississippi state line. It was the deep South, home of good ol' boys, bigotry, and Blue Ribbon beer.

After arriving, I attended a small social led by Dr. Stoney, our professor in forest mensuration, a class devoted to learning how to quantify forest products for sale. Class schedules, rules, eating times, and expectations of our summer research were presented. Dr. Stoney was not a dynamic speaker, and he gladly yielded the floor to Mr. Johnny, the majordomo at Ames. Mr. Johnny was dressed in a field uniform of tan khaki, and spoke on anything and everything that went on at Ames, including the rich history of Ames Plantation and available recreational opportunities.

"My, my, ain't this intrestin," Mr. Johnny stated with a southern accent one could gargle with. "I see this year's class looks like last year's class... one nigger and one woman...Well, anyway, let me tell y'all are on Tennessee hallowed ground. Ames, here, is the home of the National Field Trial Championship for bird dogs. Plenty of quail here."

What did he just say? It wasn't the first outright example of prejudice I had seen since heading south for college. Of course, on day one Craig was singled out as a Yankee Eskimo. He was able to brush off the "Tonto" moniker as ignorance, but I wasn't so sure I would have been able to do the same. Even after I moved on to UT, a larger, more urbane, and supposedly more progressive school, someone placed a burning cross in the courtyard of the Andy Holt apartment complex to protest the fact that a black woman was running for student government, and that racist act left an ugly scar on a magnificent university. And now a widely respected educator in our program had just singled out one classmate, a student from Africa, with a racial epithet, and another because of her gender. I was not a civil rights activist, but I never understood disrespecting people for their skin color. Mr. Johnny's comment may have bounced off my classmate's ears as no one seemed to think it was out of the ordinary... except me, a Yankee raised with my father's core values.

"There's some old nags at the barn down yonder you boys kin ride any time after supper," Mr. Johnny went on. "Check 'em for ticks when y'all done riding. There's also a skiff you boys can haul to the swamp for a night of frog gigging. Mighty fine frogs in that swamp. If ye ask nice, Mabel will fry them up for you in the kitchen. One more thing, you boys mind your manners when drinkin' loudmouth down at the Rathole, ya hear. You represent the great University of Tennessee."

Mr. Johnny seemed to look forward to giving his welcome speech and his simple country warning about the Rathole every summer to a new class of forestry students. His rich sense of country humor and bromides were a warmer welcome than Dr. Stoney's monotone discourse.

There was an older, two-story mansion at Ames, as well as a fairly new building where we bunked, ate, and had classes. The sleeping area was one large, open room with a couple of rows of twin beds. It was as close as I ever got to sleeping in a military-type environment. At the end of the day, the guys would sit on chairs—not our beds—and pick ticks off one another. I couldn't help thinking of an old movie where I saw monkeys picking nits off one another. If the tick was augered into the skin, someone would light a match and then blow it out, placing the hot tip on the tick to make the tick withdraw.

The blowtorch heat and ninety percent humidity in the dense woods and river bottoms was brutal, but the mosquitoes, ticks, chiggers, poison ivy, and copperhead rattlesnakes made it like jungle warfare against the elements. Every morning we dusted our

146

waistbands and boot tops with powdered sulfur as a defense against chiggers. Another challenge was kudzu, an Asian native commonly known as the vine that ate the South. Kudzu is a perennial, trailing vine that can grow up to one foot a day and as long as ninety-eight feet; it wound its way along telephone poles to the forest canopy, blocking out sun and robbing trees of nutrients.

The closest town to Ames Plantation was Grand Junction, population 300. It was here that I first saw black and white water fountains and black and white washers and dryers in the laundromat. After being raised in a family that believed in racial equality, I found these separations to be painful indicators of our nation's racial health. *Is racism a problem only in the South? How many black people live in Montana? What about the Native Americans?*

It was rumored that Mark Twain once said, "I spent a year in Grand Junction one day." Horrid-smelling asafetida bags hung in the window of the local drugstore to ward off germs, evil spirits, and even bronchitis. This was 1974, but Grand Junction seemed twenty years behind the times, maybe forty—and not just racially.

Near Grand Junction, located outside of town, sat the Rathole, a local watering hole used by the class to fill up on Pabst Blue Ribbon Beer. It was here that I first saw segregation in action. I sauntered in with Lester, a classmate who wanted to shoot pool. Dolly Parton belted out "Jolene" on the jukebox, a song I had grown weary of.

The front partition of the bar had the jukebox and shuffleboard table, and I failed to see the sign above my head, "Whites Only." The rear section of the Rathole had the pool table. Black people were allowed to shoot pool and be served, but they could not cross over into the front, which was reserved for white people. However, whites could cross over and play pool without retribution. Lester and I stood at the threshold where two black guys, Sonny and Woodrow, pulled us to the pool table. Sonny, who had just slapped his thigh in delight, handed us cue sticks.

"We gonna let you boys break. How 'bout dat," Sonny cracked. "You boys put your quarter up."

"Boys!" Lester shouted out. "Y'all ever see boys with twelve-inch peckers?"

Oh shit, Lester.

147

The pool hall became deathly quiet. A moment passed... Sonny and Woodrow thought that was the funniest damn thing they'd ever heard as they couldn't stop hoopin' and hollerin' with the rest of their friends.

Do you guys know of the legislation passed in 1964 outlawing discrimination and racial segregation in facilities that served the general public—or don't you care?

Lester scratched on the break.

"There goes ya first quarta'. Play again gentlemen?"

Do you know we put a man on the moon five years ago? Do any of you know who Martin Luther King was?

Segregation made me uncomfortable, but no one else was upset. It was the South. Time crawled there. Sonny, Woodrow, and their friends treated us great, and I felt good about that. Barriers were broken, and a few games later, I paired with Sonny and Lester paired with Woodrow, and maybe it was the first time that mixed doubles played together at the Rathole. The Rathole didn't burn down.

I likened the Rathole to an arena, just as much as Clad Metals was an arena. Once outside the bar, there was no sign that kept blacks and whites from fraternizing, and they did. And just like Clad Metals, once men stepped out of the arena, they seemed like normal guys.

After Lester and I fell victims to the Great Rathole Hustle, we were invited to join the yearly Squirrel Stew feast prepared as a thank you to all the forestry students who spent tons of cash on Pabst Blue Ribbons. All the stew ingredients were thrown into a big, black cast-iron kettle that sat on top of a hot charcoal fire. Besides squirrel, we were told that locals had emptied their freezers of raccoon and opossum. The more Pabst you drank, the better the stew tasted. I had bitten down on a piece of squirrel skull with my first bite.

"Hey," a local black guy called out. "Ya know what to do when that happens? Ya gotta take that skull 'tween your fingers and suck da brains out'a it."

With courage from Pabst, I obliged, to the howls of the crowd. I knew eating squirrel stew in rural Tennessee was far removed from my Montana Dream, but I also knew it helped me be a better person by understanding tradition and respecting the differences in the family of man. I always believed the world was my classroom. A better person is what I had vowed to be, and that was equal to or greater than any dream… even if I had to eat squirrel stew.

One afternoon, Dr. Stoney invited a guest speaker, Dan White, a Tennessee state forester, to talk to the class.

"The biggest problem I have here is fire suppression. The poverty level is so bad that locals intentionally set the woods on fire so they can be hired on as firefighters," he told us.

When someone in the class asked, "Hey Dan, what's the salary of a state forester?" we all were numbed by his answer:

"Eight thousand dollars a year is your yearly income. I've been here three years."

What had he just said? Eight thousand dollars. I could have made that much cutting lawns.

This was a paltry salary even by 1974 standards. The average income was close to fourteen thousand dollars, and Dan said it would take three years for a forester to make a measly eight thousand dollars. This announcement was all the more reason to get to Montana after graduation.

Another class took us to Johnson Brothers, one of the largest furniture makers in the South, where we talked with the procurement forester while we toured the plant. What we saw caused heated debate once we left the premises. The segregation at the Rathole had been dismissed by my classmates, but they were enraged by the work practices in the furniture plants. The managerial overhead was all white, and the black workers, many spraying varathane and other wood-product finishes, worked in confined spaces without respirators or masks. It was the same situation at a plant that treated railroad ties with creosote. Only black workers were actively involved in the pressurization of creosote into the ties.

This trip forever cured me of any intention of looking for a career in the Southern wood-product industries. This field trip showed me how black people did the shit jobs and white people were managers. I didn't need a forestry degree to see that. Montana was coming in sharper focus with each new day. Graduation was six months away, but my thoughts of moving west started to influence my lifestyle.

Chapter 35

Rock 'n roll was my diet, but Willie, Waylon, and the boys played music about cowboys and good-hearted women. That was my kind of music. *Would Montana be my kind of place?*

This music had caught my ear, and I left the university area music scene to dance and cruise the honky-tonk joints outside the city. Thoughts of Montana also affected the way I dressed.

"I would like to try on a pair of Levi straight leg jeans, size 34 waist," I told a sales clerk at a western store, bypassing the more familiar flare-bottomed Levi's.

My well-worn hiking boots, now worn only for hiking, were replaced by a pair of Tony Lama factory-rejected cowboy boots. Food tastes changed also. The next time I made chili, I used red chili beans. Pinto beans were too Southern for me.

For quick reads, there was Louis L'Amour and his storytelling about the authentic West. I went through a "Western Transformation," and it felt so right.

Finally finding my academic groove in western wear, I made the Dean's List on a regular basis.

There was a new catalyst, too, a chalkboard that had been hung in the forestry school's administration office. Professors listed their planned vacancies from the university. Several professors had written that they would be attending conferences at the United States Forest Service Region One headquarters, which was in... Missoula, Montana.

One day, I noticed that Dr. Dimmer, a wildlife biologist, was going to be in Missoula for a week. I stopped by his office soon after he returned.

"Hey, Dr. Dimmer. I saw that you were in Missoula, Montana, last week. How did you like it?"

He slowly looked up from his paperwork, raised his reading glasses to his forehead, and put his clasped hands behind his head. "How was Missoula, is that what you want to know, Loring?"

"Yeah, how did you like it?"

"Well, the short version is that I found it tough to come back to Tennessee. It is what they say it is: God's Country."

"I knew it, I knew it, Dr. Dimmer."

Summer classes were staggered, and I worked part time for Elkins Landscape Services. Frank Elkins, a UT grad student, had started a small landscaping company and had secured lawn-mowing contracts in the prestigious Sequoia Hills area—a five-minute drive from the UT campus. Frank was in need of someone with experience in lawn mowing.

"I'm your man, Frank," I told him one day in the hallway of the Plant Science Building. "When I was in high school, I caddied a lot at a country club, and some days I cut the fairways and greens. I know my way around a lawn mower."

"You can start tomorrow."

Frank assigned a company van, loaded with a brand new Ariens riding mower, a very familiar 21-inch Lawn Boy mower, and the newest of all landscape tools, a weed eater. I mowed estates, like the one owned by the president of the Blue Diamond Coal Company. Sitting on that mower in the warmth of the Tennessee spring and summer, I dreamed my favorite dream of cool streams, towering mountains, wild trout, and children born under the wild Montana sky.

Chapter 36

After the Great Rathole Hustle, I grew closer to Lester, a Tennessee native from Unicoi. His wife, Charlene, a bodacious, red-haired Tullahoma girl, was in nursing school at UT. Lester was at least six foot three and had a head of hair that closely resembled that of the Lion from the Wizard of Oz. He and Charlene were also intent on moving west, though they were not focused on Montana like I was. Lester and I both shared a great passion for outdoor adventure and planned a float down the Hiawassee River. Floating the Hiawassee, with its Class 2 and 3 rapids, rock ledges, and swirling eddies would be a challenge in an open canoe, but it was an adventure worth dreaming about.

Buying a canoe in Montana was on the top of my wish list. The canoe would be first, but then I also needed a new rifle for elk hunting. I'm a Remington man, but I liked the Browning .308 lever action, and it won out over the Remington 30.06.

Early one Sunday morning in mid-August, a Tennessee summer day that was at its brightest and sunniest, Lester called. He'd listened to the radio report on stream flows that morning, and the Hiawassee rapids looked good to ride.

When I stood at the launch area at the Appalachia Powerhouse two hours later, I felt the river's rhythm kept time with the breaking of the white water over the rocks and ledges.

"You take the bow," Lester said, laughing. "That's where the action is."

The water was clear and warm, running fairly high from the dam's discharge. Within a few minutes of paddling, I heard the roar of "Thread the Needle," the first set of rapids.

"Remember, we always have to be paddling faster than the river so I can steer," Lester yelled from the stern.

The next four sets of rapids were only precursors to the final set at the four-and-a-half-mile point, called "Devil's Shoals." In the crowded river, Lester and I came to a resting spot in a small eddy as we waited our turn to shoot Devil's Shoals.

"We're up," I yelled above the roar of the water, and made a powerful forward stroke to free us from the eddy. Within a few seconds, I found that we were a little right of where we should have been. We did not have enough speed, and were now at the mercy of the river. We launched off of a rock ledge. There was no way this boat was gonna land flat in the water. We were really screwed.

At the base of the ledge, there was a large curler, a steep wave that curled back into its upstream side. The bow had angled sharply down into the water, landing on the nose, and threw me out of the canoe, earning me a raspberry the length of my left forearm. Lester was launched forward out of his seat, and his head just missed a rock outcrop. The canoe filled with water, and one oar had already floated out of sight. We both clung to the upside-down canoe, riding it downstream until we approached shallow water, where we righted it, bailed it out, and released the spare oar.

Standing on the banks of the Hiawassee, a river totally worth being designated as Wild and Scenic, I shook the last drops of water from my ears. The only thing hurt was our pride, and we relived those white-knuckle moments all the way back to Knoxville. The last chapter of my Tennessee outdoor adventures had come to an end.

Chapter 37

Well, gentlemen, welcome to the RW," were the last words Dr. Welk, a cigar-chewing, nattily dressed forest economics professor, spoke at my final lecture. Dr. Welk resembled a croupier at a Las Vegas casino and I wondered if he was giving odds on the three percent.

"Dr. Welk, Dr. Welk," a student called out. "What is the RW?"

Dr. Welk stopped, turned to the class, and slowly removed his unlit cigar. He looked long and hard at the cigar before speaking.

"You ask what the RW is. The 'real world,' gentlemen, the real world."

Dr. Welk... I know a little about that.

Graduation was on a gray December day, where thousands of graduates lined up according to their college. To speed the commencement exercises, degrees were handed out by college. Forestry was in the College of Agriculture and first to graduate. A sense of victory seethed over me when it was my turn to walk on that stage and receive the diploma in my left hand and shake the dean's right hand. A graduate. A Volunteer for Life. The Tennessee chapter of my life was closed. My Montana chapter was about to open. The *Boys' Life* article that I read nine years earlier was a calling card, inviting me to a land that I could be happier in. *Darn it, I should have sent Smoke a graduation announcement.*

Gathered in front of the Torchbearer, UT's official symbol, I explained the importance of the Torchbearer to my parents and Katie, and why it was a great place to take a picture.

"The statue holds up the torch of enlightenment in the right hand and wears a sword as a symbol of security. In his left hand, there is a globe with Winged Victory, a symbol of success and the individual's ability to make the most of his opportunities despite the world's challenges."

It was a proud moment to stand with my parents in front of the Torchbearer, still dressed in my cap and gown. I was the first in my family to graduate from college, and my father was overcome with emotion.

"Son, you had your challenges," he said, shaking my hand with both of his. "But look at you, look what you accomplished, and what we all went through to get to this day at this incredible university. This special day, this special moment. Your mother and I are so proud of you. Let your adventure begin."

Westward ho! I was ready to go.

Chapter 38

Graduation left me both disconnected and in limbo. Gone was my access to the university library, the aquatic center, or cheap football tickets. I was in the RW, and looking for work while my application for federal employment was processed.

I lived in Townsend in a rental cabin on the banks of the Little Pigeon River, just thirty miles from UT and one mile from the entrance to the Smokys. Lester offered me a job working with him for a heating and air conditioning company. Lester had some experience and I had none, but I soon learned the complex art of stapling fiberglass insulation to wall studs. How strange it was to have a degree in forestry and pack insulation or snip tin while assembling ductwork for minimum wage. *The Forest Service has to be reviewing my application by now.*

All the limboness disappeared one morning in early April, when the telephone rang.

"Hello, is this Loring Walawander?" a man's faraway voice asked.

"Yes it is; who's this?"

"Bill Stearns here with the US Forest Service on the Umatilla National Forest in Pendleton, Oregon."

This shocked me. Oregon was Region 6. I knew I marked Region 1, which included Montana, and not Oregon on my application.

"Congratulations, we have selected you for a career position in fire management and control."

"Wow, sure Bill, tell me more."

"The Umatilla National Forest is located in the Blue Mountains of southeast Washington and northeast Oregon. The forest has some mountainous terrain, but most of the forest consists of v-shaped valleys separated by narrow ridges or plateaus and heavily timbered slopes. It can get pretty darn hot here in the summers," he concluded.

This was the call that I was waiting for.

"Yes, Bill, I'm interested." I was euphoric and confused simultaneously.

How could I get selected for Region 6? Fire management was not my first choice, and it was not Montana, but I accepted the position with the realization that this could be my only offer.

Two days later, the phone rang early before I headed out to snip tin. Another faroff voice was on the line.

"Loring, Hank Westfall here. I'm with the US Forest Service on the Wisdom Ranger District on the Beaverhead National Forest in Montana."

This has to be a prank call set up by Lester.

His voice was relaxed, raw and craggy as the mountains he was near. I could hear the drawing in of a cigarette, and envisioned the Marlboro Man. Montana was calling, and my breath slipped away. *My ears could not believe it. The Montana Dream was happening.* I knew a lot of Montana geography but had never heard of Wisdom. Hank's voice was one that embodied wisdom.

"Wisdom is an hour south of Butte and located in the Big Hole Valley and ringed on the west by the Continental Divide," Hank continued.

Is this really happening? Who knew that this is my dream? This had to be a prank. Hank was not talking about just anywhere in Montana, but the Big Hole Valley! The Continental Divide! The Big Hole River! Ten-thousand-foot mountains in the Pintler Wilderness! *Tell me more, Hank. Tell me more.*

"Wisdom is a small town, about a hundred people, but Beaverhead County is bigger than Connecticut. I have a trail maintenance position open, though the high country doesn't open up until mid-June, so everyone is involved in tree planting operations at first. Once trail work starts, you will be out in the wilderness for ten days at a time. I wish I had a career position to offer, but this offer is for only nine months, maybe ten months a year. But working here will get you a well-rounded foundation of forestry practices."

I was going to be paid to work in the wilderness, just like Smoke. All right.

"When do I report Hank?"

"Monday, May seventeenth. I'll put the paperwork in the mail today."

After hanging up with Hank, I realized I had accepted a career opportunity in Oregon and also a position to work ten months a year in Montana. I couldn't do both, so I called Bill back. The conversation went very well, and Bill understood my Montana desire.

"You'll like Montana better," Bill added at the end of the conversation.

Bill was correct with that assumption.

Part 5

The Lodgepole Pine (Pinus contorta)

A pioneer species, they are among the first trees to repopulate areas after a fire. The cones have a resin between their scales that only breaks when temperatures reach 113 to 140 degrees F. Native Americans used the straight and slender poles of the trees to support their tipis. These pines can grow up to 150 feet and live up to 400 years.

Chapter 39

Wow, how happy I was to be on the road again. Almost six years had passed since I first heard of four-peckered billy goats in Nashville. May, 1976, and I was Big Sky bound. I wanted to visit my parents first.

There were family changes at home. Marke had married Nancy the previous summer, and my father was laid off from the mill. The first thing I did after I arrived home was to make my father relax with a cold beer while I put the Lawn Boy in action. I bettered my high school mowing time of four hours by fifteen minutes. The lawn was not as big as I remembered it.

"I still don't believe you can cut this lawn in under four hours," my father cracked.

"I had lots of practice, Dad."

"And here is your bonus," my mother said laughing, as she handed me a pint of fresh, cold, carrot juice.

"How is that Dodge van running?" he asked while I sipped the fresh carrot juice. "Is it ready for Montana?"

My father had an uncanny sense and already had detected my disillusionment with the Dodge van.

"I'm not happy about the crappy performance, Dad. After the engine blew on my way back here for Easter, the factory rebuild was not right. It's still under warranty, but it's burning way too much oil for a new engine. It took two quarts on this trip. The dealer in Tennessee found nothing wrong with it."

"Well, maybe we should go down to Burgunder Dodge, and talk to Greg. He was the salesman, and we should take it up with him. There might be different options than to stick with that van."

My father always watched my back. Years before, he knew that I drove to West Virginia to drink beer. He also knew that by giving me challenging books to read, my life would be broadened. I never thought far enough ahead to think that a van was probably the most impractical and stupidest vehicle to have in rural Montana. I believed that he had already met with Greg Burgunder and talked about the troubles with the Dodge Caravan and had already perused the lot, looking for options.

"Let's go to Burgunder's," my father beckoned the next Saturday morning. "They have been in business since I was a boy. I trust them."

From the beginning, my father took a back seat and allowed me to handle the problems with the van with Greg, who let me tell the whole story of the engine failure. Greg was a young man who had tried to let his hair grow longer, but could not commit to the part down the middle and still parted it on the left side. In spite of his youth, he had already been taught a successful business model from his father: if you don't take care of the customer, someone else will.

"When I bought this van, Greg, you told me that it had one of the most dependable engines on the market. Well, the engine blew while still under warranty, and the Tennessee dealer's rebuild was shoddy. It just burns a lot of oil."

"I hear you're headed for Montana."

Did I tell him that?

"Look Loring, I want to make this right for you. Dodge makes tremendous, reliable engines, and I'm sorry you had a bad experience. What would you like me to do?"

"I can't rely on this van in the Montana boonies and would consider trading it in," I said, while I turned to catch my father's approving nod.

"Well, let's go see what we have on the lot," a smiling Greg said while getting up from his desk.

The first truck I came to, a Dodge Power Wagon, drew me like a magnet to a nail. The metallic green paint glistened in the morning sun. Power Wagon, just the name gave me a level of comfort about heading west. Power. I loved it. The truck seethed with testosterone. It was so Montana, and I saw myself driving on a back road to my favorite hunting spot, or hauling a canoe to ride the waves of a wild river. I took a seat behind the wheel and put my right hand on the gear shift. Four on the floor. All right. Manual shifting.

"Here's the keys. Let me get a dealer plate, and you and your dad can take it for a test drive," Greg told me.

It took running through the gears one time on the highway and I was in love with the truck, and my father could tell.

"Let's head back and see if we can make a deal," he said.

Back in Greg's office, a deal came together rather quickly, I thought.

"Okay, Loring. I'm willing to take the van back at top trade-in value. As it sits right now. Leaking oil and all."

"Well, that's a good place to start Greg because it's still under warranty. How about the Power Wagon? Will you take five grand and the trade?"

"I need fifty three hundred."

Out of the corner of my eye, I caught my father's discreet, gentle nod. "Well, that makes me feel good about Dodge again. Thanks, Greg. Where do I sign?"

"I hope you enjoy it," Greg said, as he handed me a voucher for five gallons of gas at the Shell station next to the lot.

What was not to enjoy, four-wheel drive in mountainous terrain? It didn't have a radio, which was no big deal. I would continue to use my portable Zenith transistor radio like I had done with the van. Early pioneers needed a good horse to make it out west, and I now had the equivalent of one hundred fifty horses in the 318-cubic-inch V-8 motor.

"Let's take a drive to Finleyville before we head home," my father said, with a broad smile that showed his perfect set of teeth.

Finleyville? What the heck. We never go there.

He had me drive to Huffy Trailer Sales, where I pulled to a stop in front of the row of Uni-Cover pickup toppers.

"I think you'll need one of these to protect your dream belongings, don't you?" he said with the same smile.

He seemed ecstatic to be able to set me up for my Montana Dream, to freely give without reservation because he believed in me. I thought I needed to repay all the money that was invested in me, but I came to learn that he would never accept it. The lesson he taught was for me to do the same for my son someday.

That Saturday morning I purchased a dream truck to load my Montana Dreams aboard, and now it was covered to keep them from blowing away. My parents had sacrificed a lot for my Montana Dream. I saw it as another challenge my father set before me: make something of this Montana Dream. The stakes were high. My father was a good poker player and had opened the round of betting. I called his bet.

What was I taking to Montana? I didn't have much besides lots of jeans, and the navy-blue North Face down coat that I bought on sale in Tennessee in preparation for Montana. I reread the label on my North Face sleeping bag. It said that I was good to twenty below. Cold never bothered me, but I never had been that cold. Then Rob's army coat... It went everywhere. There was a two-man tent, a well-seasoned No. 10 cast-iron skillet, some unmatched Melmac plates and bowls, a couple Louis L'Amour books, an Eagle Claw spin/fly combination fishing rod and reel, and my Remington 870 shotgun. My mother held a box in her arms when she came by to see how it was going.

"Almost packed up, dear?"

"It's getting there, Mom."

"Here, this is for your new Montana home."

Opening the box, I found that I was now the owner of a stainless steel Acme Juicer, so I could make my own Montana carrot juice. It was a very cool gift, and not one that many young adventurers headed west with.

"Don't let me forget, we need to go to GNC and get you stocked up on Vitamin C and a good multivitamin before you leave. Maybe some peppermint tea, too."

"Hey, Mom, do you want to go for a ride in the new truck? Hop in."

"Sure, dear. Where to?"

"I'm going for a haircut."

It was pretty cool to take my mom for a ride. I never envisioned her in the front seat of a pickup, but it thrilled her to see me run through the gears while climbing the hills around home.

Chapter 40

Tuesday morning was my launch day, not at the crack of dawn that I would have liked because I had opted to have a family breakfast before leaving. My grandmother had spent the weekend with us, and I wanted to spend some time with her. *But now it is time again for my familiar exit scene: Loring is off again.* I wanted to put everyone in the back of the truck and take them to Montana. There would be no returning to my native Pennsylvania after college graduation as my mother had hoped. My father sipped his coffee while my mother, her mood now a notch above somber, heaped scrambled eggs and six linked breakfast sausages on my plate. Now, I would be a three-day drive away and not ten hours.

Time had come. Ten years had passed since I read about Smoke Elser and his trip into the Bob Marshall Wilderness in Montana. There were challenges, broken hearts, and mended hearts, and now I had my covered wagon, full of dreams and fuel, ready for the highway to roll under its new set of Goodyear tires.

"Can we get a picture in front of the flowering plum tree, please?" my mother pleaded.

The flowering plum tree, when it bloomed in the spring, was her most-favorite tree in the yard. She worshipped it.

"Wait, wait, we need to take it again. Grammy wasn't ready," my mother insisted.

I climbed into the driver's seat, and reached for my Foster Grant aviator sunglasses on the dash. My father came alongside the open window and reached in to shake my hand.

"Good luck, son, and remember to call your mother. When you get to the Wisdom Ranger Station, walk in like you own the joint."

Words of a steel worker, but I was blue-collar branded, and he always seemed to be on point. Pulling out of the driveway was the hardest thing I ever did. In my rearview mirror, I saw my family all huddled together under the plum tree, waving me goodbye. In a minute, exhilaration replaced sadness as I felt the excitement of twenty-two-hundred miles of adventure. Big Sky Country was waiting for me to stake a claim for my future in a state I had only seen in pictures. And Hank was the only Montanan I ever had talked to.

In five minutes I drove through the coal town of Hendersonville, my mother's hometown, which still smoked from depressing coal fires that burned underground. Then my high school, high on the hill above the interstate, which overlooked a disappointing time in my life. Three hours later, in Columbus. *Did OSU ever get his life together?*

My new truck was like a trusty steed of the old West. *I will take care of you, so you never let me down like my other Dodge. We have miles of roads to explore, and you are now part of my Montana Dream.* The Dodge never did let me down; in sixteen years and 280,000 miles of highways and byways, it always got me home.

Untypical spring weather, searing hot with only strands of high cirrus clouds in the sky, followed me west. I had been driving with my window open, and the left side of my face and my left arm were getting deeply tanned so that I was half red and half white.

Another hour passed and I hummed a few lines of Willie and Waylon songs to pass the time. My humming sounded as flat as the country I was driving through.

Driving alone left me time to think on America's westward migration as I felt I was driving my own Conestoga Wagon.

Why would those settlers just stop here in Iowa, and clear all of its timber to plant corn that grew over eight feet tall? *Look at that corn! It is three feet taller than Portman's Farm. And over there… soybeans as far as I could see.* Was it the same reason my ancestors stopped in Pennsylvania to mine coal? *What makes a man stop?* And what made a man leave everything he had, and all that he knew, to keep heading west? I knew one thing: I was tired of seeing all the flat land. Montana's mountains were getting closer with every mile.

South Dakota was even flatter than Iowa, and that landscape suited my loneliness. The Badlands were appropriately named. One hundred Wall Drug signs were lined up one after the other. And then the Corn Palace signs. I had gotten the message to stop at both.

At a Conoco station, somewhere west of Mitchell, stood the most weather-beaten, sunbaked man I had ever seen. His skin was so dry, I thought it would crack like plaster if he started talking.

"Hey there, partner, I'm heading to Montana and wondered when I'll get to see some mountains.

"Mountains you said, son," he said, squinting his eyes in the bright sun. "This country is flatter then my ex-wife's chest."

Parched and road weary, I pulled into Chamberlain and looked for lodging.

I was in luck. There was an air-conditioned hotel with a vacancy, and a pizza joint next door. There would be no truck bed for me that night. Beer, cheesy pizza and air conditioning. This was good medicine for ten hours of needed sleep.

My morning shower left me smelling like a truck stop restroom from using the motel's Irish Spring soap. Fifteen minutes later, I realized I was also allergic to that soap and broke out in a rash.

After three days on the road, I began to feel a change deep within me. I was alone. Five years had passed, almost a lifetime it felt, since I was alone on that Sunday morning sidewalk in Nashville. So alone, I remembered, I convinced myself of it. However, I now thought I wasn't so alone at that time, that it just was my mind telling me that I was.

My aloneness was short lived. A hitchhiker stood on the side of the road in the most forlorn section of highway in South Dakota. The Dodge was gassed, and I was still nursing a cup of truck stop, dishwater-strength coffee twenty miles west of Rapid City when I slowed down to a crawl. Sizing him up quickly, I decided to stop. The hitcher was a tall, lanky, college-age guy with shoulder-length blond hair and aviator glasses, but no hat. On his shoulder he had slung a well-traveled day pack with a thin sleeping bag bungie-corded on.

"Where you headed, my man?" I asked.

"Anywhere west."

"Well, I'm headed west, so pile in."

"Nice truck," he told me after stowing his bedroll in the back.

"Yeah, I know, I love it. It's six days old, and I've driven it over fifteen hundred miles already. How far west you headed?"

"I'm David by the way, David Guilford. I'm heading to the San Juan Islands."

Even though I minored in geography, I drew a blank with this area and confused it with San Juan in Puerto Rico.

"No," he said, "I'm going to Orcas Island, one of the islands that make up the San Juan Islands. Going to do some missionary work there."

"Oh, that sounds really cool. Do you plan to go into the ministry? I thought about seminary when I was very young. I never got that call, but I did get the call of the wild."

"Ha-ha. That's funny. Yeah, someday, maybe, I'll enter the ministry. Say, what route are you taking to Wisdom?"

"I-90 to Butte or Anaconda, then there is a fifty-mile road, Mill Creek Pass, to Wisdom," I told him.

"I think we can do Yellowstone tonight and still wind up in Butte or Anaconda at a good time."

"Well, there is no way we can pass up the park, then."

David talked like water gushing from a pump, and he flooded my ears with welcome conversation. I was convinced he was born to preach.

The town of Buffalo was nestled in the foothills of the beautiful Bighorn Mountains. In the distance, snowcapped peaks jutted on the horizon, soaring high into the clear blue sky. I was no longer anxious when I first viewed my newfound joy… the Rocky Mountains. They were real. They were my dream. Mountains… finally. I had arrived.

A weary, dusty, hot day across eastern Wyoming was our itinerary. We talked and we talked, and our words flew out the window and filled the emptiness of the Wyoming prairie. As David talked, I counted antelope in my head.

We reached Cody, Buffalo Bill's old stomping grounds, shortly after five, but there was an hour's drive to Yellowstone. Cody sat in the scenic Wapiti Valley with panoramic views of the Absaroka Range. The mountains were breathtaking, and I felt my dream unfolding in 3-D on a big screen, just like I remembered in *How the West was Won*.

"Hey, David, let's stop in that grocery store and get something I can cook for dinner," I offered, eager to get my cast-iron skillet seasoned in the West.

"If you cook, I got the beer," David quickly volunteered.

My menu was simple: a couple of potatoes and an onion and a green pepper that I could fry in the skillet and a package of Polish sausage that we could grill. David held up a six pack of Coors from across the aisle.

"Will these work for you?" he asked, then flashed a bright smile with beaming white teeth, and nodded his head up and down several times.

Coors beer, although famous in the West, had just become known in my college days, as friends would bring some back from western travels.

"Let's get a bag of ice, so they'll be chilled when we get inside the park," I added.

"Smart thinking, buddy."

It was mid-May and the park was mostly empty of tourists, with snowdrifts still covering shady areas among the trees. Snorting bison wandered along the roadside, grazing on new grass at the road's edge.

"David, there's a campground and an empty spot."

"I'll get on the fire," David offered, "but first let's pop a top on one of those cold Coors's. They have a weird type of pop-top, I heard. "

A weathered, gray log was my seat, and I sipped a chilled Coors. And then another. Potatoes sizzled to a golden brown in the skillet, while sausages grilled on a stick, dripped grease over some hot coals. *Pffft, pffft*, each drip would sound out when it landed on a coal. The sounds of food cooking, mixed with the crackling of the dried pine burning, and the distant howling coyotes meant our Yellowstone Symphony of the Senses had climaxed.

The night sky was full of stars and formed a beautiful canopy to our wilderness symphony. *Good weather tomorrow*. David stared blankly into the fire, hypnotized by the dancing yellow, blue, and orange flames, as if they would reveal answers to what lay ahead on his journey of missionary work. I had never asked. We were two intrepid travelers, lost in our thoughts. Tomorrow, I will finally cross the Montana border. *Has it been only three days since leaving Pennsylvania?* Now, I was sitting near a campfire in Yellowstone Park, cooking on an open fire, just like my scouting days. It was unbelievable.

Chapter 41

The pitter-patter of rain drops played a wilderness reveille on the tin roof of my pickup's topper. This was the first rain that fell during my trip, and the low-pressure front that had moved in overnight brought not only rain but spring snow to Yellowstone.

Climbing out of my warm and cozy North Face bag, I reached for my army jacket. Outside the truck, I quickly pulled the hood up, as the rain had turned to fat snowflakes.

"You up, David?" I yelled towards the tent that I let David use for the night.

"Yeah, I'll be right out, I'm tying my shoes. Man, who turned winter on?"

"It is winter; we're getting covered with snow." I told him. "Don't bother to pack the tent, just throw it in the back of the truck to dry. I'll get it later."

As the truck warmed up and the windshield defrosted, I looked again at my road atlas.

"There are a bunch of different roads to get to Wisdom, but if we head for the North Entrance, we'll be in Montana. Looks like we can reach I-90, and that will help you hitch a ride west."

David nodded in agreement while he rubbed his hands together, then exhaled his breath on them for warmth after handling the wet tent.

We had fifty miles to drive through the park yet. The morning rain, snow, and fog near Yellowstone Lake dampened the scenery but not our spirits. *I'll be back here sometime soon, but today was my day to achieve Wisdom.*

And then... just minutes after leaving Yellowstone, we passed a billboard that read, *Welcome to Montana. Big Sky Country.* I saluted my entry with three honks of my truck's horn.

"Wahoo! I made it. Only took me ten years. I'm in Big Sky Country at last, David."

"Good for you, buddy. I'm happy for you."

My body relaxed to a never-known peace after I crossed the border. Montana just felt different, and it surrounded me with an aura of calmness, peace, and achievement. It was how I dreamed about it as a young boy. My Montana Dream was a good dream, one filled with good intentions, and with a lot of help and support of others, I had just made it come true.

Windshield wipers were synched with my heartbeat... both at high speed. A spring rainstorm had turned to slushy snow as we approached Anaconda, and Wisdom was an hour away.

"There, up ahead on the left, I see the Mill Creek sign," David shouted out. "You can pull over."

There were large slag heaps and one tall smokestack at the turnoff. The map said it was a smelter.

"Well, this is the end of the line, buddy. I hate to leave you out in this crummy weather."

"I'll remember you for a long time. Don't worry about me. Bet I catch a ride in ten minutes. Adios amigo. I'll send you a postcard."

Fifty miles. *I could feel Wisdom.* It was great to have David along, but now I centered my thoughts on arriving in Wisdom by three as planned.

Chapter 42

My hands were full of wheel as I tried to negotiate the curvy, winding ascent of Mill Creek. The road wasn't quite two lanes wide, had no guardrail, and was unpaved in spots with axle-deep potholes. What kind of country had I signed up for? All the hills had no trees, just charred stumps from a fire long in the past. The map showed Mill Creek Pass to be twenty miles long, and I hoped for a change in scenery.

Standing in the shallows of California Creek, there was an adult bull moose, nibbling on the tender spring shoots of willow growing along the creek's edge. I cursed. I was out of film.

It was hard to keep off the gas as I felt I was almost home. Welcome to Montana. Moose on the loose.

My first Wisdom sign said to turn right onto Highway 43 that bordered the Big Hole River. Only thirty more miles. Screaming in delight, I laid on the gas.

The weather was still socked in, and I could not see any mountains or the Continental Divide from the floor of the Big Hole Valley. Then there was another sign that stated I was in the "Land of 10,000 Haystacks." More like monster loaves of bread, these haystacks were surrounded by many wooden contraptions that looked like large slides on skids scattered throughout the flood-irrigated valley.

There's Wisdom. Dead ahead. The town's cemetery is on the right, just a mile from town. Boy, Wisdom looked small and a place out of time.

Immediately upon entering Wisdom, I saw the ranger station. "United States Forest Service: Beaverhead National Forest: Wisdom

Ranger Station" the sign read. My eyes could not believe it. There it was: an isolated ranger station, miles from nowhere, marked the pivotal point of my Montana Dream. Never was I more prepared to step out my truck, take a deep breath, and charge into my daring, new world.

Walk in like you own the joint. Got it, Dad. Twenty-two-hundred miles from home and family.

Standing at the door was a tall, blue-jeaned, Gary Cooper-looking stunt double. He radiated the appearance of the western man I had seen in movies. His Camel was smoked down to its last drag, and he stubbed the butt into an ashtray with his left hand. When the smoke cleared from around his face, a deep-set pair of attentive blue eyes scoped me out. He threw out his open right hand. His long, lanky legs bowed out a little. But mostly, he struck me as a man who would take no shit, a lawman who would have been good company for Wyatt Earp at the OK Corral.

"Hank Westfall," he drawled in the seasoned voice that I remembered from our phone call.

"I'm your new man, Loring Walawander from Tennessee. We talked on the phone."

"Ga-w-w-d damn, you sure look like a forester," was his Wisdom welcome.

I had on a Woolrich buffalo-plaid shirt and a new pair of Levi's. *How is a forester supposed to look?* I wondered, but I enjoyed the immediate acceptance of a Montana man by passing the dress code.

Hank talked rough and crusty, and used plenty of expletives. His outward disposition was no façade.

"Let me show you around and meet everyone. Barb will get you some keys to stay in the bunkhouse over the weekend. You can room there if you want till you find a place. Like I told you on the phone, housing is scarce outside of the bunkhouse."

Bunkhouse living was in my past, and I was on my own to find an alternative. By the end of the next hour, the staff had closed the office and everyone headed to the Antler Bar, directly adjacent to the ranger station. It was happy hour, and I was invited.

Not once in my life had I experienced anything like the Antlers. A painted, wooden Indian guarded the entrance. Inside the small, cozy bar, antlers of moose, elk, antelope, and deer were mounted on the walls. There were head mounts, mining lanterns, crosscut saws, traps, beaver pelts, and other western relics hanging from the ceiling. In the corner stood a quiet Wurlitzer jukebox and a pool table with well-worn felt. The bar surface was once a giant Douglas fir tree that had been sawed lengthwise, planed, and coated with verathane.

Surrounded by Rich, Dave, and a few other guys from the station, Rich introduced me to Gena, his mother-in-law and the widowed owner of the Antlers. Gena, a perky, smiling, middle-aged woman, beamed with delight as the bar started to fill for happy hour.

"How's my boys today? Who wants to shake first?" Gena asked while rattling the dice in a black cup in front of us.

This happy hour was blowing my mind. The Antler Bar was my launching pad to all things western. My Montana Dream had gone to live action. The jukebox came to life with Mickey Gilley singing about "how all the girls get prettier at closing time," and the smell of a baking Tombstone Pepperoni Pizza filled the air. Jars of pickled eggs and turkey gizzards that looked like they were brined in embalming fluid rounded out the bar menu. I saw this food as palate cleansers, not real food, just something to make the next drink seem fresh or make you throw up.

Gena handed me a black cup with three dice inside it.

"Well, big boy, you get to play your first Shake a Day."

"Shake a Day. What's that all about, Gena?"

"Best two out of three rolls for a beer. You can play once a day. Roll the dice, partner."

"Three fives, Gena."

"Two sixes," Gena said after her roll. "Horse on me."

Horse on me, what is she talking about? I wondered until I saw the similarity to the game of horse, a playground game shooting a basketball.

Gena took the next roll with four threes.

"Horse a piece," she said.

I rolled for the third time and threw three sixes, which was good enough to beat Gena's last roll.

I won my first Shake a Day in Montana!

Gena reached into the cooler and brought out a frosty can of beer and handed it to me.

"It's *Lucky* when you live in the West, Loring," was her remark that resonated deep within me. "It's *Lucky* when you live in the West," I repeated under my breath.

I looked down at the white can of beer, with its name, *Lucky Lager*, scrolled in red across the can. Yes, it was, oh yes, it was Lucky, and I called home to tell everyone how Lucky it was.

Chapter 43

The morning sunlight peeped in the bunkhouse window and woke me from a deep slumber. Slowly cracking open the bunkhouse door, I was breathless with what to expect.

My eyes bugged out. During the night, the weather pattern had shifted, moving clouds and rain away, leaving in its place the most spectacular blue morning sky. Silhouetted against the southern horizon, stood Ajax Peak, like a giant molar that had been crowned with snow. To the west rose the Continental Divide and the forty-mile-long Anaconda-Pintler Wilderness, with the towering pair of East Goat and West Goat peaks jutting into the sky to the north. My soul had just gotten sucked into the Anaconda-Pintler Wilderness.

This wilderness straddled the Continental Divide in the Anaconda mountain range of southwest Montana. Time would stand still until I climbed the high and rugged peaks, cirques, and glacial moraines. Sparkling lakes and tumbling streams and waterfalls, fed by icy water running off the snowfields above the timberline, would invigorate both skin and soul, much like Cummins Falls had done. Rich had told me that was where the majority of the work would be. Wow! People paid to vacation there, and I'm going to be paid to work there. Rich also suggested that I look for Dale Conwell, the owner of a new and used store and also four apartments in Wisdom.

Wisdom was the smallest town I had ever been in. *What do one hundred people do here?* The town consisted of a tiny grocery store, a sawmill, two gas stations that were full service, a K-8 elementary school, a post office, a Masons Hall, and a volunteer ambulance and fire department. The eye-catching lime-green building, Conwell's New and Used, sat in the center of town. It was here that I found

Dale, a fortyish, gray-haired wheeler-dealer kind of guy sipping a fresh pour of coffee. His store sold everything from rifles to hair curlers, both new and used, like his sign said.

With a firm handshake, I introduced myself and asked him about his rentals.

"You know, I have one apartment left, top floor on the right," he said, pointing down the street. "Hundred bucks a month. Washer and dryer are in the basement. You're just getting started out here, so I'll let the deposit go since you're working for the Forest Service. You can move in today. I see you have a new truck. How about a bumper sticker? Guys need a bumper sticker in this country."

Fingering through a pile of stickers, I finally found one that pushed the edge and matched my new Montana swagger: "Cowgirls Are Better Without Spurs."

In the middle of one of Montana's most-isolated towns, I had secured housing before noon and a snappy bumper sticker. *What a Lucky man I am*. I had better keep on rolling those dice.

"What do people do for food in Wisdom?" I asked Dale.

"Well most folks have venison or an elk in the freezer, but if you can't live off the local store, then you have to drive seventy miles to Butte to get what you want."

Thanking Dale, I moseyed over to the Wisdom Market. There was milk, bread, a few shriveled apples, two brown spotted bananas, and some frozen hamburger. One item stuck out like a sore thumb in the freezer case.

Tater Tots!

Tater Tots had invaded Montana. My stomach cringed from memories of Tater Tot casserole or Tater Tots slathered in brown gravy… or white gravy. Besides frozen hamburger there were boxes of Banquet chicken and Tombstone pizzas.

My grandmother, an ardent follower of organic foods and raw vegetable juices, always preached to me to treat my body like a temple, (although I shook the temple pillars a few times at UT) and eat more fish that was good for the brain. Doctors at Presby made a remark that my diet had given me the edge in surviving. After I saw the available local culinary provisions, I headed my chuck wagon to Butte.

Chapter 44

Monday... fingerprints taken. Driving test given. Forms signed in triplicate. I was now employed by the US Forest Service. Later that afternoon, Dave, a well-seasoned, gray-bearded forester who worked in timber sales administration, approached me.

"I noticed on your SF-171 application that you have some mapping and mechanical drawing experience."

"Yeah, back in high school I was pretty good at map drawing in my geography class, and I had one mechanical drawing and surveying class in college. I'm proud of my printing, and I have never used cursive after sixth grade."

"Well, I can use your talent. I'm a little behind, and I have the Johnson-Schultz timber sale map that needs to get done. You can work on that all this week, then join the tree planting crew next week. I'll get you lined out with ink and the pens in the morning."

My first week with the Forest Service and I was going to be inside an office drawing a map on a large sheet of Mylar, when I secretly wished to be standing on top of Ajax Peak instead.

The bunkhouse started to fill late in the week with additional seasonal help. Some of these guys would work on the fire crew, supervised by Hank, the Fire Control Officer. Dave supervised tree planting, and Rich would oversee trail maintenance and range management. Ted, the district ranger, was always in his office, hardly mixing with the staff but staying plugged to the phone talking forest politics.

Due to Wisdom's isolation and its designation as a hard-duty station, the Wisdom Ranger district was permitted to hire local

179

residents to help to fill the tree planting and trail maintenance rosters. Seven women of various ages were hired and were historically referred to as the "hen crew." They had their own assigned vehicle, an older International Harvester carryall, and it was referred to as the "hen wagon." Roberta was the youngest at twenty, and then there was Lill, who was in her seventies and was tough as leather.

"When you hire on with this outfit, you hire on tough," was Lill's daily pep talk to the crew.

After years of tree planting, she knew the physicality, skinned knuckles, sciatica, and ground-off fingernails that came with the job.

"Grab your hard hats and load up. We're going to the tree cache first," Dave told us after everyone had assembled in the warehouse Tuesday morning.

The tree cache was a very large highway culvert that had been mounded over with eight feet of snow, an additional foot of woodchips from the local sawmill, and several large canvas tarps. An insulated wooden door was jury-rigged for the entrance. Once inside, I shook my head in shock. The light shone on hundreds of boxes of bare-root stock from the Coeur d'Alene nursery, all kept cool within the confines of the cache.

So this is where it all starts. Boxes of lodgepole pine and spruce packed in damp vermiculite, ready to be planted in logged areas where natural regeneration was not successful. Hank was right. I would learn forestry from the ground up. My wish of regenerating America's forests had just begun. *Plant a tree, plant a new life. One wish achieved.*

"Let's go with three boxes today," Dave told me.

That was three-thousand trees, or a little more than two-hundred trees per person.

Once loaded, our caravan of three green, four-wheel-drive pickups and the hen wagon headed for Big Swamp Creek, approximately thirty miles away. Dave picked truck 16802, a short box Chevy with a winch on the front bumper, and waved to me to climb in.

"You ever need that winch?" I asked Dave.

"Ha, shit, in this country do you know what four-wheel drives can do? Get you a mile further and a mile deeper," Dave shot back with the voice of winching experience.

The drive to Big Swamp Creek was the first time I experienced seeing the exquisite Big Hole Valley up close and personal, and it felt more dreamlike than real. I had learned from my week in the office that the Upper Big Hole was the widest mountain valley in southwestern Montana, with much of the valley floor above 6,000 feet in elevation. Wisdom was 6,200 feet, and had seventeen frost-free days a year, with rhubarb the only garden crop that thrived. The surrounding mountains sustained a wealth of wildlife, from the rare wolverine to moose, elk, and deer. Grizzly bears had been pushed out of the Big Hole a hundred years earlier.

We turned off the main road and drove for miles on gravel, winding through sagebrush meadows, rumbling over cattle guards, and crossing rickety bridges above the west fork of the Big Hole River. Golden eagles perched atop telephone poles, searching for prey. This terrain was often called prairie, where sagebrush grew in the dry areas, and its enticing smell of turpentine filled the truck. I was on a sagebrush high. Jackleg fences went for miles in every direction along property lines of ranches and grazing allotments. We passed a turn for the trailhead to Ajax Peak, and I wanted to jump out of the truck.

Scattered throughout the valley floor, I saw more of those wooden contraptions that were close to the humongous stacks of hay.

"Hey, Dave, what are those things used for?" I asked. "They're everywhere."

"You sure do ask a lot of questions. Well, here's lesson one of your Big Hole education," he said, laughing. "Those contraptions are beaverslides, the official symbol of Big Hole haymaking. They have been around since 1910 and originated in the Big Hole. Ranchers used available wooden poles and planks to build them to stack hay."

"How does it stack hay?" I said, still confused.

"Well, when they start haying, it will be easier to understand. That frame supports the inclined plane while a load of hay is pushed to the top. Old timers still use draft horses, but many are switching to tractors. The hay is pulled up, maybe around thirty feet, and then drops through a large gap. That loaf of hay right there, is about twenty tons and can last five or six years."

Big sky. Big bales. Big slides. Big dreams. Everything here was big, and I was stoked.

"Let's all huddle up here and go over the basics of tree planting," Dave ordered.

While he talked, I cast a gaze over the planting unit. Dwarf subalpine fir that survived the slash fire gave off an intense fragrance, somewhat like a Christmas tree. There were still tiny patches of snow in shady areas, where an abundance of glacier lilies, with their frail, sunny yellow petals, appeared to float along the forest floor.

"You know you can eat those," Lill told me. "The deer and bears love them, and so do I. They taste sweet, almost like green pea shoots. Watch me."

"You eat the flowers too?"

"Yeah, those are the best part."

My mother would have to hear about this, I thought as I grabbed the nearest flowers and munched away.

The terrain was rugged with slopes that ranged from flat to thirty percent. This unit had been clear-cut several years earlier, and the residual logging slash had been burned, leaving large charred logs scattered among large rocks. Beargrass thrived, and their tall white heads bloomed throughout the hundred-acre unit.

"We used to plant with a hoedad with trees that had trimmed rootstock, but we're starting to plant untrimmed bare-root using augers. Studies are showing better survival with the untrimmed roots." Dave rambled on. "We are going to auger plant," he said, unlocking the large work chest in the bed of 16802.

Dave pulled out three augers, small gas engines mounted on a frame with shoulder straps. The engine powered a five-inch, carbide-edged auger to drill holes in ground that was more rock than dirt.

"Let's demonstrate. Loring, let's get you set up. Put these earplugs in first."

I didn't mind shouldering the auger while at rest, but once Dave pulled the cord on the small Tecumseh engine and the engine fired, my body vibrated from head to toe. I pulled back on the throttle and drilled my first Montana hole, a cylinder about eight to ten inches deep. The granitic soil, abundant with cobble-sized rock had tossed the auger and dirt in all directions before I finished. *This'll make a man out of you. Only four hundred more to go.*

My father encouraged me to get a college degree so I didn't have to work with my back. Five years of college and my first job was drilling holes.

"Let's get two more augers ready. The rest of you, fill a planting bag with trees, and try to keep those roots from drying out," was more direction from Dave. "Grab a scalping tool too. And remember, the green side up, roots straight, and compact the soil back into the hole."

Three augers roared to life, and twelve planters followed, planting the nine foot by nine foot spacing created by the guys on the augers.

Each tree I planted, I took personally. *Keep those roots straight. No air pockets. Tamp that ground. Scalp the grass away. Put a piece of shade material on the southwest side of the tree.* The reforestation of this unit was more complex than logging it. Up, down, up, down was the tempo as planters moved from hole to hole, bags of seedlings swinging from their hips, while the augers' gas engines fractured the mountain's serenity.

I was in the arms of good luck, but tree planting was not a way to garner fame nor fortune. It was brutally beautiful to look at the fruits of our labor at the end of the day. My inner terrain reveled in living a new way and becoming the new man with the raised consciousness that Charles Reich wrote about. My physical body had regained its vitality and endurance since my surgery. The tics were still present, but I never thought about them. Montana was so big that my tics seemed to be swallowed up in the mountains' grandeur. *Yes, this was all going to plan.* My dream was unfolding each day, and although I didn't need a college education to plant trees, I found the experience was a metaphor for my life. *To grow tall in spirit, to be able to bend, and not break.* When I stuck my hand into that cold planting hole, and became intimate with the dirt, rocks, and roots, I was spiritually grounded to Montana forever.

Chapter 45

G o grab Jake, Loring, and meet me at the corrals," Rich hollered one morning.

Jake, a rough-and-tumble, tousle-haired kid, was just out of high school. Together, we would pack into the Anaconda-Pintler Wilderness and clear the trail of all downed trees, repair any bridges, and install water bars as needed to halt erosion along the trail.

"It's time for you two guys to meet Evelyn, Evvie for short, and learn something about mules and packing for the wilderness."

Evvie was the line back dun mule that Jake and I would use to pack into the Anaconda-Pintler Wilderness. Evvie stood close to fifteen hands and made a noise that was a cross between a horse's whinny and the donkey's hee-haw when we walked into the corral.

I had ridden horses when I lived in the country and occasionally rode the nags at Ames Plantation. I knew how it felt to be bucked off, but I didn't consider myself a seasoned horseman who could whip and ride... or know a darn thing about mules.

"We've had Evvie for over five years, and she's been great to work with on packing and doesn't need the maintenance of a horse," Rich told us. He approached Evvie's neck and expertly slipped a halter over her head and led her to a hitching post outside the corral. "Always show her the halter and come to her from the side. I'm gonna show you two the bank robbers' knot to tie her up, and then have both of you catch her, put the halter on, and tie her to the rail," Rich ordered.

Later that day, Rich took me aside.

"Loring, I want you to know you're in charge out there."

My first supervisory position with the Forest Service was being in charge of an eighteen-year-old kid and a mule. I didn't know which one would be the bigger challenge, but I felt confident about my abilities.

While Jake and I worked on our mule skinning, Rich went inside the barn for the panniers and a pack saddle.

The panniers would hold our ten-day food supply and hand-powered work tools: two shovels, two double-bit axes, a felling wedge, and two pulaskis, a combination tool that was half axe and half adze. There was also a crosscut saw, often referred to as the "misery whip." These were the only tools we had to clear the trail of downed trees, build water bars, or repair bridges. But Evvie couldn't take everything. Jake and I would still need to carry backpacks with tent and sleeping bags into the wilderness.

Rich had Jake and me clear sixty miles of lower elevation non-wilderness trails that week before we headed into the Pintlers. One thing we would miss in the wilderness was the red Homelite chainsaw because they were prohibited.

"Don't reroute the trail unless it is extremely necessary," Rich instructed. "Remember to clear the trail wide enough for back-country horsemen and outfitters. The guys last year thought only hikers and backpackers used these trails. I don't want to deal with that issue again."

On Sunday night, I grasped the reality that my long-awaited trip into the wilderness was just hours away. I could never have enough nature. It was a spiritual necessity. The Smokys had given me solace and stillness after my illness and the loss of Gail and Dixie. The Cherokee believed in the restorative powers of the mountains. My Montana Dream was not too big for the Anaconda-Pintler Wilderness, and I hoped that I would find the same tranquility there as in the Smokys.

It was risky to have a big dream, but to not believe in it could have left me with remorse. I had come face-to-face with the tenacious win/lose duality that usually was associated with big dreamers.

It was with these thoughts that, the next morning, I shouldered my thirty-five-pound pack, shook Rich's hand, and led Evvie and Jake into the Pintlers.

Chapter 46

Jake and I hiked along a trail that was seldom visited in 1976. We passed through high-mountain meadows of tall, lush grass, pockets of giant spruce, and other areas in the wilderness that seemed untouched by the "hand of man." The primordial beauty of the Pintlers was light-years away from the manicured grass fairways, pruned shrubs, and flower beds of Valley Brook Country Club, or the landscaping of Knoxville's prestigious homes. It was easy for me to thrive in those surroundings, except for the dense fog of blood-sucking mosquitoes that swarmed my face and up my nose all day.

"Shit, Hip, do you have any bug dope?" Jake asked when the chill of the morning left and the mosquitoes buzzed to life.

"Yeah, here in my shirt pocket," I told him.

I tossed it back to him.

Jake was a heck of a good kid with a great attitude. He worked hard and was good company, but he was eighteen and our conversations never quite evolved. Two things about Jake that I always remembered were that he referred to me only as "Hip," preceded by "Shit," and could imitate the voice of Donald Duck to perfection.

"Shit, Hip, this bug dope really works."

"It should. This stuff is almost one-hundred percent pure DEET. Look at the little green bottle. It's army surplus from the Vietnam War. It says it's safe for your skin, but it melted the frame of my sunglasses and ate the paint off my pencil. Watch your eyes."

Wisdom had the distinction of being the only Forest Service District that had work halted because of mosquitoes. I wore a long-sleeved denim shirt saturated with the repellant for protection while blocking out fears of what this bug dope was doing to my skin.

We hiked at a brisk pace, and Evvie gave us no problems. And then, in the shadows of giant Douglas firs, broken rays of sunlight highlighted the carved lettering on my Holy Grail: the Forest Service sign that said we were now entering the Anaconda–Pintler Wilderness. It was another Kodak moment, and I had Jake capture it. First, there was the sign welcoming me to Montana, then there was the sign for Wisdom, but this was the sign of my early hopes, my present dream, and my ultimate destination. Stopping for a moment, I let all my senses record that long-awaited moment... Clark's nutcrackers noisily harvested seeds with their raucous kraaa-kraaaing call that disrupted the stillness of the moment. Evvie had a good sweat on, and mule sweat coupled with a leather pack saddle filled the air with an odor that only could be described as wild. Mosquitoes buzzed my ears, and a large horsefly landed on my wrist. Rich had told me that the air shed above the Pintlers was among the purest in the world, and he hadn't lied. I was in the wilderness, a place devoid of pollution, congestion, and mayhem. Even with noise from the nutcrackers, the wilderness seemed quiet and in balance... quiet enough for me to hear my heart beat. There was no television and the rants of crazy politicians. The smells of modern life—the factories, and the exhaust fumes—were replaced by the fresh scents of spruce and fir trees.

The wilderness trip of my own to remember. I wish that I could have called Smoke at that instant and told him of my entrance into the wilderness, but he was probably in the Bob. I was on the Continental Divide Trail, and after crossing the wilderness boundary, I knew I could never leave Montana. I no longer had to read books to travel vicariously through the wilderness. I was immersed in it.

Our destination was Mystic Lake and the guard station that sat at its edge. We ate the remaining miles up in quick fashion and arrived by early afternoon. Our first night was to be based out of the guard station, a small cabin, complete with a wood stove, bunk beds, kerosene lanterns, and official US Forest Service plates, bowls, and cups left from the Civilian Conservation Corps days.

"Let's unsaddle Evvie and get her in the corral. I wanna get my Eagle Claw fly rod put together and hook a rainbow," I told Jake. "Remember, Rich said we were to report on the fishing conditions of all the lakes. Heh heh."

New to fly fishing, I had only read a dime-store introduction to the sport and had not attained the artistry of working my rod with the magical four-count rhythm. As a result, my fly line was a mess of wind knots because I had not let the line completely roll out behind me. I tried too hard, casting into the wind, thinking that I had to get the fly twenty yards out into the open water.

Then, a rainbow jumped to an insect that was preparing to land on the lily pads that were much closer to shore. *So that's where they hang out.*

I stripped out fresh line and tied a #16 Royal Coachman dry fly to my seven-foot leader. "The only fly you need in the Pintlers," Rich had told me.

Starting to think like a fish, I cast shorter distances among the lily pads where the trout were feeding. On my third cast, a lunker snatched my fly right before it landed on the water.

"Keep that rod tip up, work him out of those lily pads," I told myself with great jubilation.

"Shit, Hip, that's a keeper," Jake said as he grabbed my net, waded into the shallows, and netted my first rainbow, a beautiful blue-green torpedo-shaped fish with a pink streak along its sides.

"That's dinner, Jake. Cast out your line. You catch more fish when you have your line in the water."

In a half hour, Jake and I had caught our limit of twelve- to fourteen-inch rainbows, and we retreated to the guard station with a stringer of cleaned fish, ready for the cast-iron skillet.

That evening I tried hard to hang onto the memory of my first day in the wilderness. *See, Smoke, it took me awhile, but I have my wilderness trip to remember now, and I can check that off in my book of dreams. You can reach your dreams if you really want to. I was custom made for this job, a real mule skinner.*

From within the comfy confines of the guard station, I looked forward to the morning cup of coffee brewed cowboy-style...fresh grounds thrown directly into the boiling water. When the grounds sank, the coffee was ready. That would be a good cup of coffee.

"Jake, wake up. Where'd you stash the radio? Evvie's gone from the corral!"

"Ah, over there, in the outside pocket of my pack."

I did not look forward to calling the station, even though it was a morning and evening requirement. I was in charge of one crew member and a mule, and the mule was missing.

"Wisdom, trail crew, over."

"Trail crew, Wisdom, over."

"Barb, you gotta tell Rich that Evvie has broken out of the corral and is missing."

Everyone in the office burst out laughing. *What's so funny?*

"Loring, are you reporting that Evvie is missing?"

"10-4."

There was more laughter. It sounded as if the whole town was there.

What was so damn funny?

"Rich has loaded Evvie and his horse into the stock truck. Evvie doesn't like to be away from Mule Acres, so she high-tailed it back to Wisdom last night. He said to start cutting some new poles, and he'll help you two fix the corral this afternoon. Wisdom out."

"10-4 Barb. Trail crew out."

It took the rest of the morning before I stopped feeling like a true greenhorn. I was still a young pup, unwise to the ways of the wilderness, and a long ways away from being a woods-savvy mule skinner.

Evvie in one of her more cooperative moments.

Jake and I started fresh the next morning, leading Evvie, who was now back on the job after her breakout. We traveled over a mile before we had to tackle our first challenge, a very large, ancient, weathered whitebark pine that's roots had finally let go of its centuries-long hold to the Earth and had come down lengthwise on the trail. This once-majestic tree would require many chops with the axe and plenty of pulls with the "misery whip" to clear.

"Well, here we go, Jake. Take the panniers off Evvie, and I'll wax the saw. We'll be here for a while."

Our saw was professionally sharpened, and the edges of the teeth glistened as I removed it from its sheath. I had to be careful because I was on a lifetime regimen of blood thinners for my heart valve. If I had cut myself on previous day trips, medical help was reasonably close. But now... in the wilderness... a serious cut could be life-threatening, so I wore leather gloves and saw chaps.

After I rubbed tallow on our sharp saw, Jake and I started our first cut. The saw buckled before completing one full pass.

"You gotta pull the saw, Jake. Don't push it. You saw what happened when you pushed it. It buckled. We gotta get in rhythm like tuned guitars, man."

"Shit, Hip. How do you know about that stuff?"

"Oh, back in college, while some students were studying molecular biology, forestry students competed in hatchet-throwing and wood-chopping competitions. Don't get me wrong, forestry was

191

one of the toughest curriculums in college, but we had to protect the old ways of working in the woods, and drink lots of beer after the contests."

Later that evening, I relaxed around the campfire and stared at the unclouded moon that rose in the east, with its slanted beams of light intersecting the blue, licking flames of our campfire. In the firelight, Jake whittled away on a piece of weathered whitebark pine, and I saw Evvie, hobbled and hungry, munching away on mountain meadow grass. Staring upward, I fixated on the handle of the Big Dipper, imagining it full of all my Montana Dreams. Never had I seen the Milky Way with its millions of gleaming stars so clearly.

My wilderness experiences started to add up: landing rainbow trout, chasing runaway mules, watching mountain goats walk five feet below a rock I sat on, and seeing lightning blow an ancient pine to smithereens the previous day. Walking and climbing for miles every day left me feeling how fortunate I was to be able to endure the physical trials of wilderness work with an artificial heart valve. When you hired on with this outfit, you hired on tough.

Maybe, because I had grown up kind of lonely, I needed to prove myself both to myself and the outside world. I understood that most fears were born of loneliness. The facial tics just seemed to set up an invisible barrier to people who did not know me well. Well, no moss grows under my feet. Perhaps my Montana Dream was part of a divine plan to test me: emotionally, physically, and spiritually... to not let anger manifest within me, to handle feeling alone, to not retreat from facial tics and grimaces, to become better, not bitter, to set my dream as high as those stars.

Why was I always in a relentless pursuit of high achievement? Is that why others noticed my leadership potential? My faith was strengthened the first time I saw the sunlight break into prisms of light at the Twelfth Station. The Pintler Wilderness was my new church, and I felt like the priest I never was.

Chapter 47

I'm gonna put on a clean shirt to go home today," I told Jake. "This shirt is toxic waste, saturated with all that bug dope after ten days."

Only a pack on my back left me with the feeling that I was fully dressed.

"What's the first thing you gonna do in Wisdom, Hip?"

"Well-l-l first, I'm gonna throw all these clothes in the washer, then climb into the shower and scrub all of the bug dope off of me with that stinky, rusty Wisdom water. And then I'm gonna head to the Antlers and have a cold Lucky with the other guys. I'll just head back to my place and lay on the couch and dream about Mystic Lake trout while Emmy Lou Harris sings me to sleep."

Jake never had a chance to answer as our two-way radio crackled to life.

"Trail crew, Wisdom, over."

It was Hank.

"Wisdom, trail crew, over."

"Loring, we just had a spotter plane fly over some smoke to your southwest. That lightning storm the other night got a small fire going. About a quarter acre in size and growing. Unload Evvie and tie her to a tree. Rich will come get her. You and Jake head to the fire and start building a line around it. The fire crew will be there in a couple hours."

"10-4 Hank. Trail crew out," I signed off while I buckled the radio to my belt.

I swelled with pride, realizing Hank had just given me the order to head to the fire and take action until the fire crew arrived. Jake and I would need to work together to make a big contribution in our initial attack. Hank was counting on me, and I wanted to be at my best when my best was needed.

"Let's go, Jake. We've just been called to a fire. You take a shovel and an axe, and I'll grab the canteens and a pulaski."

We left the trail and started bushwhacking to the southwest, where on a small ridge line we spotted the smoke column. It was less than a mile away, but with no trail, we slowly climbed over boulders and treacherous downfall on the ground.

"A good hour hike in this terrain," I told Jake as I scanned the steep uphill route ahead.

But Jake was eighteen and broke the first rule of fighting wildfires. He raced to the fire and covered the terrain like a shot-at mule deer. In a minute, I was at least a hundred yards behind.

"Damn it, Jake, I told you to stay close," I shouted out.

I scrambled for the next quarter hour and started to smell the smoke, but I couldn't spot Jake.

Another five minutes passed, and I was in view of the fire starting its run up the slope.

Groaning sounds. I stopped. It had to be Jake.

"Jake, where are you?" I screamed.

The moaning came from the direction of several large boulders, where I found Jake lying spread-eagled, clutching his chest, clenching his eyes, and gritting his teeth.

"Aw, shit, Hip, I think I cracked some ribs. I'm hurtin' bad."

Oh boy, was I pissed, but now was not the time to tell him and rattle him further than his injuries had done. I would let him know how he disobeyed my instructions and how it resulted in injury. I was his supervisor and had to let Jake know he was responsible for his own safety.

"Did you crack your head, too?"

"No, ahh, ahh, just my chest."

Armed with extensive first aid knowledge from scouting and college, I examined Jake for broken bones or open wounds.

"Gotta get you closer to the fire, Jake, so I can watch you. Help is on the way. Can you walk?"

"I think so, ah, ah, if you help."

Leaving the axe and shovel behind, I held the pulaski in my left hand as a cane and supported Jake with my right arm and shoulder. Jake was stable, and I treated him for shock by propping his legs up. His hands clutched his chest in agony.

"Just stay calm Jake. You're not spitting up any blood, which is good."

Grabbing my pulaski, I started to scratch a fire line. Smoke swallowed me, and my lungs started hacking in defense. My eyes burned. Snot ran in strings out my nose to my chin. Alone… with a wildfire raging out of control. Another hour passed before Hank and the fire crew arrived.

"What's up with Jake hunkered down over there?" Hank asked me, squinting his eyes at him while taking a drag on a Camel.

Camel could have benefitted from an ad showing Hank drawing in a drag from his cigarette, standing on the fire line of a smoky wildfire.

"He fell on the rocks and is complaining about his ribs, but he's not in shock and his color is good. He said he can walk out with some help."

Hank was an EMT; he examined Jake, and concurred with my diagnosis.

"Okay, I'm sending Fred with you, and you two get Jake to the Mussigbrod Road. I'll call Rich to drive the road and look for you. When you get back to the station, you and Fred take Jake to Butte to get checked out."

I was Jake's supervisor, and while reluctant to leave the fire shorthanded, I knew the responsibility of caring for Jake fell squarely on my shoulders.

It was two a.m. when the doctor finally released Jake from the emergency room.

"He has one broken rib and hairline fractures on two ribs. He's bruised pretty deep in the chest wall. He'll be sore for a while, but he can return to work on Monday doing light duty," the doctor informed me. It was four in the morning before I helped Jake to bed in the bunkhouse. It was the longest day of my life.

Friday was my scheduled day off, but I was required to stop by the office to fill out the accident report on Jake.

"You got some mail while you were out," Barb told me.

The bold handwriting of my father was easy to recognize, and there was a letter from my grandmother. There also was a postcard of a pod of whales... postmarked from Orcas Island, Washington. David didn't forget.

Chapter 48

Not much sleep for me last night," Fred confessed as I shared a frosty Lucky with him at the Antlers after returning again from Butte, that afternoon for a blood test.

"Certainly not the evening of relaxation I planned. I haven't pulled an all-nighter since college."

"Say, are you up for heading out on your days off for an overnighter to Hamby Lake? Seven miles in, and some good fishing. Milwaukee Mike heard about it the other day when some guys stopped in for a beer. He said he knows where the sign for the trailhead is. Hamby is not in in the Pintlers but in the West Big Hole Primitive Area. There is another small lake, Geneva, I think he said. We can fish that one too."

"You bet, I'm in. I gotta unload some food, and I'll be back in a bit."

There were over a hundred mountain lakes on the Wisdom District alone, and I had been only to a dozen so far. After ten days in the wilderness and one short night of sleep in my bed, I was going to head outdoors and hike fourteen miles on my days off. I was just living my dream.

The next morning at Hamby trailhead...

"There's seven of us, but I don't think the three girls want to carry any beer," Fred moaned, looking at me for help.

"C'mon Fred, even Megan, the college girl from Washington? Your home state."

"Yep, even her. A little too cosmopolitan for this job, I think. And dig this. She's complaining that we're just packing Luckys. For

197

some strange reason, known only to God, she's in love with Great Falls Select."

"You're kidding me! Only a father could love a daughter who drinks Great Falls Select. Guess they never heard Lill's speech about hiring on tough. All right... Let me think... I'm sure they'll drink Lucky if we carry it for them. I can pack one more six-pack of Lucky, if that will help. You guys can split up the other two sixers."

The pack felt good on my shoulders, but the extra weight of the beer made me feel like I was walking on my knees. *Do I really need to show this group how tough I am? My doctor's instructions were to set my own pace, but we never talked about backpacking a case of beer seven miles uphill either.*

The morning wore on as we gradually climbed one major ridge to the top, only to be rewarded with another ridge to climb. At about what I thought was halfway, the trail became very steep, but provided us with unconceivable views of the West Big Hole. It was then that I realized we were hiking on a fire trail and not one for recreational hiking.

"Hamby must sit on the other side of that ridge," I told the group during a rest break. "Keep on truckin'."

Pulling a large garbage bag from my pack, I started to fill it with some crusty snow that still hid between the larger rocks on the north side of the trail.

"What are you going to do with that snow?" Gwen asked me, somewhat dumbfounded by my actions.

"Well, Gwen, there's not enough for a snowman, and I don't like warm beer, do you?"

"No!"

The bag with seven cans of Lucky was packed in as much snow as I could fill around the cans.

By mid-afternoon we came into view of the placid waters of Hamby Lake, and it was bigger than I thought. Then our eyes focused on a spectacle that was born of poor planning by Milwaukee Mike.

"What the hell, Mike?" Gwen screamed.

"You are such a dumbass," Fred let loose with both barrels, as tempers erupted from the exhausted and thirsty group.

Milwaukee Mike was not stung by the barbs hurled at him.

"I'm going fishing," he told us. "Beers are on me."

Around the edge of the lake was a campground with pickup trucks, camping trailers, and tents. A blue canoe was on the water. After six hours of hiking, we found out that we could have driven to Hamby.

Chapter 49

My Montana Dream was unfolding to plan, but I was only half-awake to discovering more when I hooked up with Ellie, a tagalong friend of Lester's and Charlene's. The three had driven up from Idaho to visit me in Wisdom in late August. We were all having beers at the Antlers when I noticed Ellie's sparkly blue eyes and a voice that was as pretty as a lark when she sang along with songs on the jukebox. She wowed me over when she sang "Me and Bobby McGee," a capella in a soprano voice, tossing her long, blond hair along with the beat.

Lester saw the pool table open and asked Ellie to grab a cue stick, leaving me a chance to chat privately with Charlene.

"How long have you known Ellie?" I asked Charlene between sips.

"I've known her for a couple years. We used to waitress together at the Cracker Barrel when I was a sophomore. She graduated two years ago and was working in Virginia, and we kept in touch. She decided she needed a change and loaded her Mustang and came to visit us."

"Why did she need a change?"

"Oh, if I remember it right, it was about three or four years ago she lost her family in a horrific accident. She got hurt pretty bad, too, but she lived and her family all died."

"That's terrible. I mean is she doing okay? She looks good after what you just told me."

"Yeah, I think she's doing okay. I promised her I wouldn't talk about it in detail. Come on, Loring. You think she's cute, don't you?"

Lester and Charlene stayed the weekend, but Ellie and I hit it off, and I asked her to stay for a couple days longer. A couple of days transformed into us living together. Ellie was quick to find work in a neighboring town, and I found myself in a live-in relationship with a woman I barely knew.

Ellie came into my life at a needy time, and I wasn't completely sure if she was right for me. I had physically recovered after my illness, but my internal decisions about Ellie were not based on a rational process. It was all emotional, and the catalyst to wanting to get involved may have been the fear of being alone in a small western town with the darkness and cold of winter near. My illness had left me wanting more than what I was ready for at times. I had witnessed how life could be short, and I wanted to marry, and have a family. I thought marrying Ellie would resolve the unsettled feelings that I had ever since Gail had passed away. After two months, I told my father I wanted to marry Ellie.

"Don't marry, yet," my father said in warning. "You don't really know each other, and you're not ready. You don't understand what changes you will go through in the next few years, let alone forty or fifty. Take your time, son. Believe what I tell you. Your mother and I feel you're acting on impulse. That's not like you."

"Yeah, yeah, yeah, Dad. You know everything. If Gail hadn't died, maybe we wouldn't be having this conversation."

"Exactly my point, son. She was a good match for you, and we got to know her."

He had hit the nail squarely on the head.

My father seemed to have a treasure trove of wisdom that was complemented by giving me the freedom to live as large a life as I could build, but he now sensed I was making a mistake. I had only known Ellie a very short time, and we married on a whim. More than likely our marriage was an emotional Band-Aid for two young people who had suffered incredible losses in their lives. I lost a girlfriend—a piece of my heart—and a dog. She lost her family. I had a life-threatening illness. Ellie was severely injured during the course of losing her family.

Love had hurt us. Did it matter whose loss was greater, or were all losses created equal? How deep did a hurt have to be before it would hit rock bottom? *Or is there a bottom?* It was my utmost wish to get my life to the next level and finally release Gail, finish my grieving process, and climb back into the real world. Oh, how I missed the simple day-to-day talking with her and making each other laugh. But what I ached for most was the way that she would rub her hands over my naked chest and stroke my face, bringing a calmness to my body that temporarily slowed my tics. She had a way about her that even my mother knew was special. It was so hard to finish my grieving because I never would have all the facts about why she wanted to see me. Her memory continually played like a broken record.

How can my dream grow if I make my box of rocks any heavier?

"Move on, Loring, be the man in motion and release me," she would have told me. "Look for the goodness in Ellie and follow your bliss."

After some serious soul-searching, I realized that I had overlooked many of Ellie's special qualities, but it was still with a wistful resolve that I proposed marriage.

Ellie hesitated with uncertainty, then accepted. I believed her hesitation stemmed from similar feelings. She needed not to be alone.

"Let's drive to Reno and get married," she said. "It'll be easy and fun."

"Yeah, sure. We can drive down on a Friday, get married Saturday, and be back in Wisdom on Sunday. You can meet my parents when we drive to Pennsylvania for Christmas next month."

"No, no," I said to myself later. Thoughts of my family and my church overwhelmed me. Others had told me of how a Nevada quick marriage happens, and I kind of knew what to expect. My dear brother would not be the best man, replaced with a rent-a-witness, a complete stranger. A justice of the peace would probably have our names clipped to his reading to help remember who we were.

My hasty decision to marry shortchanged my family of participating. I didn't feel right that I skipped having my marriage performed in my church and officiated by Father Ben... the church of the Twelfth Station and the priest who had administered Last Rites of the Church to me.

The wedding was over before it started. The justice of the peace had our names clipped to his binder like I had heard he would. After tipping our wino witness five dollars, Ellie and I made a quick exit of the Reno courthouse to attend our wedding luncheon at a drive-through taco joint. I choked down three. No chapel bells rang that morning in the small, gambling town of Reno. Yes, it was easy, but there was no fun, no celebration, no ode to joy, and no family in attendance. No one was home when I called my parents to tell them the news. Ellie and I drove the next twelve hours in numbed silence.

Chapter 50

Layoffs happen, and it was an experience that I was familiar with growing up when my father was occasionally laid off from the mill. But now, my college degree was not going to help me find work in the frozen cattle country of the Big Hole after I was laid off. Knowing it was going to happen prompted me to find work, any work. It was during a Wisdom Community Social in early December that I had met a familiar rancher, Calvin Barkley, the owner of Wild Prairie Land and Cattle Company. Tall and lanky, wearing a powder-blue silk neckerchief and Stetson hat, Cal looked the real cowboy, but he had left the ranch to take care of itself for an evening of fun. He had driven over twenty miles of icy, back roads from his ranch that sat on a bench overlooking the North Fork of the Big Hole River. His wife Colleen was with him, and together they came to "cut the rug" on some country western music. I had a sad country dancing ineptness, never learning the two-step or swing.

Polkas were in my blood, being from Pittsburgh, and I was an accordion player in my youth. But, if I was gonna live in Wisdom, I better learn these steps. However, on that night, my logging boots, with a thick Vibram sole, only accentuated my ineptness with the new steps, and I squashed Ellie's toes several times.

There was a moment that I caught Cal alone at the buffet line, and I worked my way through dancing cowboys to ask him about work.

"Hey Cal, I'm going to be laid off before Christmas and wondered if you're needing any ranch help the first of the year."

"Well, my brother Ray and I could use some help feeding and moving cattle down south to our winter ranch in Dillon for calving.

The winters there are not as rough as the Big Hole's. Can you ride a horse?"

"Yeah, I can ride a horse, but I'm no roper or steer wrestler. I'm not afraid of hard work or the cold."

"How about tractors?"

"Yeah, I'm familiar with tractors. I helped my friends bale hay and cut silage back in Pennsylvania during high school."

"Can you drive an eighteen-wheeler full of cattle?" he added with a chuckle, while slathering ketchup and mustard on his hot dog.

"Ah, got me there. I never drove an eighteen-wheeler, but I'll learn."

"That's okay. Well, I can't pay much for a 'green hand' like yourself, but I'll hire you for two hundred forty five bucks a month. Colleen will feed you good, and you can eat all you want. You're welcome to stay in the bunkhouse for no charge. You do your own bedding."

"Thanks, Cal, I just got in married three weeks ago, and I'll keep my apartment in Wisdom. I can start right after the New Year."

The wages were an insult, even for a green hand, but I would be fed, and I was a hungry boy then.

Chapter 51

Ellie and I were returning to Montana after being back to Pennsylvania visiting my family for Christmas. What I had envisioned for my Joyeux Noel in introducing Ellie to my family was awkward. Ellie was withdrawn, and she was not the smiling or the charming woman my parents had witnessed with Gail. I was very uncomfortable and reconciled that a new family with differing cultural mores must have been hard for Ellie, after tragically losing hers. Ellie was modest and quiet, reluctant to kid with my father like Gail had done. I wanted to go home.

Somewhere in the middle of South Dakota, on a snow-packed highway that night, Ellie confessed, in a cold, brittle tone, "I won't be living in Wisdom with you, Loring. I found an apartment near my work."

"What!"

Surprised at first, I thought further that this could be a logical statement. Ellie had found work in a neighboring town an hour away from Wisdom, and commuting over a mountain pass in winter could be a hardship. A small apartment to stay in on bad weather days seemed logical.

"No, not just for the winter or bad weather days," she told me emotionlessly, turning her head away.

"What are you talking about? We've been married seven weeks. I was gone for two of those weeks on that fire near Glacier. There has to be more to this story than what you're telling me. Well?"

The transistor radio was dead. Ellie gave me the silent treatment. Silence. More silence. Silence, for the next seven hundred miles. Terribly upset with Ellie's mendacity, I found relief behind the wheel of my truck. The road was in my blood, and the feel of the snow-packed highway that crunched under my wheels allowed me to mind travel back to my utopian dream of living in Montana with all of its magical beauty and grandeur... and no heartaches. How Pollyannish was that.

Chapter 52

S hattered! Outside my apartment window, the dark, freezing Wisdom night left me numb with the cold. Inside, my heart was dazed from despair. Facing the incandescent truth of being separated in a hasty marriage to Ellie, a woman I hardly knew, a moment of clarity came to me, and I sensed there were possible unexplored grief issues between us that we had chosen to ignore. Another heartache. Married. Seven weeks. Alone again. Walking out of the Pintler Wilderness by moonlight would have been easier than finding my way in the parallel wilderness of my marriage where I was really lost and confused, and had no map.

This shocking marital development was similar to my feelings about Ajax Peak. There was magic with Ajax Mountain in how I viewed its strength and beauty, but the magic I expected to find in my marriage was not there. From the valley floor, Ajax was stunning, free of imperfections, cracks, crevasses, or other mountain perils. However, up close the peak was anything but blemish-free. Loose rock and scree called for extreme caution, scrutiny, and focus before taking the next step. The greatest growth came from climbing over rocks, cracks, grass, and snow… obstacles that would only strengthen me for the climb to the next summit. The view from the top widened my view of Earth and didn't let me see it through a set of myopic eyes. The mountains provided the solitude and lack of distractions for uninterrupted meditation.

There was silence and solitude—and loneliness—in my apartment that night, but instead of peaceful meditation, I felt a poverty of spirit deep within me. *Recommit.* The hours dragged by as I anxiously awaited the sunrise and the dawn of a new day.

In the morning, I realized that Montana was a land where people that were drawn into our lives could share the dichotomy of beauty and harshness. I planned my route to the high summit of Ajax, but I did not plan a walk three steps up to an altar. My father was right. My marriage started like the view of Ajax from the valley floor. It was my mountain temple, all so pretty and wonderful. But there was also harshness that I didn't expect.

Though the emotional and geographical distance was consistent, Ellie and I still spent time together on some weekends trying to navigate to some sort of normal. Several weeks later, Ellie needed an emergency wisdom tooth extraction. Despite our unusual situation, I couldn't imagine not being the person to get her to and from the appointment and help her while she was incapacitated. We were driving back to her place, her mouth full of gauze and pink drool coming from the corners of her lips. She was still groggy from the sedation when she tried to talk to me, but I couldn't understand a word she was saying.

"Are you saying that there is no coffee at your place, and I can stop to get some if I want? Is that what you said?"

"Ah-ha."

I didn't need or want any coffee, and even if the anesthesia was still causing her fogginess, she had the presence of mind to think of me getting up in the morning without coffee. That one single moment of time, that one ah-ha, found a soft place in my heart, but it did not define our lives together.

There was a later time in my Montana Dream when Ellie's caring was replaced with acrimony.

One evening before supper, I was making fresh salsa when Ellie flew into a rage.

"I can't take any more of that grunting or those goofy faces that you make all the time. I've had it. I wish I could shake them out of you."

Whoa! I felt like the end of a cracked whip after she told me that. I was perfectly aware that my tics were not easily accepted by everyone. Maybe that had contributed to me feeling alone a lot. People feared what they didn't understand, and Ellie, if no one else, should have accepted my human condition. I couldn't explain my

209

condition any better to Ellie than I did to Gail. Ellie offered an apology, and I accepted but never forgot the way it made me feel. It was hard for me to see the truth in Ellie's eyes. I was hurt, but I would not let it spoil my life. As harsh as Ellie's statements were to me, I packed them away in a place for forgetting. To ease my pain, I retreated and reopened Gail's box of acceptance, which rekindled my emotions for her once more. The memory of Gail was my "fraidy" couch. When faced with ugly situations, I would hide behind the comfort of her memory.

Chapter 53

Uh-h-h-h-h. Uh-h-h-h-h. That sound was the most I could coax out of my Dodge the first day I was to report to Cal. My truck seat was hard as a brick, and my tires had flat spots on the bottom.

Uh-h-h-h-h. Uh-h-h-h-h. The battery just couldn't get the motor to turn over at twenty below zero.

Jimmy, my seldom-seen neighbor and grade school teacher, who lived in the other upstairs apartment was going to work early that morning.

"Loring, you're gonna have to get this rig ready for Big Hole winters. You gotta go down to Buddy's Conoco and have him put a tank heater in so you can plug your truck in at night. Look over yonder, that's what all those outdoor plugs are for. Have Buddy drain all your lubricants and replace them with Conoco Polar Guard. That's the crap they use on the North Slope. It doesn't thicken in cold temperatures like motor oil. Now let's see if we can get that Power Wagon to start."

Jimmy reached behind the seat of his pickup and pulled out a large can of ether, with a squirt tube attached.

"We gotta be careful with this stuff, so we don't bust your crankshaft. Get inside and I'll squirt some ether down your carb. It should turn over."

On the second crank my engine came to life, with flames shooting out of the carburetor. Then the engine sputtered and came to a rough idle.

"Gee, thanks, Jimmy. What do you think Buddy will charge for all that," I said as we waited inside the apartment entrance for our trucks to warm.

"Oh, you're looking at about fifteen for the heater, twenty in labor to install and drain. Maybe another twenty for the Polar Guard. Do you have an extension cord? You'll need one of them."

More expense, keeping my truck warm. But Buddy, I heard, operated like every other business in Wisdom. Lucky beers, gas, and Tater Tots could all be put on your tab, payable at the end of the month. Beers on credit. Now that was Lucky.

Cal was not anxious to start hauling cattle that day with the temperatures hovering at ten below zero.

"Pray for a Chinook," Cal suggested, referring to the strong, dry, warm winds that sometimes blew from the mountains brought quick temperature changes. "I don't like to haul in this weather. Cows will swish their tails outside of the trailer, and they'll freeze off. Supposed to be warmer tomorrow. We have some flooring work in the horse barn to do today after feeding. How about you fire up the Ford tractor and take a big, round bale down to those calves on the south side of the road."

Cal and Ray, who moved from Colorado, were relatively new to the Big Hole and did not put their hay up in the traditional method of using beaver slides, but preferred to round bale their high-quality hay of timothy, blue joint, and nut grasses. These nutrient rich native grasses did not require additional feeding of grain or silage during the winter. With a 700 pound bale on the front forks of the tractor, I felt more connected to my Montana Dream, and I realized that I was a Montana-experience-junkie at heart.

Maybe I'll write a story of my life someday. Swirling clouds of snow above Ajax Peak were backlit by the deepest blue sky. The tractor ride was bumpy as hell as I drove over piles of frozen cow manure. The wind turned my cheeks numb, and snot-cicles hung from my nose and moustache like ice daggers. My eyelids were freezing shut, and that helped me temporarily overlook my marital dilemma. I wanted to take a time out and live a large Montana moment of ranch life and warm my hands near the exhaust.

Between those brief moments of concentration, my mind never wandered too far from the separation. *Should I leave her?* That didn't make sense because she already left. *Should I stay? Give a chance to a dream-buster? How about my chance?* It was all so crazy. I had never felt so confused and torn like this before. This separation was not part of my Montana Dream, and I did not want my destiny to be crowned the King of Pain, ruling over a most-desolate kingdom.

"Lunch," Cal yelled after I parked the tractor and closed the gate held together with the common Big Hole-style of using a horseshoe on a chain.

Ray's son, Buck, joined us, and Colleen had put a hot lunch of meatloaf and mashed potatoes and apple pie for dessert on a red-checkered table cloth. It looked like a setup for a Sunset magazine photo shoot. If this was lunch, I wondered what was for supper. Colleen had already started cooking again after lunch was served.

"Say Cal, what made you all move from Colorado to the Big Hole?" I asked in an attempt at creating small talk.

Cal, in between bites said, "I think that's Ray's story."

"Well, Ray?"

Ray did a double take on being asked, and raised his eyes off the dinner plate to glare at Cal. It was obvious to me that this story was one that Ray preferred to keep private.

"It was three years ago, and Cal and I were moving cattle out of the high country near the Gore Range in Colorado. The day was clear, but thunder and lightning started to move in and there were several 'bolts from the blue.' Bolts started to strike in every direction, and then a side splash of lightning landed on the pommel of my saddle, killed my horse right under me, and blew me off my horse along with the soles off my boots. I landed upside down and temporarily lost my hearing. Right then and there I had an epiphany. I believe God didn't want me in Colorado anymore, so we moved to the Big Hole."

"Holy smokes, Ray, I've never heard anything like that before. When I was fourteen, I had an epiphany too about moving to Montana."

Am I being spun by the grand master of western yarns?

213

"The story's all true, and he still has the boots," Cal said, and forked another slab of meatloaf onto his plate.

It was uncanny to find that Ray and I both shared a Montana epiphany.

Cal and I drove the eighteen-wheeler to the Dillon winter ranch the next morning. The shitters were unloaded into a large pen, where Ray brought out a propane torch, a branding iron, a box of syringes filled with a vaccine, and a box that looked to be jam-packed with large rubber bands. There was also some kind of lopping shears.

"Everyone has a job to do here," Ray told me. "Buck here will move the bull calf into the squeeze chute and lock him down. Loring, you get that branding iron hot, not cherry hot, just about the color of gray ashes, and brand him on the hind quarter. I'll show you on the first calf. Their coats are pretty dry, and that will give us a good brand. It'll smoke, but we don't want to make an open wound, just to kill the hair follicles. I'll do the vaccinating and put these bands around the calf's scrotum. Not as messy as castrating. Cal will lop off any horn growth. Got it?"

"YEEHAW. Let's get western," I heard Buck yell after getting the first calf into the Powder River squeeze chute.

It all worked like Ray said, and after I branded the calf and Cal lopped off the horns, we sent that balling, smoking, bleeding calf to the winter pasture. Within a minute, the calf was munching on hay. We finished that load and moved inside and took our cowboy hats off at the door. Cal went to the oven and brought out the piping hot hamburger casserole that Colleen had sent down with us. She sure knew how to cook for hungry men and did not use Tater Tots.

Payday. Cal didn't take any taxes out, and I had a whopping two-hundred-and-forty-five-dollar check. Pay Buddy. Pay Jerry the grocer. Paying the rent left me with less than twenty dollars to spend, but the twenty dollars was all mine. Ellie had a job and was living on her own. I was poor in the pocket, but not in spirit. All I needed was for my rich uncle to get out of the poorhouse.

"Hey Loring, how's the cowboy life?" Don, also laid off from the Forest Service, called out as he was filling his blue, rusted Jeep to only half full at Buddy's. "Cherie and I are pretty broke, but I heard there's a logging sale on private ground up Doolittle Creek and they need some guys to set chokers and stuff."

"Heck, I can saw and fall timber. I can't go back to ranching. Twenty dollars is not going to carry me through the month."

"Well, let's go up there Monday morning and check it out."

"I've never quit a job before, Don, but I think Cal will understand."

Cal did understand, and I left my Resistol cowboy hat and life on the range after a month to go logging, with no guarantee of being hired.

Chapter 54

Don and I four-wheeled up Doolittle Creek to Roy Harmon's logging camp. An idling, metallic-blue cab of a Peterbilt logging truck had "Roy Harmon Logging, Salmon, Idaho," stenciled on the doors. There was a small work trailer with wood smoke coming out of the stack. Next to the trailer, a D-3 bulldozer was parked next to a Caterpillar cable skidder that was not running, while a bunch of rough-looking woodsmen were fiddling with some action involving the winch on the skidder. This skidder selectively pulled sawn trees out of the woods and was also used for pulling tree stumps and pushing over small trees.

Don and I sauntered up to the group, looking for the woods boss or even Roy himself.

"What do you two assholes want? Can't you see I'm busy?" said a greasy, grimy, hawk-nosed, pipsqueak of a man.

"We're looking for Roy; we wanna see about work," I said.

"I'm Roy. Come see me tomorrow. I'm busy."

I pushed back. "We can't come tomorrow."

"Told you I'm busy."

"We can saw, set chokers, whatever you need. You have to be down at least one man, all those logs on the landing haven't had a knot bumper yet, and your truck isn't loaded."

"I fired that knot bumper's sorry ass on Friday."

"I'm ready to work today."

"Me too," Don piped in.

Roy Harmon gave me the creeps. I had never met such a scrawny, foul-mouthed peckerhead like him before in my life. He was a gyppo logger, one who didn't work for a company or lumber mill. Gyppos worked for themselves and ran their crews on the thinnest of economic margins and safety regulations. Employees had no grievance procedure involving working conditions or pay. It would be Roy's way or the highway, but I knew I was tough enough and skilled enough to not expect any trouble.

"You," he said pointing at me. "You seem to know so gawd-damned much, you wanna work, go get your ass bumping knots on the deck. And you, you long-haired hippie bastard," pointing to Don, "Follow me."

The Homelite saw on the log deck was a piece of junk. Just like the name said. They're for the home, and they're light. I had used a Homelite for clearing trails and knew their eccentric qualities quite well, but I was disgusted by the condition of this one. The chain was dull and hung loose on the bar, the air filters were plugged, and while there was a can of mixed gas, there was little bar oil left in the jug. Thanks to a season of trail work, I had that Homelite tuned and sharpened within an hour, and before Roy came around again.

I started bumping knots, logging lingo referring to sawing off the remaining limbs and branches that the sawyer was unable to get in the woods. Don walked behind the now operating CAT skidder, preparing to unhook the choker cables from the logs the operator had skidded to the landing.

"I miss the Forest Service," Don yelled above the roar of the super-charged diesel.

"So do I," I said as I pulled the throttle back on the saw to attack the fresh load of logs.

When I got caught up on bumping knots, Roy suddenly appeared from the trailer as if on cue.

"Get your ass behind the D-3 and set chokers. This outfit is the shits."

Speak for yourself, Roy.

I heaved on the winch line, dragging it through a foot of snow out to the logs. Sixteen-foot choker cables ran free along the winch line, and I needed to set each choker around the end of a felled tree, so that when all the chokers were set and the winch line reeled in, the logs were attached and delivered to the deck in one turn. There was no big timber involved, just lodgepole and Doug fir in the fifteen-inch diameter class.

Each job I had in Montana kept getting more physical, but I was dirt poor for all the work I had done. *See these clothes, son. How hard...* My father's words jarred my memory. Were dreams made of this? Men like Roy Harmon didn't earn my respect, but hunger had me overlooking his character in exchange for food money. I tried never to think about the Bjork–Shiley valve clicking away in my chest. No, I wasn't playing offensive tackle for the Steelers like Dr. Zap said, but I think my Montana work would have left my Presby doctors speechless. I was always alert for the saw to kick back and cut me. Roy did not provide safety gear for chainsaw use like the Forest Service. There were more hazards in a logging operation than clearing a trail with a chainsaw or swinging a double-bit axe in the wilderness.

Chapter 55

It was so cold, my jaw muscles were slow to move. Alone, in a phone booth, I breathed the steam off my ungloved hand as I called home one Sunday morning.

"Hi, Mom," my voice crackled into the frosty mouthpiece of the pay phone. I blew on my hand and tried to get my gloves back on after dialing. Stomping my feet to keep warm shook the inside of the frigid phone booth that sat in the center of Wisdom.

"Are you still eating well at the ranch? I'm worried that you aren't getting enough vitamins. And how about your blood test? It's time isn't it?"

"Aw, no, Mom. I'm eating really well. Work's going okay, got a new job, logging. It's just really cold here. Don't worry, I'm going for a blood test this week."

After six weeks, I needed to tell my parents about my current living arrangements, and I was glad my mother had answered the phone. I was at a loss on how to break the news, then thought I'd soften the blow by using a popular line from a country song.

"Mom, most days the past month I've been sleeping single in a double bed."

"Oh, no, no."

"Yeah, I know. I feel like I fell off a cliff, but I'm doing okay. Really. I don't understand anything though. I feel she is a completely different person than I first knew. I called her last Saturday, thinking I would drive to see her."

"Well, what did she say?"

"She told me 'No, I'm not up to seeing you today,'" I said.

"And then?" my mother wanted to know.

"'Come if you want, but I may not be here,' she said. It's really screwed up Mom. I got into something I know nothing about."

"Katie, go get your father," I heard her say. "Loring, would you like a visit?"

"Mom, that's okay. You don't have to come. I know you and Dad weren't happy about me getting married, but I'm doing okay and I'll figure this mess out. It's really cold here right now, but I'm healthy and working."

"All right. I'm sorry that you have to go through this. Give it a little time. You jumped into this marriage way too quickly, and maybe Ellie is scared what she got herself into. You know how I feel, and I am not surprised. I'll fill your father in."

My mother had only met Ellie one time and never formed a solid opinion of her. She had been concerned enough to tell me that she thought Ellie seemed distant to me during Christmas, and that had worried her. I had noticed it, too. Now, she found it hard to believe a woman would leave a marriage without giving a reason. My mother, although one to let her boys fight their own battles, was a fierce combatant when it came to protecting her children. She was a young warrior as a child, having to survive a brutal father, and wanted us to be strong. She had started with selecting my name. Then there was the time she told UT Security how to do their job on an Easter morning, the time she was ready to jump on a jet and attend Gail's funeral, and now she wanted to come to Montana to support me, even after I did not heed her or my father's advice.

Chapter 56

E very day Don and I went to work, we never knew what to expect. One day no skidder operators showed 'til nine, after they had slept off a drunk. Another day, there were no fallers, and the skidders had no logs to pull. On a Friday of our third week, nobody showed to skid logs and the cutting unit started to have logs jackstrawed all over the woods. On the way home, I asked Don if he wanted to work Saturday and Sunday.

"I never ran a D-3 before, but it doesn't look that hard, Don. It's easy to start, and I know how the levers work. We can skid at least eighty or ninety logs out, and make a hundred bucks apiece."

"I'm good with that," Don agreed. "Maybe that'll make Roy get off our backs. He caters to all those asshole buddies of his from Salmon and treats us like cow shit."

It was a rough start on the D-3 Saturday morning when I took hold of the steering controls.

Let's see, this lever to go left. Here's the brake... whoa baby. I tromped down harder to stop while I figured out the touch of the other controls.

"Fkn-a, we're logging now," Don yelled as I came to a stop to release the main-line.

The D-3 was a small machine, and it always seemed to be tilting to one side or the other as I maneuvered over logging slash. Don and I had absolutely no knowledge of diesel mechanics, short of filling it with fuel, and hoped that we could get through the day without the newly repaired steering clutch and brake breaking down. There wasn't a protected cage for the operator like the CAT had, and that

221

scared the hell out of me. It had taken an hour to really feel comfortable and gain enough faith that the little dozer would not break down.

At the end of the day, there were two loads of logs ready for the mill on Monday. Don and I had skidded everything the D-3 could handle, and we did not want to mess with the CAT on Sunday.

Monday morning, Don and I were sitting in the work trailer waiting for the machines to warm. Guys sat quietly, smoking Marlboros, sipping coffee, and sniggering when one would let out a big fart. Then another one would go, and that turned the sounds within the trailer to a Big Hole Fart Symphony.

"Good one. That woke my ass up," said one gagging sawyer.

"Bottle it and cork it," said another, pinching his nose shut.

"Lay off those damn pickled eggs at the Antlers," was the best comeback, though.

Roy finally rolled in with his Peterbilt, and that caused most guys to put out their cigarettes in exchange for a lip full of Copenhagen and bolt to work. Don and I hung back, wanting to give Roy our log tally sheet from Saturday and maybe get an atta boy.

"Roy, we came up on Saturday and skidded eighty-four logs to the deck. Here is our count," I told him.

"Ah no, no. I don't wanna hear that shit. Who told you guys to skid those logs? Did I tell you to do that? I'll be a son of a bitch if you think I'm paying you two. Get outta here. I don't need you two assholes trying to run my outfit."

Don and I turned to leave, curbing our anger, not wanting to get into a bout of fisticuffs with that peckerhead. On our walk back to my truck, we passed the log deck with the Homelite chainsaw. I had had enough, and Roy was going to have something to remember me by.

"Hey Roy," I yelled, pulling on the saw's starter cord. "Watch this shit."

The saw fired to life, and I plunged the tip directly into a large rock. I closed my eyes as chips of rock, and bits of steel flew as the teeth on the once-sharp chain were reduced to nubs.

"I'm not an asshole, Roy. Remember that."

I chucked the still running chainsaw into the nearest snowbank and never looked back. Justice for me had now been served, not asshole, but Big Hole-style.

Chapter 57

Two months, two jobs, two meals a day, and a marriage on the rocks. It sounded like an opening line for a Merle Haggard song. I wanted out of my flaky marriage, but the Boy Scout in me, and the long-ingrained Scout oath kept me committed—more than the forgotten, generic, scripted wedding vows in Reno.

My new Montana life had turned into a survival test. Physical, demanding jobs kept me fed, but my father's words echoed again. *You have a good brain son, use it.*

I was falling, free falling, clinging to hopes of a better spring. With time to reflect, I realized Roy Harmons could be found all over the world, but people like Hank, Rich, and Calvin could be found, too. They were the essence of Montana, a blessing in my new world. I was also blessed to be where I always wanted to be, even when I was hungry. My dream was still alive, and it included more mountains to climb and a family to raise.

The mirror in my bathroom reflected a face unknown to me, a face that was hardened and cold-tempered from the Wisdom winter. Looking like the Viking, Eric the Red, with a two-month-old red beard, prompted me to grab my Gillette double-edged razor and come clean. My language had deteriorated to that of a Roy Harmon. I was spiritually lethargic and oblivious to my shameful state of penury. Praying for a new beginning, I transcended once again to envisioning the prisms of light coming through stained glass. I craved clarity... and a loaded double cheeseburger and fries smothered with Heinz ketchup.

My separation mystified me. Should I try harder at reconciliation when it was perfectly clear that Ellie wasn't interested? There wasn't a significant amount of emotional attachment invested, and a divorce could be a quick escape from the reality of my heartache. Ellie's feelings about my tics had put me on notice… people who love one another should love without reservation. But heartaches were nothing new for me, and I needed to concentrate on living a day at a time and regain control of my life, first. A shower and a shave, along with putting my filthy logging clothes in the wash was a good start.

That afternoon I stopped by the ranger station to see Hank and asked him if he had finalized my return date.

"Well, I'm glad you stopped in," Hank drawled, stubbing out the ever-present Camel. "Dave's transferred, and we'd like you to supervise tree planting this year. You'll get a pay level increase because you'll be supervising a crew."

"Wow. That's good. I'll miss trails, but I know I need to move on. I want a full-time position."

"Your chances would be better in northern California or Oregon where they grow real timber."

"I'm not interested in moving to Oregon, Hank. What about after tree planting?"

"Well, the staff talked over the winter about you taking over the small-timber-sale program, any sale less than a million board feet. This country has so much post and pole material that we're swamped with administering all the sale requests. There have been too many irons in the fire, and they are all cold. We need to have one person to handle nothing else. You'll schedule and handle everything, from the onsite review, sale layout and marking, writing the contract, and administering the sale. That'll keep you busy."

"Looking forward to getting back to my career. I'm not a real cowboy, Hank; I only bought the hat. This winter has been kind of tough, but I'm ready to get back to work with the Forest Service. Do you have a date in mind?"

"Can't see anything sooner than April eleventh. Our budget keeps shrinking every year."

So does mine, Hank.

That was still six weeks away. Don and I heard that we were eligible for Food Stamps if we registered in Dillon, but I could not bring myself to that level of acceptance. I was prepared to keep eating plain oatmeal, without the extravagant accouterments of raisins, cream, or brown sugar. A frozen box of Jolly Green Giant Brussels sprouts were the main course for my twenty-fifth birthday.

Hank tapped the end of a Camel on the desk before lighting up.

"You know Loring, the Steel Creek Guard Station is available to rent this year," he said after exhaling his first drag. "Twenty bucks a month to rent, and we can withdraw that from your pay. You'll have to chop wood, carry water, and use an outhouse, but there is a queen bed, propane stove, and refrigerator that's set up. I can let you stay in the bunkhouse short term if the Steel Creek Road is still snowed in."

Steel Creek Guard Station sat at the end of Steel Creek Road that ended at the base of the Pioneer Mountains. It was old and weathered, with a faded, green tin roof. The cabin was surrounded by a fragrant carpet of sagebrush that badgers burrowed below and pronghorns pranced above. Small, scattered stands of quaking aspen occupied the foothills to the Pioneers, and that made it a perfect setting to live out my western dream of climbing higher mountains, floating quiet waters, and catching pan-sized brook trout in Steel Creek. For relaxation, I craved to read Louis L'Amour novels and *The Last of the Mohicans* by the light of a kerosene lantern within the rustic ambiance of an isolated but picturesque cabin.

"Heck yeah, I'll take it Hank. I know it's a five-mile drive out of town, but I have a good four-wheel drive. Hey, do you mind if I borrow your newspaper. I'm so out of touch with the outside world."

"Some may find wisdom in that," Hank said, laughing.

"All I know from the past two months is that the Raiders won the Super Bowl, Jimmy Carter is now president, and Gary Gilmore was executed by a volunteer firing squad. Did I miss anything?"

Hank shrugged his shoulders, suggesting I may have known more world events than he did.

Chapter 58

An article in the *Anaconda Leader* outlined plans for a new golf course being built at Copper Mountain Resort near Opportunity. It was mid-March, but while Wisdom was entrenched in winter, Opportunity, a thousand feet lower in elevation, had bare ground. There was not much other news of interest as the paper covered mainly local topics and high school sports about the Anaconda Copperheads. But the article about the golf course intrigued me. Thinking there may be job opportunities, I gave Copper Mountain a call.

"Good morning. Copper Mountain Resort. This is Anna Marie. How may I help you?"

"Yes, hello. My name is Loring, and I'm calling in reference to your new golf course. Any job openings at this time?"

"Yes, we have a tree-planting position open. Do you have experience working around golf courses?"

"You bet I do, Anna Marie. I also have experience in tree planting and landscaping, and I have a forestry degree."

"Good, good. Any experience with operating a front-end loader?"

Huh. I froze on the question.

"Well, yes, I do have some experience working around heavy equipment."

This was mostly true. It was my philosophy to always answer yes and then read a book or ask somebody. If I handled a D-3 for a day skidding logs, what could be so hard about a front-end loader? One had tracks and the other had wheels. I knew there was a way to start a machine and a way to stop it. Everything else was easy to figure out.

"Copper Mountain is looking to open their new golf course in late April and would like to have the Russian olive trees planted on the fairways before then," Anna Marie stated, upping the ante with the completion date.

Russian Olives are a thorny shrub or small tree that grow to 15-20 feet in height and thrive on the barest of soil. They were a good choice, given the location, but I had never worked with them.

After cruising through a very short interview, I was hired and would now drive an hour to work... but I was working. Work... a better four-letter word. This Montana Dream needed to keep moving forward, as I had had just scratched its surface. At no time during that winter was I ready to raise a white flag, retreat, or surrender my dream to hardships.

The only surprise was that the Russian olives were not bare-root stock but were balled trees that were five to seven feet in height and weighed a hundred pounds. That was the reason for the front-end loader. And the golf course... It was no comparison to Valley Brook, where I caddied while in high school. Valley Brook was a twenty-seven-hole championship course that sat in gentle, rolling hills with hardwoods and pines and a meandering brook that ran through it. The sand traps had imported white beach sand. Copper Mountain's fairways resembled a groomed cow pasture and had local, brown, river sand in the traps. There was just no comparison to the lush green fairways and velvety putting surface of Valley Brook. My planting of the Russian olives would be the first landscaping done on the course.

The planting was completed on time, and I managed to get the front-end loader royally stuck only once, on my last day. I got it stuck axle deep in soggy ground that required a tow truck and major ground repair afterward. My boss overlooked the incident with the loader and was impressed enough with my work to offer me a full-time position before I left. It was a very tempting offer, but April approached and I was ready for the Big Hole and more mountain adventures. I could have been dreaming, but I thought I had seen Smoke on the horizon.

Chapter 59

Not needing an apartment now that I was booked into Steel Creek, I stopped by Dale's New and Used to let Dale know I was moving out and his apartment would be vacant.

"Moving to Steel Creek huh? Hate to lose a good renter. You know that road turns to gumbo after a rain. Very muddy. I see you don't have mud flaps on your truck yet, either. It's the law in Montana, you know. How about a pair of Big Sky mud flaps. Got a pair right here."

"I'm kinda tight right now, Dale. Can you hold them till next month?"

"They'll be sitting right here."

Dale's heart was always in the right place, but making a sale was his calling.

Everything I owned could still fit in the back of my truck. Steel Creek was my new home, at least through October, and living there, I hoped, would be like Thoreau finding peace and solitude on Walden Pond. I found, like Thoreau, an exceptional wholesomeness in being alone. *Live like a monk. Chop wood, carry water*. It all was a pretty simple escape from the news of urban corruption and a broken marriage. I found comfort in my self–reliance, the quiet solitude, and not having to explain away my tics or grimaces. Ellie's attack on my tics was the first time I had ever heard someone confront me about how they affected them. I became skittish about being in public and more aware of the distance that they created with some people. I was coming to grips with reduced social acceptance because of my tics. I had noticed how mothers would shield their children from me in a grocery store checkout line. I smiled as big as I could, but the children seemed more confused. I knew that I would not outgrow this curse, but wished every morning they would just disappear, even for a day, to relieve the pain in my face and jaw. To live a temporary quiet life of seclusion like Thoreau was not an escape from reality for me, but a time to rejuvenate. From the day I had been discharged from Presby, I had run my life with a wide-open throttle, never slowing down to reflect about the goodness and fulfilled dreams that were now part of my Montana life. *Could a hurried man be a happy man?* My physical body was hard, resilient, and tough, but inside, I was confused and lost. I hoped the solitude at Steel Creek could help me find clarity on dealing with Ellie… or the strength to leave.

Work harder, I told myself, and I would look at Ellie with a new set of eyes. I had a second chance at life. Should my marriage warrant anything less? No, I didn't think so, but I had also refused to bow down to failure. I was young and proud, and I didn't know when it was time to fold and cash out.

Spring ushered in the consciousness of a new man once again. Then, as a result of reaching out over several weeks, I received a letter from Ellie, who expressed a desire to get back together again. *Did I force her into a corner? Was her decision made of free will?* Nothing in the letter mentioned anything about love.

I had always wanted to try reconciliation, but I had adjusted during the severe winter to living my life without her. Could I trust the future of my Montana Dream upon such an unstable foundation? It was hard to not feel, "once bitten, twice shy," but I was willing to push my solitude away for a chance at a new beginning.

Ellie moved to Steel Creek, and we tried to bury the hatchet and start fresh. Ellie adjusted well to the rustic and semi-primitive living conditions. I hauled water in old milk containers from the nearby campground. She heated water and washed the dishes. Candles or a kerosene lantern provided the evening reading light.

The hardest part of Steel Creek living was going twenty-five feet to the outhouse.

"I got swarmed by mosquitoes so bad, I couldn't breathe," Ellie complained.

"Oh, I forgot to tell you that you need to wear that hat with mosquito netting or cover your face with a bandana. And close the outhouse door really quick."

If anything, Ellie was tough and never whined about the rigors of life at Steel Creek.

Days slowly passed, and I still sat on a fence. Neither overjoyed about our reconnecting, nor unhappy about working on our second chance, we lived in a state of peaceful coexistence, but not growing in love. Give it some time, I thought. We were together again, and that's a start. There was one noticeable change on our first trip for groceries.

"On our way to Butte for groceries today, I think we should stop by the pound and see about getting a puppy. I think it would be good to have a dog, don't you?" Ellie asked.

"Yeah, I think that would be cool, if we find the right pup," I answered. "Only the right pup, one that is frisky."

I never thought about the loss of Dixie influencing my choice to have a dog again.

We found our way to the Butte animal shelter after buying a two-week supply of food from Buttreys. There was one young pup that caught our eyes immediately. She was a black-and-tan mixed breed, but showed some beagle cross. While all the other dogs were howling their heads off or barking, she sat quietly with a forlorn look that seemed to say, "Take me, take me." And we did.

"What shall we name her?" Ellie asked on the way home.

The pup was frisky, and enjoyed being petted and fussed over.

"I have just the name for her!" I exclaimed, snapping my fingers.

I had been surveying proposed timber sale acreage in the Ruby Creek drainage.

"Let's call her Ruby because she's our little gem."

Back at Steel Creek, Ellie opened a bag of Puppy Chow for a hungry Ruby while I hauled in the groceries.

"The fridge has never been this full," I told Ellie. "I don't know how efficient these propane refrigerators are, so I better bump it up a few degrees."

"That makes sense to me."

A few hours later, I opened the refrigerator for supper food.

"Oh my God, I can't believe this. Check this out."

231

Everything we had bought was frozen solid: the lettuce and the celery, along with the peppers, mayonnaise, pickles, and milk.

"Well, I guess the propane refrigerator really works," Ellie said, groaning at the loss while I attempted to salvage two weeks of groceries.

After sorting and recouping some of the frozen food, Ellie and I lavished ourselves with bowls of oatmeal, oblivious to the still hungry eyes of Ruby lying at our feet.

Chapter 60

George Sheffield, the new senior forester and my new boss, came to me while I was making a correction to the Johnson-Schultz timber sale map. Working with a precision that I learned in college surveying, I remembered to keep my mouth shut to prevent any spittle from landing on the wet ink. Before every stroke of the pen, I had a mental picture of the stroke; the stroke would either be away from me or toward me. There was no room for error.

"Looks like my recommendation to send you for supervisory training has been approved," George said, after taking a big sip of java.

"Um hm," I said through a closed mouth while setting the pen back into its holder. "That's great news. Are the classes at the district offices in Dillon?"

"No, I'm sorry to tell you that classes will be next week at the Regional Office in Missoula."

"Missoula." The Region One Office.

"You have a week out of Wisdom, buddy. Try not to have too much fun, and make sure you go to the Oxford Café and have a plate of calf brains and eggs. Famous eats in Missoula, and only a block west of the R.O."

After hearing that news, I hoped that by some remote chance, some UT Forestry professors would be there, especially Dr. Dimmer. I knew what I would say:

"Guess what, Dr. Dimmer? Montana is like you said it was, God's Country, but you know what? I don't have to go back to Tennessee, but I'll treat you to a plate of calf brains and eggs."

I made the circle of three.

"Remember to come back on Friday, Loring. Try not to let Missoula wrap its arms around you," were George's final instructions as I was signing out a vehicle for the week on Monday morning. "We're pretty lucky getting you in the class. Most spots are allotted to bigger districts."

Well, George, you are a few years too late on that notion about Missoula wrapping its arms around me, as I remembered the Boys' Life article that lit my fire in 1966.

"Don't worry, George. I'll be back."

It was a three-hour drive to Missoula, which seemed like a very long drive to go such a short distance. I looked forward to crossing the two mountain passes, Chief Joseph and Lookout, where winter would still be in force, before descending into the postcard views of springtime in the Bitterroot Valley. What a change of events had taken place in just a month. Now I had per diem money to eat on. My life had improved dramatically in one month and my free fall had leveled off. The Forest Service was my reserve parachute, and now deployed, I was looking to reenter my Montana Dream, smack-dab in the epicenter of US Forest Service's Region One headquarters. The memory of my winter nightmare of hunger, heartache, and poverty vanished.

Morning misty rain had fallen in stretches along the highway. Everything looked so alive. Lilacs had bloomed by several ranch houses. Pastures were greening up, and horses were starting to lose their coat of long, thick wintry hair. Spring, a time for change once again, I reaffirmed.

For a week in Missoula, I would attend a class on Introduction to Supervision. The Forest Service saw a leadership quality in me, but so did John "Lefty" Meinen, my scoutmaster, when he appointed me leader of the Flaming Arrow Patrol. And so did Father Ben while I was an altar boy, asking me after a wedding, "Have you ever thought further of seminary, my son? You are so dedicated to the church." That sense of leadership had evolved through the years but was curiously absent in high school. *Why did I suppress it then?*

Then there was Captain Maxwell at Tennessee Tech, who had tried to recruit me to be an officer in the US Army. *How do my leadership qualities circumvent the facial tics and grunts that are always a part of me?* I was thought retarded by some, and by others, a principled young man and a developing leader with boundless energy. I came from blue-collar ancestry, but I was not comfortable wearing that mantle or living that life.

Further developing my leadership qualities became a new addendum to my Montana life. If I could rise above my own setbacks—illness, loss, embarrassing tics, and a mechanical heart valve—then someone else could rise above their setbacks, too. I never thought I had to be perfect in anything, but I would push the envelope to be the best. My calling in life was to be an inspiration to others. Fighting misconceptions about my tics had toughened me, but, at times. I had to restrain myself from throwing my successes back in someone's face for doubting me.

Or maybe it was not the tics? Maybe it was my parents who instilled a higher level of expectation in me because much had been given to me. I recalled a quote that my father had underlined in a Kennedy reading from my youth: "Victory has one hundred fathers; defeat is an orphan."

I chose victory.

Chapter 61

W hat is supervision?" was the first question asked by our instructor.

"An observation and analysis of people in their work, looking for methods of improvement, eliminating time-wasting practices, being safe, and achieving your goals," I answered.

I thought I was off to a good start and smoked that response.

"Very good answer," my instructor commented, "but you failed to mention feedback, listening, and communication, perhaps the most important word of all in supervision?"

"Oh, yes. Definitely communication." *How could I miss that?*

Like a dry sponge, I tried to absorb all the new material, and it was easy to become overloaded. This was only an introductory course, but I wanted further development as a supervisor. I thrived on the challenge of managing people more than I had realized.

After classes were done for the day, I had an agenda to shop for a canoe, a priority item on my list of Montana desires. Seeing canoes on the Clark Fork River in Missoula just heightened my anxiety.

Ellie was also more excited about buying a canoe than a couch and looked forward to paddling around Miner Lake in the evenings. I looked forward to floating and fly fishing the Big Hole River.

Missoula, a town with a river that runs through it, surely would have Grumman canoes for sale.

"Go to Bob Ward's," an instructor told me. "They have the best selection of rafts and canoes in Missoula."

I wanted a fifteen-foot Grumman aluminum canoe like Lester's, the model we floated the Hiawassee with.

"I wouldn't buy a Grumman," the young, outdoorsy, college clerk told me at Bob Ward's. "Too much money."

"I thought they were the best."

"Well, yes, in a way," he corrected me. "For my money, I would look for the innovative, much cheaper Coleman canoes made out of a new material called Ram-X. Colemans glide over gravel where the Grumman will hang up; they are practically indestructible, though a little heavier. They only come in orange right now and aren't the prettiest boat in the water, but they're pretty forgiving about crashing against rocks."

"Can I look at some of those? I'm good with orange."

"Sorry, dude. We don't carry them. The nearest Coleman outlet is in Bozeman."

"Bozeman?"

I can't make a three-hour detour one way to Bozeman.

"Yeah, it will be a while before they hit Missoula."

"Well, I can't wait for that. I travel to Butte for food, so what's another seventy miles to Bozeman for a canoe."

"Go for it, dude."

The next Saturday morning, Ellie and I left early for Bozeman.

Chapter 62

"Ahhh. Tree-planting time again. Get out the Bengay, Band-Aids, and beer," I said, teasing Fred.

Tree planting was the brutal, but beautiful time of year that aroused my emotions and tied me to my new adopted consciousness.

"You're one sick dude if you enjoy tree planting," Fred sighed in between sips of his Lucky at the Antlers that night. "My fingers are still numb from running the auger last year."

"I know, but it feels so good when the last tree is planted. I think sometimes that I want to have a company and plant trees all over the West."

"You really need to sit down and have a Lucky, my man, and then check into the state mental hospital. You're scaring the hell out of me about liking to plant trees. Get real."

But this year the crew was under my supervision. The crew hadn't changed much. Lill, Rose, and Roberta were back and formed the nucleus of the hen crew. I never doubted that they hired on tough for another season. But I also had a new guy, Bob Holland, on board that spring. Bob had been in the Navy and served during Vietnam, but now, out of the military, he had dreamed of moving west from Wisconsin and yearned to be a smokejumper. Before he could train as a smokejumper, Bob needed to work on a district fire crew for a few seasons, then an interagency Hotshot crew.

Like a lot of guys I had met from Wisconsin, there were two topics they never tired of talking about: the Green Bay Packers and walleye fishing. Bob talked about them, too, but we both shared a dream of living in the West for the rest of our lives.

238

While shooting pool at the Antlers one evening, I asked Bob about trying fly fishing.

"Nope. Never tried it," he confessed, while lining up the five ball on a long table shot.

The cue ball exploded off the tip of Bob's cue stick and sent the five ball into a corner pocket. I never heard the ball sink into the leather pocket as the cue ball found its mark, dead center perfect.

"Did I ever tell you," he said, laughing while chalking his cue stick, "never shoot pool against a navy guy."

"Lily Lake is only a three-mile hike from my place at Steel Creek. We can be at the lake in an hour. I've caught some rainbows there in the pound class, really good fighters on a fly rod. Best trout fishing I've had so far. When I flick that fly into the ring on the rise and it's snatched by a rainbow…"

"What, no walleye?" Bob asked dolefully.

From that moment, Bob was christened Rainbow Bob.

Me and Rainbow Bob, spinning fishing tales at the Antler Bar in 2016.

Our friendship grew, and Bob played a key role in supporting me in my supervisory role. Bob worked like two men, effortlessly, never tiring or questioning my authority.

"Need someone to hike down to the truck and bring up more gas," I said while adjusting the carburetion on an auger. "I think we have some water in this tank."

"Got it, boss," was Bob's quick reply and down the hill he flew.

"Why do we have to work in the rain?" a summer college student moaned one day.

"Because it's your job, dumbass," Bob told him while zipping up his own rain gear. "College kids."

Bob did not have a college degree, and he sometimes questioned the intelligence of those who did have one, but never showed it. I loved it. Bob was a damn fine worker and no college degree could replace the work ethic, integrity, and common sense of the man.

The previous year, I was a worker and did not recall all the bitching and whining going on behind the noise of the augers.

"The rain is turning into snow," or "The ground is too rocky," or "I lost my scalping tool," were everyday whines. However, "Is it break time, yet?" won for number of whines, and the most hilarious was from a college guy from Santa Barbara for: "I can't wear a hard hat because it cramps my karma."

I was lucky to have workers like Bob, Lill, and Rose. The crew of fifteen may all have bitched at times, but Lill would always remind me of one thing: "A bitching crew is a working crew."

Lill was absolutely correct, as my crew earned Certificates of Merit for finishing on time and under budget.

Chapter 63

The Antler Bar after work served as a gathering place to plan evening fishing, hikes to Proposal Rock, or floating the Big Hole. It also served as a second community hall to have chili feeds or for wives to meet their husbands after work. Children and dogs played together on the floor, while cowboys and loggers drank in seamless harmony. There was one night that the tree-planting crew tried to set a record for the number of Luckys drunk to celebrate the last day of tree planting. The record must have been set because Gena ran out of Lucky.

The unwritten rule of the summer season was to spend just as much free time outdoors after work in a week as you did during work.

One night at the Antlers in mid-July, Gary, a Butte native, proposed a canoe float. With a drooping Fu Manchu moustache, he resembled a younger Yosemite Sam when he scrunched his straw Stetson cowboy hat down on his head. A rabid adventurer of Montana's hidden gems, Gary always had new ideas for the weekend.

"Anyone interested in floating Red Rock Lakes National Wildlife Refuge? It's open for floating starting this weekend."

"I'm in. A trip like that is what I bought my canoe for," I told him. "Where's Red Rock? I never heard of it."

"We head to Dillon then west on I-15. The refuge sits at over eight-thousand feet, and the ice has just melted off. We can float the eight miles from the Upper Lake to the Lower Lake. Leave early Saturday. Float Sunday and be back home by dark. I remember seeing pelicans, trumpeter swans, geese, and thousands of ducks when I went there as a kid. I have a friend, Ron, in Butte, who said him and his wife are in."

"Count me and Ellie, too," I said. This sounded like a great adventure, the kind I always dreamed of. Easy paddling, no white water, and a great trip for Ellie, a novice canoer.

"Well, Chris and I are in, too," Fred added, making it four canoes to haul.

Red Rock Lakes National Wildlife Refuge is an extremely remote refuge and was not widely known by most Montanans, except by a lot of duck hunters from Butte and Dillon. Once leaving the I-15 at Lima, the rough, rocky, potholed road looped our canoe convoy twenty-eight miles through a fairly wide valley. We passed several old homesteads that were deserted. The craggy Centennial Mountains held their heads aloft and rose over 10,000 feet, framing the view to the south. A single kiosk stood alongside the road with pamphlets and maps of the refuge. I could see why it was referred to as the most beautiful refuge in America, but no one was visiting.

Is this where the lonely go? We passed not one car along the way. *I wondered why I, a man who had bouts of loneliness in the past, had selected one of the loneliest states to live in... or hide in.*

We saw numerous creeks that flowed into the refuge and created the Upper Red Rock Lake, River Marsh, and Lower Red Rock Lake. It was here that we planned to launch our canoes into the Upper Red Rock Lake, float through a section of marsh grass, and paddle across Lower Red Rock Lake. It was eight miles of open water and marsh.

"Hey, how long is this float? It looks like there are hundreds of routes," I quizzed Gary, while I stared out, looking for the main channel.

"About six hours, maybe, if I remember back that far. Me and my dad always set up camp here at the lower lake," Gary said as we stopped to eat a late lunch and grab some chilled water from the cooler. "We can shuttle the canoes and trucks in the morning."

The campground was primitive and lacked services. Thank goodness Mother Nature was in a good mood. The next day's forecast was a floater's wish, hot and sunny, with no foreseeable change in the forecast.

The sun set, and the thermometer plummeted at that elevation. I snuggled deeper into my trusty North Face bag and zipped up for the night. Ellie had a mummy-style sleeping bag and had it zipped all the way up when her nose got cold. Red Rock was so remote that no light polluted the night sky. Through the screened flap on the tent I could see the billions of stars in the Milky Way and the full splendor of our galaxy.

How far beyond those stars would heaven be? The concept of infinity baffled me, and I decided that heaven was right here on Earth, on the edge of Red Rock Lake. All was quiet on the star-studded water. The howl of coyotes had become common, and I now heard them as my Montana lullaby.

Morning mist was still rising off the water of Upper Red Rock when we had launched four canoes. Near the shore we spotted silhouettes of the long black legs and relatively short bills of sandhill cranes, wading and nibbling on plant vegetation. The morning air was deafening with the quacking and honking of tens of thousands waterfowl. Ellie and I paddled through the mist, gliding over mixed aquatic vegetation of marsh grasses and pondweed, and dense colonies of coon tail. The floating leaves and stems provided tremendous food for dabbling ducks and fish, but left each canoe picking their own route. Our four canoes quickly became separated, and we were by ourselves.

"Have fun, see you at the truck," I heard Gary's fading voice call out as he paddled out of sight.

"Which way should I steer," Ellie asked from the bow. "There are so many different channels."

"I know. Go with the channel that is moving the fastest," I said, guessing.

The sun had burned off the mist, and we were flabbergasted by the waterfowl.

"Look at that raft of mallards off your starboard side, and wait, look, two trumpeter swans just landed about a hundred feet out," I called.

"But there are pelicans just off your port side," she answered back.

"Pelicans. In Montana!"

Dip, dip, and pulling them back, our paddles propelled us through Upper Red Rock Lake, but we still had to paddle through the marsh grass section between the two lakes. Our progress slowed because I had purchased a seventeen-foot Coleman canoe and not a fifteen footer. Canoe camping was on my agenda, and the larger canoe was a better choice. However, it was not a good choice to paddle within the narrow, twisting confines of the refuge.

"You better put on more sunscreen," I cautioned Ellie. "You're fair skinned, and at this elevation, the glare off the water can fry you."

"Pass it up," she said turning to pick up the plastic bottle of Coppertone SPF 10 off the blade of my paddle.

All of a sudden, there was a stiffening breeze and dark clouds rolled in from the west.

"Feels like a front may be moving in, but it will probably be later tonight before anything happens. Forecast called for no rain."

"Don't ask me, you're the weatherman," Ellie said. "It is getting really hot, though."

"Well, I'm not worried. Could you pass a peanut butter sandwich back?"

After paddling the length of Upper Red Rock Lake, we finally entered the marsh grass divider between the two lakes. The dark clouds had turned black, and the wind had changed from a breeze to a howl.

"You have to pull more water back with your stroke. Head into the wind," I yelled to Ellie. "The wind is turning us broadside and backward."

Thunder rumbled and roared in the distance; lightning strikes were hitting close in the bordering hills.

"I can't paddle any harder," Ellie said, gasping.

Pea-size hail started to pound us. Icy slush accumulated in the bottom of the canoe. Some pieces were bigger than marbles, and the slush became ankle deep.

"Ow, the hail is hurting my head," Ellie cried.

"Cover your head and shoulders with a towel and hunch forward. Let the hail hit you in the back," I yelled above the rat-tat-tatting machine-gun sound of hail hitting the canoe.

We had to get through the marsh grass, but the storm continued to build, and we were at the mercy of the wind. I stuck my paddle straight in the water. It was four to five feet high, and the bottom seemed firm enough to stand on.

"That's it. I'm going in and pull us through the marsh," I yelled again.

Over the side I went. Beneath the idly swirling surface was a frigid current that numbed my legs. Mud from the river bottom oozed between my toes with each step. Once again, I faced the dichotomy of beauty and harshness that was Montana.

A canoe paddle was clenched in my left hand for balance, and I reached for the bowline with my right.

The hail slacked off to sheets of sleet and chilling rain, but the wind still howled. Thunder boomed close followed by a brilliant jolt of white in the gunpowder-colored sky that branched silently to the ground bordering the lake.

"We're sitting ducks!" I screamed, but it was lost in the wind and thunder.

Please God, no Ray Barkley treatment for me today. I don't want to be lit up like a light bulb.

Once I was down on the water it was impossible to see up and over the marsh grasses, creating a maze with many routes to choose. *Pick one. They all will eventually lead you out. Go with the flow. Be the river, not the rock.*

How glad I was that my bowline was twenty feet long. I sloshed, waded, or swam the length of the line, then stopped, and pulled the canoe to me. The coldness of the water had lowered my body temperature, and I began to shake, but my face was warm and getting warmer.

"Made it," I gasped as I pulled the canoe through the last of the marsh grass. We were now in the Lower Lake, and there was more marsh grass, but there were open pathways between the large patches.

The sky had vented its fury and was now spent. I could see the dim outline of my truck sitting on the dike, still a ways off.

Ellie maneuvered to the center of the canoe. Using a clump of marsh grass for leverage, I flopped inside without flipping Ellie out, but I scared the heebie-jeebies out of her.

"Loring!" she screamed.

"We're coming back next week. I really love this place."

"No way, I want a quiet paddle on Miner Lake."

Ron's canoe was about two hundred yards away, and in the distance, was the unmistakable outline of a Dodge Power Wagon, with Gary waving alongside, his distinctive straw hat still on, but a little flatter.

"Let's do that again," he screamed when we were within earshot.

We all had made it safely back and looked like a bunch of drowned rats with lobster red faces. Coppertone SPF 10, the gold standard of sunscreens, hadn't protected us at the higher elevation, and we were in misery.

There was an old Montana adage: If you don't like the weather in Montana, just give it a minute, it will change… I found it to be true that day at Red Rock.

The early evening sun's rays had broken through the gunpowder sky, casting an unearthly glow of light pinks and oranges on the water and peaks. The water in the lake shimmered, and the geese untucked their long necks. The pamphlet was right. Red Rock Lakes National Wildlife Refuge was one of the most beautiful refuges in America. However, there should have been one more line added to the pamphlet: Thunder, lightning, and hail are always free.

Chapter 64

On a mid-December day in 1979, I received another layoff notice. I had gone through this song-and-dance routine for three years, having had to scrounge for work for three months. *See you in March. Thanks for a great job. Shake a day.* All these sentiments ran through my mind that morning before work. It was time to move on with my life outside of Wisdom. There was more to Montana. I still had to meet Smoke and tell him of my wilderness adventures. I thought often of the son who Father Ben had promised would come to me, and dreamed of the day it would happen.

But there was so much to be thankful for. I had put my heart valve to a test that Bjork-Shiley could smile about. When I first arrived in Wisdom, I was concerned about having periodic, required blood tests, but I was able to maintain timely scheduling while living in one of the most remote towns in Montana. Strong and physically fit, I climbed more mountains than I could ever ask for, even ones in Glacier National Park, the Bitterroots, and the Mission Mountains. Some could have outrun me, but no one could out-walk me. I had wet a fly in over a hundred Alpine lakes in the Wisdom District. Craig and his new bride, Maria, had visited Wisdom, and we all climbed Copperhead Peak when the wildflowers were in all their glory.

Winters had brought new adventures like snowmobiling and cross-country skiing with new friends, Mac and Adele. I had learned to ice fish, pulling up rainbow trout and kokanee salmon through a hole in the ice at Georgetown Lake.

Ellie and I had found some traction in our marriage, and I got off the fence, and we both had a grand time of adventuring and moving on from our tumultuous early years.

One Friday in September, Ellie was late to arrive home. I did not know she had located golden retriever pups for sale and had driven to Hamilton to get the first pick of the litter. Ellie's gift of a golden retriever pup was the most thoughtful and exciting gift I had ever received from her, and she won my heart back. I wasn't hesitant to have another dog after losing Dixie to an accident, and Ruby mysteriously disappearing, and I looked forward to training a hunting dog. I named him Sackett after the Sackett family from the Louis L'Amour series. After gun training him for hunting in the field, we blasted mallards out of the wintry sky and jumped pheasants in cornfields and scared up sage hens in the sagebrush.

A goose I shot on the Big Hole River was a Thanksgiving dinner. Sackett was not handsome or regal looking like Dixie. Golden retrievers have two variations of coats, either curly with honey-gold ringlets flowing along their flanks, ears and tail, or flat, like Sackett. He always looked scrawny because of that. What he lacked in appearance, he made up for with loyalty and his work in the field. Sackett was the first dog I had ever trained to hunt in the field, and he made me look so good that friends wanted me to train their dogs. I didn't know anything about gun training; I just read a book. He took to the gun without fear or trepidation and was bred to never give up on a downed game bird, methodically working in circles with his keen nose to the ground. I never left home without him.

Sackett with a mallard.

There never seemed to be enough money for that Browning .308, but I let Dale Cornwell make me a deal on a .35 Remington for a hundred bucks.

"She shoots a half keg of powder and a doorknob," Dale said, testifying to the rifle's knockdown power.

It was not the rifle I wanted, but it had been good enough to bring down a trophy mule deer just fifteen minutes from the Steel Creek cabin on the last minute of the last day of the season the year before.

My administration of the small-sales program for the district was noted as exemplary. But all these accomplishments would not have bought me a cup of coffee in January. Moss was beginning to grow under my feet, and I knew what I wanted to do.

"Well, Loring. Will we see you back next year?" George asked me in an unsure tone later that day within the cozy confines of his pine-paneled office while I handed in my keys.

"Well, uh, I don't think so George. I've lived large the four years here, but I feel I need a change of direction in my life. I hope to start a family someday soon and need to move on to other career challenges. I don't have a career here."

"Well, I know it's been tough, not getting you a permanent position here, but we'll miss you. What's up your sleeve, if I may ask?"

"You know George, I thought a lot about it, and leaving Wisdom is hard. But I've decided to follow my dream and start a reforestation company and contract tree planting, trail construction, and timber cruising for the Forest Service."

After work, I went to my last happy hour at the Antlers. It was not all that happy as I reminisced about all the good times I had there. Change had struck again. Gena had sold, and the new owners put an end to "Shake a Day." It seemed the Antlers was being sanitized when the head mounts, traps, and pelts were removed. But Gena's words from my initial welcome on my first trip to the Antlers still echoed: "Loring, it's Lucky when you live in the West." She was right, and I was moving on.

Chapter 65

Ellie needed to be closer to her new teaching job in Eagle Creek, so we rented an old, dilapidated farmhouse with a barn and ten acres in the Eagle Creek area before the 1979 holiday season. There was a dazzling view of Sleeping Chief Mountain from my backyard, and bald eagles perched on tall cottonwoods along the fence line. An irrigation ditch ran through the hayfield, and Sackett was in dog heaven.

I had no fear or anxiety about starting a reforestation company. Failure was not on my radar because I had sunk every available cent I had into the business. Startup money had come from a life insurance policy that I cashed in for ten thousand dollars, a thousand dollars in savings, and whatever money I could save from substitute teaching at a local school.

Teaching was leadership, and I felt I did well at it, that command presence that Captain Maxwell alluded to... until one day I was assigned seventh-grade classes. That one day sent me to the *Twilight Zone*, as the students had a field day mimicking my tics. It wasn't much fun, but it went with the territory of being a sub.

I had no prior knowledge of running a business, but I was undaunted by the challenge because I knew the scope of the work required. Time was money, and I needed to secure a tree-planting contract by March, the official start of the contract season, if I wanted to eat.

In the short time I had to relax, I read and finished national bestseller, *The World According to Garp*, by John Irving during the Christmas holidays.

I didn't find it a good Christmas read as the author mentioned that "we are all terminal cases." Throughout the book, the Garp character seemed to be obsessed with death, both in his writing and in his personal life.

Garp, Garp, I thought. I saw something significant in that name, and I played with the letters, looking at possible acronyms. *Why am I drawn to this name?* What was so significant about a man obsessed with death and the death of those close to him? And then the answer jumped at me like a jack-in-a-box that had reached that one, magical note. There was no need to reconfigure the letters. I had it. Garp. Greener Acres Reforestation Projects. And in that instant, a company was born. I saw no death with this connection, only life in the form of regenerated forests. The next day, my mother called to inform me that my Uncle Frank had passed away unexpectedly, but peacefully, in his sleep.

Chapter 66

I was four years familiar with planting bare-root seedlings in power-augered holes. Forest Service interest continued to grow since I first planted trees using this method in Wisdom in 1976, mostly due to the higher survival rate and more rapid growth.

There was excitement in the industry about the new development of a lightweight auger powered by a chainsaw engine that replaced the cumbersome and unsafe backpack version. The Forest Service was willing to pay higher costs for auger planting per acre in exchange for better survival and growth rates. I wanted to be part of this transformation of tree-planting contractors and thought I had a chance to corner the market.

I read the bullet points on one contract from the Deer Lodge National Forest. Three-hundred acres in Ham Gulch. Near the town of Maxville. Three-hundred-and-twenty-five acres in Cottonwood Creek near Deer Lodge. Terrain flat to thirty percent slope. Clear-cut, dozer piled, and burned. Auger planting only. Now, that's what I was looking for. Six hundred and twenty five acres, over a square mile of clear-cut forestland to plant.

How many chainsaws to buy? How big of a crew? How many augers? How many spare drills? I nitpicked through my budgetary process to cover every known contingency I had witnessed while with the Forest Service. Makeshift budgets were constantly refigured based on this process.

One Thursday night caught me deep into number crunching when the phone rang unexpectedly. It was my mother.

"Do you watch *Quincy, M.E.,* dear? It was just on here."

I had a twelve-inch, black-and-white Sylvania television that I hardly watched, but I did watch Quincy sometimes because I was still intrigued by the world of medicine.

"It's only seven o'clock here, Mom. Quincy won't be on till nine. Why Quincy tonight?"

"I think the show tells us what your tics are, something called Tourette's syndrome. A young man in the show had what you have, and Quincy discovers it is a neurological condition that is not being researched enough. Quincy talked about orphan drugs, those drugs that remain undeveloped or untested or otherwise neglected because of limited potential for commercial gain. Please, please, watch it tonight. Do you have any neurologists in Missoula?"

"I'll check it out, Mom, and call you back."

Tourette's syndrome was a high-class name for such a socially embarrassing condition. If it was this Tourette's syndrome, at least it was referred to as a neurological disorder and not a mental disorder. My mother could now unload the heavy sense of guilt she had carried, thinking that eating organic food and drinking carrot juice caused my tics.

"Well, you sure do have an extensive medical record," Dr. Sullivan, a neurologist, pointed out. "And remind me, why am I seeing you today?"

Dozens of doctors and chiropractors had examined these tics, but this Dr. Sullivan seemed unhappy, unfocused, and uncaring about my tics. Maybe it was that his arm was in a sling.

"Skiing accident," he mumbled. "So you watched a television show and now diagnose yourself with Tourette's syndrome?"

"Yes, I have had these facial tics and vocalizations since I was twelve. No doctor has been able to diagnose me."

"Well, if you have Tourette's syndrome, you will be my first case. We have to take a blood test first to rule out Wilson's disease."

The blood test ruled out Wilson's disease.

"So do I have this Tourette's syndrome, Dr. Sullivan?"

"That would be my guess."

"Is there any treatment for it?"

"No, but here is a pamphlet that describes the symptoms and an address for a support group in New York."

It was ridiculous that a television actor could articulate Tourette's syndrome better than my doctor. Dr. Sullivan could not relate to me on what life was like with Tourette's, and I had thought me being his first case would generate more questioning. Dr. Sullivan had rated my Tourette's from mild to moderate in severity. I sensed he was uncomfortable dealing with me and quickly dismissed my exam, letting a pamphlet do his work.

The pamphlet was: *Tourette's Syndrome by Elaine and Arthur Shapiro.* I read that in the past fifteen years, the Shapiros had seen a remarkable increase in knowledge and interest in Tourette's syndrome. *How come any doctor or chiropractor that examined me had never heard of this Tourette's syndrome?* A disorder they called it. Hmmm, not a disease. And my mother thought it was carrot juice. One section explained me pretty well. Repetitive movements or unwanted sounds that can't be easily controlled. That was me. Blinking eyes. Another yes. Facial tic. Yes. Whole head and shoulders may be involved with chronic multiple tics. Yes. Tourette's patients are able to do complex arithmetic and run numbers in their head. Oh yeah, that was me, too. Functioning at high levels with little sleep… After reading, I learned that these tics had a highfalutin' name, but nothing could be done about them, but it helped me understand why I had episodic bouts of loneliness and feeling excluded.

The pamphlet had described me to a T. There was relief in knowing that Tourette's was not life-threatening. Nothing else changed. I had an elegant, French-named disorder, and no treatment.

I was a "one and done" patient of Dr. Sullivan and thought he would never make the staff at Presby.

Chapter 67

Taking a nerve-shattering dive into the RW of owning a business left me feeling like I was up against a wall. GARP was mired in layers of insurance interpretations of the work that was to be contracted. Continental Divide Insurance was my last chance. Two previous agencies had turned me down in purchasing a worker's compensation policy for my employees because of insufficient collateral. After I had met with Jill at Continental Divide, our chatty policy talks had come to the point of almost being argumentative. Jill was young and persnickety, and had presented me with a quote that was unreasonable, sticking to the company line. I couldn't back down, no matter how meticulously, though ridiculously in my case, she interpreted the company's policy requirements.

"Jill, why is my policy being rated for logging operations, one of the highest risk categories there is? There is no way I can afford this coverage," I asked, pleading.

"Well, Loring, Working with chainsaws automatically places you in the higher-risk policies that we cover," she told me, while pointing her pen to a set of metrics.

"No, Jill, you are not understanding that while we have chainsaws, we are only using the motor. The cutting bar will be removed and a converter will be mounted so that the engine will turn the auger."

"But that is still using a chainsaw, correct?"

I was getting nowhere with Jill. She had convinced herself that a chainsaw was a chainsaw. At that point, I asked her to appeal my determination with their home office. Two weeks passed, and I was feeling very uneasy about my appeal. *Have faith, recommit. They will do the right thing.* At the end of the second week, I received a call from Jill saying that the company had reversed their position and placed GARP in the classification of nursery workers, a class that had one of the lowest premiums. By prevailing in my appeal, I had saved a thousand dollars with no loss of coverage. And that was a thousand dollars I did not have. Everything I owned was used as collateral, including the best truck that Dodge ever assembled.

I later stopped by the insurance office to sign some papers and hand Jill a check.

"I'm glad it all worked out for you, Loring," Jill said happily while she fiddled with keeping the policy papers in order. "By the way, do you need a bookkeeper? I have someone in mind, and I talked to her about you. Here is her number. Her name is DeeDee."

Was I ready for another DeeDee to enter my life? DeeDee was not an ordinary name, and for me to have had two DeeDee's touch my life was not coincidental. *Does she study the stars, too?* Or maybe it was nothing. I had never believed in coincidence, and I felt anyone named DeeDee had to be a good sign.

Another issue surfaced when it came to purchasing scalping tools, a tool that each tree planter would need to scalp grass and debris away from the drilled hole. My father had instilled in me that you only get what you pay for, and available scalpers, like the ones the Forest Service used, were cheap and inefficient. I decided to try and make a better model. My low-budget operation was no excuse for poor quality.

With no knowledge of welding or working with metal, I was lucky to find out that a nearby high school was offering evening welding classes. Before the first class, I had sketched how I wanted the one-quarter-inch-thick steel blade to look attached to a sixteen-ounce hammer handle. After two weeks of practice welds, I went for the real thing; welding the blade at a right angle to the collar. After a few practice chops and swings with my first tool, I knew I had built a winner at half the cost of a cheaper, less-durable model.

Chapter 68

Hey, Rainbow, I got that tree-planting bid I told you about. Could sure use you in April to plant trees. You know you love it."

"Tree planting, eh. Yeah, love it like jock itch. I'm due to report at Greybull, Wyoming the end of May for the IR fire crew, but I can help you till then. I've got a buddy here in Wisconsin named Brad, and he's heading to Greybull. Can you use another body?"

"Definitely. Is he any good?"

"You'll like him. He works like me, no bullshit."

I was off to a flying start. Bob worked like two men, and if Brad did, too, I basically had four hires. There was uncertainty in hiring friends because I would have to maintain that fine line between boss and friend. And then there were Don and Cherie, who lived in Missoula. Don had worked four years in Wisdom, also, and had decided to travel in new directions. Reaching out to seasoned tree planters made sense, and Don's wife Cherie had worked on the hen crew. They both jumped at the chance, and recommended their friend Alicia. Don had just bought a teepee from Blue Star in Missoula and was ready to pitch it. Don also loaned me a large utility trailer to haul most everything we needed.

GARP had ten people who had planted trees in Wisdom or had friends with planting experience. Chris, an Iowa farm boy who left his forestry dreams behind in Wisdom when he moved to Hawaii to become a breatharian, trying to live on sunlight, air, and the Hindu life force known as *prana*, decided that the call to tree planting superseded his desire to remain in Hawaii and meditate. It was time for him to embark on a gypsy adventure and earn a paycheck.

I would also embark on a gypsy lifestyle for several months, living out of my camper and seeing Ellie on weekends when she came to visit.

I told the Forest Service we would be ready by their planned start date of Monday, April 7. I had three weeks to prepare for my plunge into the business world, but it gave Chris three more carefree weeks of Hawaiian sun to soak up, and Bob and Brad enough time to fish for their limit of walleye. Don's work trailer now had tree-planting equipment, fuel, and shovels, buckets and axes to be compliant with Forest Service regulations.

"Let's have a pizza party at Tower Pizza on Friday and kick off this funfest," Bob suggested.

The crew voted unanimously in favor of a party. Tower had the best pizza in Missoula, and the beer came in frosted mugs. It was hard, but Chris gave up sunshine that night as an energy source.

"I'll have a large Tower Special. Pepperoni, Canadian bacon, green pepper, mushroom, red onion, double cheese. No olives."

"No olives, Chris?" I kidded. "Come on."

We were ready to rock.

Chapter 69

Whether can we get the show on the road, boss? We're burning
daylight,'" Bob, chomping at the bit, wanted to know.
"Do you think those Forest Service guys can't find Ham
Gulch?"

"Well, 'near Maxville' is kind of vague directions. We can rock
and roll as soon as the Forest Service contract administrator gets
here and reviews the contract with me."

"More government bullshit, huh? Hurry up and wait. Just like the
navy."

"I guess. It is weird having an official meeting here to make sure
that my Equal Employment Opportunity Poster is displayed. That's
all this is about. But they also should deliver two days' worth of
trees."

"This is not your first rodeo, I can tell."

"I know, but I'm on the other side now."

Waiting for the Forest Service to arrive on an unseasonably warm
April morning gave me time to gaze at the background of
wildflowers in the field next to Don's teepee, which sat in an open
grassland meadow above the rest of our wooded camp. My view
expanded towards the John Long Mountains, a small mountain
range just northwest of Philipsburg that still glistened with snow-
crusted peaks. The Pintlers rose majestically to the south and east.
The Flint Creek Valley was greening up and could be seen sprawling
in both directions far below. Budding willows outlined the
meandering course of Flint Creek with its healthy population of
brown trout. There wasn't an office in the world that could beat that.

Sackett was at my side and brushed against my leg for attention, anxious for me to throw a stick.

Okay, just one, as I tossed a stick far into the woods. Throwing anything for Sackett to retrieve was like eating potato chips: you just couldn't throw just one.

Ham Gulch was a lot of real estate to plant, but I remembered how it always was at first, looking at a clear-cut. The land was daunting—rocks, unburned logging slash, bear grass clumps, and carpets of wildflowers—but we would plant this mountain, one tree at a time, every nine feet, until it was done.

The contract administrator finally arrived, dressed in a sport coat and penny loafers, and wearing too much of some unrecognizable fu-fu cologne that clashed with the fresh mountain air. He was joined by an older, weather-seasoned, uniformed Forest Service representative from Philipsburg who went by the handle of Bud.

"Any question about the contract, Loring?" the administrator asked after a round of introductions.

"No, not right now. I'm familiar with the requirements. Spacing nine by nine. No J or L roots. Piece of shade material on the southwest side of the seedling. First payment to me on twenty percent completion."

"Well, that's good. Let's have a look at your equipment and let you get to work. Spark arrestors on the new Stihl 045 chainsaws. That's good. Augers are correct diameter. I see you invested in the carbide tips."

"I hope paying the difference will make a difference on wear. I have a lot of holes to drill."

"Good golly, look at these," Bud interrupted, while picking up one of my scalping tools. "I've never seen such a tool like this. Where did you buy them?"

"I didn't buy them, Bud; I made them."

"You made these?"

"Yeah, I did," I said, with a voice that swelled with pride. "There was nothing available in the catalogs that I liked, so I drew the design and took a night course on welding at the local high school. I bought some sixteen-inch hickory hammer handles and attached my scalper blade and collar to them. Then the edges were ground just fine enough to withstand the daily use of scalping soil and rocks away from the hole with a minimum number of swings."

"Well, they sure have a nice heft and balance; maybe you should market them?"

"It was all luck, Bud. I never welded before in my life."

"Just one more thing before we go," the administrator interrupted. "Loring, where is your Equal Opportunity Poster posted?"

"It's nailed to that tree beside my truck."

Bob turned away, so that no one could see him laughing his ass off.

"Okay, Bob and Brad, start your engines. You guys know the pattern. Keep making nine by nine foot squares. Everyone else, bag up and grab a tool. Half of you behind Bob and the other half behind Brad. Chris, bump the gas along."

The Stihls roared to life, and GARP was in business.

My own company. My own dream. My own shoulders to carry that weight. All I could see from the rear were elbows and butts as the crew members bent over, planting. It was a moment, a big Montana moment that I had dreamed of for years. This cleared, deforested land was undergoing a transformation that would benefit future generations. It would never be a case study in biodiversity, but it would be reforested.

Someday, I thought, I would bring my children to Ham Gulch and show them the legacy that GARP had left, and how with hard work, dreams could be fulfilled. I crossed one dream off of my list, leaving two to go. Smoke was out there somewhere, and one day we would meet. I had always believed that. And then there was the son that Father Ben had said I would be blessed with...

Bud checked on our progress by flying over us in his Piper Cub. He tilted his wings if he thought things looked good, but one day he didn't tip his wings. We were done with Ham Gulch and were tearing down our worksite when Bud arrived.

"You finished at the blue-painted boundary line, Loring? It didn't look like it from the air."

"You bet, Bud. We're packing up to head to Cottonwood Creek out of Deer Lodge."

"Not so fast. You haven't planted to the boundary line yet."

"I'm sorry Bud, but there is the end of our planting, right to the line," I told him as Bob joined us for a very long hike downhill to inspect.

"You see that that's an old blue boundary line. You have at least seven more acres to plant to the fresh blue line farther down the hill."

"What new blue line? The contract specified the blue line was the boundary, and there it is. We planted to the blue boundary."

"But you can see that is an old blue line. The new blue line heads off down the hill."

"The Forest Service should have blackened out the old blue line then."

"But you haven't planted it yet."

"Well, I think we're done."

"But you haven't planted it, yet."

I was a little slow in catching on to Bud's drift, and then I had a sudden insight to Bud's gift horse. Bud was asking me to make an effort to plant a basically unplantable area, thereby enforcing the contract with little impact on my business. Bud knew that area should never have been included in the contract. Back at camp, I gave new orders.

"Bob, gas up an auger. Everyone else finish packing and head out. Chris, take my truck and wait for me and Bob down on the highway. Bob and I will bushwhack our way down and ford Flint Creek instead of walking all the way back uphill."

I grabbed a tree bag, stuffed about fifty trees in it and grabbed a scalping tool.

"Let's go, Bob."

"I'm telling you, Loring, that's why they call it the Forest Circus," Bob said, heckling on the way down the hill.

The seven acres in dispute was mostly unplantable because of heavy brush and thick patches of ceanothus, a waist-high shrub. Bob drilled scattered holes as we searched for plantable spots. My tree bag was soon empty.

"It's planted now, Bud," I yelled after planting the last tree.

Bob had already shut the auger off and was hightailing it to the highway.

Chapter 70

The crew needed to stop in Deer Lodge to stock up on supplies, and I needed to buy a Mother's Day card. I was always a stickler on cards, never picking a card that was gaudy or had a verse that did not fit the person or the relationship I had with them. At Keystone Drug, a historic drug store on Main Street, I found the perfect Hallmark card for my mother. I walked three hundred feet to the post office and bought a fifteen-cent stamp.

My intentions were to fill the card with the prettiest wildflowers, a Montana bouquet that would mean more to my mother than a dozen roses from a flower shop.

I placed the card under my sun visor, intending to pick the flowers that evening. On Monday, I planned to give it to a Forest Service rep to mail for me.

Sackett, one tired retriever, sprawled across my front seat, his head in my lap as we drove the twenty miles of rutted, back roads up to our new camp.

"Sorry, I gotta shift," I said as I brushed Sackett's head going from second to third gear. "Yeah, keep wagging your tail. No wonder you're tired. You have a crew throwing sticks for you all day."

Our Cottonwood Creek acreage did not come close to matching the surreal beauty that surrounded Ham Gulch. It was steeper, rockier, and had more unburned slash to work around. It was three-hundred-and-twenty-five acres of ugly, except for the wildflowers I picked to press.

Bud was no longer our contract administrator because we now were in the Deer Lodge district. Vick was our new guy, and he arrived early Monday morning with our trees.

"What's your best guess on finishing here?" Vick asked.

"I'm hoping for mid-June."

"Well, I don't have a problem with that schedule. The soil moisture is holding up, but a few hot days could change that. Your crew really did a great job over in Ham Gulch. Bud thinks highly of your work. If no questions, I'll let you get to work. I'll see you tomorrow."

After Vick left, clouds started moving in. The temperature dropped rapidly. A cool rain fell. By evening, the rain had turned to snow, and we awoke the next morning to eight inches of white slush. This spring snowfall was just like the one I had shared with David four years earlier in Yellowstone. There was only one thing GARP could have done in this situation, and we did it. We built a snowman and dressed him up like a tree planter with a bag of trees around his waist and a scalping tool in one hand. By mid- afternoon, most of the snow was gone from the clear-cut, and sunshine had melted our snowman.

I had looked upon the earlier spring seasons in my life as times of dramatic changes. Two days after the snowfall, the familiar law of entropy and its swing to disorder struck once again. Early one morning, Brad shut off his auger and brought it over to me.

"Check this out, boss. This anti-vibration handle was set up for sawing wood. The constant pounding against rocks beat the shit out of the unit, and the handle is coming off."

"Let's look at Bob's."

The same thing was happening to Bob's handle. What I thought was a better alternative with the anti-vibration system was backfiring.

"Crap, I didn't know this could happen. I gotta run to the Stihl shop in Missoula and buy new bushings. Go with the spare saw, and I should be back in less than four hours."

Four days after the handles were fixed, Bob noticed the carbide-tipped auger bits, the most expensive piece of equipment, were chipping away in the rockier soil. GARP was falling apart.

"Bob, grab the spare. I'm gonna run to Deer Lodge to see the only man I know who can resurface these. I don't have a thousand dollars for three new bits."

Mac was a welding instructor for the Job Corps who I had become friends with several years before. His wife, Adele, had worked with Ellie at one time, and we stayed friends. In the evenings, Mac kept up a steady business of welding and metal fabrication, and at times invented new ways to work with metal.

I interrupted Mac on a Sunday afternoon while he was celebrating his new daughter's baptism. Mac had his "The Incredible Mr. Fix-it" T-shirt on, and nothing besides a new daughter could have made Mac happier than working in his shop.

Mac's ordered shop was loaded with welders, welding rods, drill presses, a compressor, and vises. If it had to do with metal, Mac had it. He reminded me of a Swiss Army knife, always sharp and ready for anything metal.

Mac resurfaced my augers with hard surface rods, and, while not pretty, the base material was now protected while drilling.

GARP was back in business.

Chapter 71

Sundays were usually an off day, but we had suffered significant downtime between the snowfall and getting the augers back to full operation. I thought I would ask the crew to work six hours, so we could make up for lost time. The math was simple. If we didn't work, we didn't eat.

If we worked Sunday, the crew could have a three-day weekend next week. The crew loved the idea and looked forward to time off to rest their beaten bodies.

There was some magic in the air that morning, possibly emanating from a Montana spring day that dawned fresh, clean, and invigorating. Our equipment had been repaired and refurbished, and I felt less stressed. It was mid-morning, and I chatted with Kevin, a new hire to replace Bob and Brad, and a friend of Don's.

"Yeah, Loring, I'm kinda glad you hired me," he said around a pinch of Copenhagen in his cheek. "I was in Missoula last week to visit my mother on Mother's Day, and Don had left word where he and Cherie were working."

"Oh, no. Last Sunday was Mother's Day!"

My morning had just turned upside down.

"Bob, take the crew to noon then knock off. I gotta run."

I peeled off my tree bag and ran up the hill like my pants were on fire. I reached my truck totally winded, gasping for a breath. Lowering the sun visor, I knew what I would find. My Mother's Day card, filled with dry flowers in a packet, had fallen to the seat. Dainty purple columbines, yellow cinquefoils, shooting stars, and glacier lilies had dried to a majestic mat of Montana wildflowers. Instead of receiving a card with a little bit of Montana and a piece of my heart, my mother had received nothing. Not even a phone call from her son. How could I have forgotten to give the card to Vick to mail two weeks ago? I had to find a phone... quick.

The nearest phone was twenty miles away, twenty long miles for me to think about how I was able to remember columns of numbers and ledger sheets in my head but forget Mother's Day.

"Number please?"

"Yes operator, I would like to call collect 412-745-0969. My name is Loring."

I felt sick enough about not mailing a card; calling collect a week late was even worse, but there was no place close to get five dollars in change to feed the phone.

"Hello," I could hear my mother's cheery voice answer the phone.

"Yes, I have a collect call from Loring. Will you accept the charges?"

"Yes, operator."

"Go ahead, sir."

"Mom, I can't believe I forgot to send a card for Mother's Day. I had a special one, with dried Montana wildflowers I picked, and it sat in the truck, and I never mailed it. It's sitting on my dashboard right now."

The card's inscription read, "Mothers Always Understand."

"It's all right, dear. I don't need a card to make me happy. Knowing you are okay makes me happy. I know you have a lot going on. How's the tree planting going?"

"It's going good. Some days are diamonds, some days are coal, like you always said. But I love it, and I'm happy."

Phoning home and talking with my mother had been a weekly event since my college days. But that day she sounded more concerned, more involved, more comforting, almost unearthly. It was like she was finally giving me a blessing on my Montana life.

"Are you taking care of yourself? I worry sometimes that you overdo it. I read that pamphlet on Tourette's syndrome. Now I know why you are always on the go and like to get things done. Promise me you will take some time and rest."

"I promise."

"And always make sure you take care of your loved ones, and remember Marke and Katie in your prayers."

Now, that was a new directive.

"I will, Mom. I wish you could see Montana someday and look at what I'm doing."

"Maybe someday, dear. Maybe someday your father and I will come and see your big sky."

"Goodbye, Mom. I love you. I'll send the dried flowers this week."

"Everything okay, boss?" Kevin asked.

"Yeah, everything's okay now. It's taco Sunday, isn't it?"

"I'm glad you're back. I want you to know I'm trying for the seven club tonight," Bob warned. "My last chance for seven."

Sunday taco fests were an important tradition for Don, Cherie, Bob, and Chris from our Wisdom days. On some Sundays, the taco fest could reach a taste bud explosion as we all mixed our favorite salsas and hot sauces together.

Today would be no different as we cheered Bob on to eat his seventh taco.

"I'm still looking for the taco that scares me," was his signature ending to any taco fest.

Our taco fest ended when Sackett ran out of the woods, howling like a banshee.

"Look at his face. It's full of porcupine quills," Brad cried out.

I rushed to get the first aid kit under the seat of my truck and grabbed a pair of scissors and pliers from my toolbox.

"We gotta get those quills out, but I have to snip the ends off to deflate the quill first," I said, speaking like a trained veterinarian, but the procedure was something I remembered from reading a trapper's journal.

Sackett was not going to lay quietly and let me pull a dozen quills, including those that were embedded in his nose. Bob held his back legs, and Chris held his front legs while Brad held his head and flinched when Sackett tried to bite him.

Be prepared was the Boy Scout motto, and I followed one unwritten Montana outdoor requirement on preparedness... always have a few feet of parachute cord available. Brad clamped Sackett's jaws together, and I quickly wound several loops of parachute cord around them. Sackett was now immobilized, and I went to work with the scissors and pliers. Even hog-tied, his body convulsed with every extraction.

"There, I think I got them all out whole, except I broke one off in his nose. I'll put some first aid cream on it."

We slowly loosened our hold, while rubbing his flanks and unwinding the parachute cord. Sackett rolled to his feet, stood up, shook his head several times, and was ready to play fetch.

That evening, the sky turned into an uncommon, brilliant red sunset.

"This beats any Hawaiian sunset I've ever seen," Chris confirmed, as he sat cross-legged, yoga-style, around the fire, trying to coax three consecutive notes out of his new Indian flute.

The crew was taking in the sunset, marveling that that we had never seen anything so vivid before, when a few specks of dust landed on my jeans.

"Just space dust," Kevin said without a doubt. "Definitely cosmic."

"No, it looks like ash from a fire," I told him.

"Probably the Forest Circus doing a prescribed burn and it got away," Bob snickered.

Kevin tried his Zenith transistor radio for news, but only static filled the channels.

"Nothing to worry about. I'm exhausted. Think I'll hit the rack," I said, adhering to the words of my mother about rest.

Sackett climbed into the rear of the truck, and I put my White's boots outside to dry out. It was a big day, but I felt better knowing my mother was happy.

Part 6

The Flowering Plum (Prunus cerasifera)

The plum blossom has been an important symbol in Chinese culture... the value of endurance as life ultimately overcomes through the vicissitude of time... and rightness in its maturity—all of which embody the characteristics of heaven. Mount St. Helens is a cultivar developed from cold-hardy varieties and is characterized by a sturdy, straight trunk and broad, very-dark-purple leaves.

Chapter 72

The outdoors always made me sleep like a log, except for that night when I tossed and turned and anxiously awaited first light.

When I opened the rear hatch and climbed out, I realized that this was not cosmic dust that covered the ground. I now stood on a blanket of fine-grained ash, at least a half-inch deep, and I wrote my name on the hood of my truck. My boots were filled with ash. The air was still. My teeth were gritty. *What was going on?*

Slowly, the crew woke up, and we gathered near the fire pit. Some expressed fears that a nuclear war had started.

"We can't work in this boss. We don't even know what it is. Maybe it's nuclear fallout," Don blurted fearfully.

"I know; I know. Everyone just wait back in your tents or campers 'til we hear. I'm sure Vick will be here soon to give us an update on this ash... or nuclear fallout."

Two hours passed before we heard trucks rumbling up the rutted road, later than usual.

Finally, Vick's here with some news.

The crew started to reassemble on Vick's arrival, but Vick was accompanied by two other Forest Service employees who I had never met.

Vick looked for me, and when our eyes met, my knees crumbled.

I knew that look... I knew that walk... Faces without expression, eyes that looked down. The bearer of bad news was always circled with their own support group. I flashed back to May of 1973 when I saw that same look, that same walk, in doctors surrounding my mother when she notified me of Gail's death. No, no, not again. Keep on walkin' Vick.

"Loring, I need to talk with you alone… We just received a call from your wife. Your mother has been in an accident, and your family needs you home immediately."

"She's dead isn't she, Vick? Tell me the truth, damn it."

"We didn't get that confirmation, just that she was in an accident and for you to get back home. I'm sorry, Loring. I wish I had more to tell you to calm your fears, but I don't know anything else. Believe me."

Maintain your center. Look at the white light coming in through the stained glass. Breathe in, breathe out. Keep it together. Your family needs you. My mother is gone.

"I also need to tell you that all this ash is from the volcanic eruption of Mount St. Helen's yesterday. All airports in Montana are closed today, and the interstate is closed westbound. You're leaving, but we need to suspend all work 'til further notice. Please use my office phone for calls. Loring, if there is…"

Milton Bradley could not have invented a more horrific board game.

"Thanks, Vick. I'll be gone in fifteen minutes. I'll be okay."

My immediate plan was to drive south to fly out of Salt Lake City. Bob was leaving, but I needed someone to drive my truck back.

"Chris, get an overnight bag together. You're coming with me. Don, I'll get you the account book, and just call DeeDee with your time when you get back to work. All the info's in there. Call my home number in two weeks and let me know what's going on. Can you take Sackett?"

I was holding up, but I let Chris take the wheel. GARP stood in a circle, covered with ash and numbed by my loss as Chris put the Dodge in gear. I couldn't look back, but in the side mirror, I saw hands waving me a sad goodbye.

Chris had a developed sense of spirituality and calmness about him, and I was thankful to have him with me in my hour of need.

I had taken Vick up on his kindness and stopped in his Deer Lodge office to make some calls. Ellie answered on the first ring.

"I'm so sorry, Loring."

"What do you know, Ellie? What happened? Is my mother dead?"

"Your brother didn't say that. He just said accident, and for you to get home immediately. I don't know when I'll be able to leave."

"Look, I need you to pack my suit, shoes, and all of my spring clothes that will fit in a suitcase. And all my meds. All I have is my dirty work clothes that I'm wearing. I'm heading to Salt Lake. You try to get on the first plane out of Missoula when the airport opens and call my home number when you land. Someone will pick you up within a half hour. I gotta go."

There was no answer at my parents' home.

It had been less than twenty-four hours since I had talked with my mother about a Mother's Day card, and I was now sitting on the passenger side of my truck for the first time. *This is where she sat when I took her for a ride to get a haircut.* The card still sat on my dashboard, the dried bouquet still intact. She was happy, and now she was gone.

It was supposed to have been a celebratory week of new beginnings for Katie, along with an addition to the Walawander family. Katie's senior prom and graduation were that week, and Marke was preparing for the baptism of Marke Jr. on Sunday. These would have been more debits against my Montana Dream account, but I would be with them now, joined in sorrow.

I felt so ripped off. Gail at twenty-one. My mother just one month away from her forty-sixth birthday. Not even a gray hair. Ellie's family lost...

Chris snapped me out of my stupor.

"Tell me more about your mom's cooking. You always talked about that. Were those poppy seed rolls that good?"

"Oh, yeah. Nobody ever could make them like her. The recipe was in her head. Using sour milk was her secret. We had them every Easter and Christmas."

It was conversations like that which helped the miles roll quickly by. We passed the exit for Red Rock Lakes National Wildlife Refuge. I saw it as just another emotional toll booth along the way to a Montana Dream that I paid a high price for. There would not be another chance to send a Mother's Day card on time. I had done the impossible by living through my illness, but my mother did the unimaginable by keeping me safe in her arms of love every single day. Day after day, without fail. My mother was a child warrior, a teenage bride, and a woman of boundless heart and loving kindness.

"We need gas. Can I get you anything?" Chris asked as we pulled off I-15.

"Thanks, maybe a tall boy. Whatever they got."

Chris came back to the truck, clutching a brown paper bag in one hand and a bag of chips in the other.

"They only had quarts of Bud."

"That'll do."

I unscrewed the cap and quietly went to work.

"Chris, Chris, look out your left window. It's a Southwest Airlines jet coming in for a landing. We're close to Idaho Falls. I forgot all about that airport. That saves three hours of driving to Salt Lake. Look for airport signs. Wait, over there is the exit."

"Nothing else open today. We can get you on the morning Southwest 7:10 flight, arriving Denver at 8:15, connecting to Pittsburgh on United Airlines at 9:40, and arriving Pittsburgh at 2:40 p.m.," the Southwest ticket agent confirmed.

With all the schedule delays because of Mount St. Helens, I was lucky to get a reservation and not fly standby.

Chris booked a cheap room at Motel West that was only three minutes from the airport. There was an old J.C. Penney store across the street, and I knew I had to buy something to wear besides what I had on. Dirty jeans covered with volcanic ash was no way to arrive.

J.C. Penney's was not my brand, but the chain was famous for issuing young people credit cards. There was a card in my wallet that I had never used, but now I saw it as a godsend. I tried on a pair of black slacks that fit okay, grabbed two darker, coordinated shirts and a pair of inexpensive, black loafers. A pair of black socks rounded out my mourning wardrobe.

Back at the motel, I slumped into the only easy chair in the room.

"Tomorrow is gonna be hard on you," Chris said in a soothing, comforting voice, while sitting on the bed.

"I'm only dealing with one thing at a time," I said, which was not my nature.

"When I was in Hawaii, I studied Rolfing and chakra therapies. I want to start doing more yoga, too."

"Chakras?"

"Yeah, it's a Hindu approach to working on the seven spiritual centers in the body. I think I could help you right now. I won't do deep-tissue massage because that can hurt, and you don't need any more pain. Massage might help ease your physical pain and working on your heart chakra may help the pain deeper within you."

I laid on the cheap, shoddy motel bed and let Chris perform an amazing act of kindness that I could never forget. There were no vanilla-scented candles burning, sandalwood incense smudging, or taped ocean mood music playing. For two hours, in the quiet of a dingy motel room, I felt the roughened hands of a tree planter gently massage me from head to toe, smoothing out the pockets of pain that had started to build within me.

Chris started working on my back first. My lower back, still sore from tree planting, responded quickly to the massage. I groaned with the release of pain. And then he worked on my neck, shoulders, and jawline.

"Ahh-ahh," I quietly exhaled as Chris worked on the tightened muscles and tissue that had formed from years of grimacing and facial tics.

These pains were close to the surface of my body and responded quickly to his touch.

"There is a lot of tightness in your chest also. This is the area of your heart chakra, and I feel it is closed."

"What caused that? I don't feel pain there. My heart checkup was good."

"Think of it as a river of energy flowing through your body. Loneliness over time may be one reason a heart chakra may be blocked."

I had an open mind and was hip to try alternative healing practices, like taking a sweat in an Indian sweat lodge along the Jocko River in Arlee. But this chakra therapy was new to me. Loneliness, however, was not a surprise factor. Maybe Chris was on to something. Did past loneliness from being different with the tics of Tourette's syndrome block the free flow of the river of energy that ran deep inside my body? I wished to find more out later.

"Keep relaxing. Think of the time you saw your mom the prettiest ever," Chris suggested.

"At my cousin Elaine's wedding. 1972."

"What was her favorite perfume?"

"Chanel No. 5."

My heartbeat slowed. I wanted to drift away, float on a cloud high above Ajax Peak because I felt it was still a bad dream. While on my stomach, I buried my face deep into the sheets, trying to dry my eyes. This wasn't a dream. My mother was gone, and I didn't know why or how she had died. Two thousand miles away, my family was mourning, and the reality would sink in for me the following day.

Chapter 73

T he first thing I remembered on Tuesday morning was finding my window seat on the Boeing 727 in Denver. The memories of Chris, my truck, my clothes, and the ride to the airport were just faded memories that never came back into focus.

Heavy metal thundered across the morning Colorado sky as the three engines of the 727 roared to life, leaving me just three hours of solitude before I landed in Pittsburgh. While the 727 headed east over the Great Plains, I was hypnotized by the view far below... the grayish-brown volcanic ash cloud from Mount St. Helens.

The eruption of Mount St. Helens and my mother's death would be forever linked as I saw the similarity between the two. Mount St. Helens was a rupture in the crust of the Earth that allowed hot gases, steam, and lava to escape and bring loss of life and suffering to anyone close. My mother's death was a rupture, a giant tear along the thin membrane of the nucleus of the family planet,which caused pain, grief, and a flood of tears to all that were close. I thought about our family's future. We were a close family and did not socialize much outside of visiting relatives during the holidays. My grandmother was our sun, and everyone revolved around her. She was a rugged individualist, a nurse who had been widowed for twenty-six years and who lived a simple life of meditation and prayer and thrived on raw vegetable juices. My mother and grandmother were very close, and I knew my grandmother would be sad to lose my mother. She possessed an iron will and was resilient, so time would be her eventual comforter.

My father would slingshot out of his stable orbit and wander aimlessly, lost in time and space, I feared.

Marke would see my mother's death as God's will. It was Katie who worried me the most. I had seen how a loss of a mother affected Ellie, leaving her with a mortally wounded soul. Katie was graduating from high school that week. She would not have a mother to buy her a clock with a snooze alarm for college. She, like Ellie, could suffer the most.

Feeling like an electrical transformer being flooded with too much electricity, I exited the plane. One hour... I would see my mother.

My cousin Stan was waiting at the gate.

"What happened Stan? Where is she?'"

"Aunt Mary was coming from work and she was in a head-on collision on Boyce Road. I heard she died instantly. My mom said the first viewing would be around four at Fryar's."

Boyce Road was only three miles from home. We had traveled that road all of our lives. Why? Why? She had just gotten a new Citation car that she was so happy with. Why?

On the notice of the deceased outside of Fryar's, I saw my mother's name, Mary Jane Walawander, in bold, white letters on a black background, making it all real. I had passed Fryar's thousands of times but never imagined I would see my mother's name on it while I was so young. I made my way to the door among the many guests who had started to arrive.

I don't know if I can go inside. This is real. No, it's a bad nightmare. You have to go inside. Your family needs you.

Summoning all available physical and emotional strength, I entered the parlor to find that it was full of grieving relatives and friends. There was not a sound above that of a sob. Floral bouquets were arriving, filling the air with the weird scent of flowers that one would only smell at a funeral home. My dried bouquet of Montana wildflowers were still in my truck, once again forgotten.

Oh, God, I forgot her again. How beautiful they would have been, laying in her hands.

280

My mother's light-colored mauve casket was to the right. I could not look at her. Not yet.

A male relative came to my side and put his comforting arm on my shoulder, his fingers massaging my neck.

"It's okay to cry, Loring; go ahead and cry, crying will help."

My body, the electrical transformer, had just received that one surge, that one energy spike that caused me to blow up inside.

Get your fucking hands off me. Don't touch me. Don't tell me to cry. When I cry it will be in private, in the shade of towering spruces in the wilderness, near a cool, Montana stream, where its icy water could rinse the salt of my scalding tears away.

My brother was busy setting up a stand with a poster that had his poem to my mother written on it. I read the poem but only remember the last three words: truly loving mother. I left him to his work.

My grandmother sat alone in a corner, her staunch faith keeping her composed, but she wasn't able to hide the grief in her face or hold back the tears in her eyes. My arms opened wide to embrace her small, but sturdy frame. She struggled to stand, came to me, and looked up into my eyes.

"My dearest grandson, you're home."

"Yes, Gram, I'm home," I said as I wrapped my arms around her and gently rocked her.

"Your beautiful mother. Why? Why?"

"Only God knows, Gram."

My sister had walked into the parlor. The coming week was to be her special week with her high school senior prom and graduation. Pomp and circumstance had no importance now. She and my mother had been extremely close, and now, their relationship had moved to one of eternal separation. The life force had been sucked out of her, and she stood quivering and crying at my side.

"Oh, Lor, our precious mother."

"I have no answer, Katie, only that God called her name. We need to be strong. She raised us to be strong."

"I'm not as strong as you."

I looked away. It was time. There could be no more disinclination, disbelief, or doubt. I had to see my mother.

Standing at her head, I stared into her face and noticed that her eyelids were sewn shut. *I know you can see me Mom; you're in this room, and you're up above. You're in a different world, one without pain. We are in pain. Oh, how I wish you could hold me now.*

I heard only sounds of sobs, but then the mournful wailing of my father filled the room as he was escorted by my uncles. How I first wished that this man, who had given me dreams, love, and support beyond measure could be stronger, but he was inconsolable.

In that most horrible moment, I recalled something my father said years ago. It was the day of Martin Luther King Jr.'s assassination, and my father was taking me for my driver's exam when we heard the news on the radio.

"Good God Almighty son, they shot him. Remember what I told you when we lived next to colored people in Heidelberg? You are not to judge a man by his color or position in life. The difference between you and the man who doesn't have two nickels to rub together could be the difference of a missed phone call. Your job is not to judge; yours is only to love."

Now, I was faced with adhering to those words, those golden nuggets of wisdom that he shared with me as a teenager. I went to him, thinking at first that he had an absence of faith that caused him to lose all control. But my father was a man of good work and good deeds, and never wanted more than what he gave. It was not a question of faith, but a question of how he could live without my mother. He needed her. He could not live alone. Who would pick out what shirts to wear? He was faced with bearing the unbearable. I would not judge him, only love him.

Ellie made it to Pittsburgh on Wednesday, and after receiving guests at Fryar's home throughout the day, my family grieved at home that evening. All of us faced the bitter reality that we were motherless children. My father, unable to carry the weight of his horrendous loss, had finally passed out upstairs in his bedroom. He was in so much pain, he continued to find relief the only way he knew how, as his father and grandfathers before him. He had turned to the magic elixir for numbing the heart, mind, and soul. A fifth of Beefeater gin was his emotional rescue.

Marke, Nancy, Katie, Ellie, and I sat in our living room and tried to console one another and find strength for the next day's funeral. Detached from the others, I took a moment to soak in the memories of that room from my spot on the plush, olive green carpet. In one corner of the room, near the large picture window, sat the Steinway piano that Marke and Katie played. And there… right next to the piano bench: the exact spot where, eight years ago, my mother hugged Gail and me on Elaine's wedding day. There were no herbal or earthy scents now, but I saw them there.

Flashing further back, I remembered a day when I came into that room, and Marke was playing "Colour My World" by Chicago, a song of great love that was cool to slow dance to. However, Katie had taken that piano to more complex levels, and had replaced Chicago with Chopin. A copy of Chopin's "Mazurkas" laid open on the piano bench. On one wall hung a large, biblical print of Jesus and his disciples on the walk to Emmaus. This print originally belonged to my grandmother, but she gave it to my mother when we moved to the country. My gaze wandered across the room and came to rest on a print that hung on an adjoining wall. It was an inexpensive print, almost cheap in fact, but it was my mother's favorite, even though it clashed with the overall décor of the room. The print was a fall scene of a bushel of red apples sitting near the tree, its leaves resplendent in fall colors.

"Do you know why Mom loved that print so much?" I asked everyone.

"I don't remember she ever said," Marke answered with a shrug.

"Well, she liked it because she told me that it reminded her of when she picked apples as a young girl on the farm," I explained.

All eyes came to focus on the print, and, within a moment, without any disturbance in the house, the print fell off the wall where it had hung without incident for fourteen years.

We were frightened at first, and then we smiled, as we all agreed that the spiritual presence of my mother had just passed through that room.

We were to be at Fryar's at nine o'clock for the last viewing before the casket was closed and carried to the church.

"This eastern funeral process is so barbaric and cruel," I lamented to Ellie. "Viewing my mother's body for three days is so hard on my father. Why don't they do it like out west with cremation and a memorial service, then spread the ashes?"

"Tradition," she answered in a voice tempered by her own horrific experience.

Sleep did not come to me that night, and, at dawn, I looked out from my old bedroom window. The new spring morning had broken with clouds and rain, and the strip of lush, green grass where my father had stopped mowing when the police came was prominent. It was the line of demarcation, before mom, and after mom. Two whitetail deer chewed grass on the edge of the lawn, bordering the woods. A cardinal landed in the large cherry tree. It was a typical spring rain shower, which was over in a few minutes.

When we left the house for the funeral home, my family walked into a day full of sunshine, the best medicine we could have received. On the way to the car, we passed the flowering plum tree, so fragrant, so fresh after the morning rain, I could see why it was my mother's favorite. It was the same tree where, four years previously, my family celebrated my departure to Montana.

"I'll be just a minute," I told everyone in the car, as I retraced my steps to the flowering plum and broke off the prettiest stem of blooms.

Later, at Fryar's, when all the prayers had been prayed and it was time for the family to form the cortege to All Saints Church, I hung back to be the last to see my mother before the casket was closed.

"Here, Mom, these were always your favorite," I said as I first shook the remaining raindrops from the bouquet over her. "This water is just as holy as that from the church that the priest sprinkled on you."

I laid the fresh bouquet of plum blossoms in her hands. The fragrance floated above her and pervaded the air inside the casket, bringing a pleasant sensory moment during my most difficult goodbye.

It was time for me to leave.

All Saints Polish National Catholic Church. The cornerstone of my family's faith for seventy years would now conduct the mass for my mother, who had been married there thirty years before.

The hearse had delivered my mother's casket several minutes before my family arrived, helping shorten my father's exposure to my mother's coffin. Marke and I struggled to get my father up the church's steps into the narthex.

"You got him, brother?" I asked as I supported my wailing father under his left shoulder.

"Got him," Marke said, supporting his right shoulder.

My father remained inconsolable, even when met by the open arms of Father John at the entrance to the narthex.

"Joe, Joe, let your family help you. You must believe that Mary is still alive in heaven. Let the Lord give you some comfort..."

Father John, just a year older than me, was new to the church, having replaced the ailing Father Ben who had medically retired. Despite his youth, Father John embraced of my father's human condition, trying to share the grief and lighten the load that my father was now enduring. His words of faith and love were blocked by the overwhelming grief and despair that not even a bottle of gin could knock out.

Upon entering the sanctuary, I saw my mother's casket in the center near the altar. Some votive candles had been lit nearby, flickering with the prayers of family and friends who sat in the pews.

Yet, there was a more intense white light than just that from the votive candles. The protective light of my youth, as if on an emergency call, beamed once again through the stained-glass window of the Twelfth Station of the Cross. The bright sunlight broke into dancing prisms as it reflected off my mother's casket... My mother's light was still shining, even though she was gone. Light particles, of all the colors of the rainbow, were bathing the first three pews of the church, those pews that were reserved for family. Once again the restorative power of the white light served me through my darkest of times. But there was another light in my life, and it was the light of the Montana wilderness that would make me whole again. *Montana, I'll be home soon.*

We all tried to pick up our lives and carry on without my mother. I finished cutting the grass where my father left off. There was no more line of demarcation of before Mom. Katie was stronger than she thought and attended her senior prom. While she was putting the finishing touches to her hair, I answered the doorbell. It was her prom date. I immediately forgot his name, but I remember the words we exchanged.

"I want to thank you for still wanting to take Katie to the prom. She wants to go, but she has been through a lot. It may be a long, tough night for you. She may not last long."

But this young man, whom I would probably never see again, replied, "I understand what Katie is going through. I'll do the best I can."

I never found out how the evening went, but I was so impressed with Katie's date. What a standup guy.

Two days later, we all attended Katie's graduation ceremony. I saw Ms. Holly on the podium. How I wished I could have told her something about my Montana life and how she contributed to it.

Marke and Nancy baptized Marke Jr. on Sunday, giving the family a death and a spiritual birth of baptism in the same week.

By the end of the following week, my father had not given up his steady diet of gin, and Marke and I took him to be admitted for detox at the same hospital my mother was taken to after the accident.

"Get me outta here, son. There's nothing wrong with me."

"Then how come your skin is blue? Come on Dad. Work with the doctors. You can't keep drinking the pain away. You have grandchildren who need you. Retire. Come to Montana. We can buy a small business and work together. We can't lose you like this."

"I know, son; I know."

He only knew he wanted more gin.

Ellie received a call from her elderly Aunt Phoebe that week. Her Uncle Jack was to undergo cancer surgery, and her aunt needed help to care for him. She left two days later.

I was concerned about Katie. I talked with my grandmother about the state of her grief. She was seventeen and was now alone with my father, who could barely take care of himself.

"Gram, do you think you can help out and get Katie to Montana once I leave? She needs to get away for a while, and I think Montana will help her."

"Just call me, and I'll give you the money for her ticket. *Niech cię Bóg błogosławi.*"

"God bless you too, Gram."

Don phoned on a Friday afternoon. GARP was out of sight and out of mind until Don's call.

"Hey, boss. How are you doing? We're thinking of you."

"I'm hanging in there. It's hard, man. What's happening with the volcano ash?"

"Well, I talked with Vick today on the phone. We're back in Missoula. Vick said the Forest Service still has the forest closed. The ash is pretty thick, and no one knows how hazardous it would be to work in. Three guys resigned today."

"Well, it seems like you are on top of things. Don't worry about the resignations. If we're not working, we don't need them."

"When do you think you will be back?"

"I don't know, Don. Soon, I hope, but my family needs me, and I need them. You gotta hang in there."

"I'll try, but man, I'm not a boss. I'm a worker and don't know the first thing about running this business. Vick wanted me to tell you that GARP was awarded that fuel break contract you submitted before leaving."

"Well, that will keep us going 'til the snow flies. It seems like you are doing a good job, staying in touch with Vick. Call me when the forest reopens."

Six weeks later... still in Pennsylvania.

Time had come. GARP had been cleared to resume planting. The same old song played without fanfare outside of the family home, where my father stood sober but in relentless grief. The detox trip to the hospital scared the shit out of him, and now he had cut back to a self-imposed maintenance dose of alcohol, that delicate balance of gin that was enough to ease his pain but kept him standing and coherent.

My grandmother was near tears, and Katie seemed devoid of any emotion. We stood near the plum tree, the scene of so many happy memories.

Big Brother is leaving again. He always leaves. Why can't he stay? Why does he have to go back to Montana? First it was Tennessee. Now Montana. Leave everything for Marke to deal with. Go climb your towering mountains. Go swim in your cold rivers.

Following my dreams to Montana had left me feeling selfish. *Profiles in Courage* had stepped to the plate. I'm up, and team Walawander needs you to hit them in. They were stranded on the bases, wanting to score. Just a little hit. Come on, big brother. We don't need the home run yet. Stee-rike three! You can go home now.

Part 7

The Douglas fir (Pseudotsuga menziesii)

This climax species will remain essentially unchanged in terms of species composition for as long as a site remains undisturbed. Douglas fir is an important timber tree with strong, durable wood. They are the most shade-tolerant species of tree to establish in the process of forest succession. The seedlings of climax species can grow in the shade of the parent trees, ensuring their dominance indefinitely.

Douglas fir grows to more than 200 feet tall in its native habitat in the West. It has been transplanted successfully throughout most of the North American temperate zone.

Chapter 74

Totally strange, but it was the first time I felt good about not wanting to plant trees. My hands were healed, but my heart was raw, and, for some reason, I was not anxious to reconnect with Montana dirt and rock, or hear the augers drilling away the precious silence of a Montana morning. I didn't want to do it for a day.

Chris had picked me up at the Butte airport, which was closer than Missoula to Cottonwood Creek. I was relieved to be back in my holy land—Montana ground, sitting in my Dodge, feeling the freedom of the West again. But something had changed. The last time I was with Chris, he had cared for me, he had comforted me and massaged my pain. Now, he seemed disconnected from our past as we rode back to Cottonwood Creek in a distancing silence that told me something had changed, and not for the better.

The crew was no different than Chris. They all seemed to have aged and changed, no longer the gung-ho crew I remembered. *Why is there tension in the air?* Somehow I felt I was being blamed for the work stoppage. Knowing their work and personal lives were in limbo for over six weeks, I gave them some space while I met with Don for an update.

"Thanks for hanging in there, Don. Only seven in the crew? What's Vick saying?"

"Yeah, well it's been rough. Everyone camped at my house in Missoula for the past month. The crew is a little squirrely. Some ran out of money. A couple guys left to find other work. I'm glad you're back because it's not the same without you. Like I told you, I'm not a boss. Vick wants to talk to you in the morning."

"Okay. Don't worry about those guys leaving. We can try to finish without them. You did a great job. And Sackett looks well fed."

Vick arrived early in the morning with only one box of trees.

"Loring, I'm sorry about your mother. I lost my mother three years ago, and I know what you're going through."

He stared at me like a boy who'd lost his mother, not like a fellow forester.

"Then you know there's no words to explain it. It sucks."

"I know. It takes time. Let me grab a cup of coffee from my truck. Want some?"

Being back in Montana was a relief. I thought of the pain that still lingered in my Pennsylvania home. It was not that I didn't have any pain, but it was pain that I could bear by myself, in a state where I could find freedom to grieve where I was most comfortable. But reuniting with Vick and my crew rekindled the memory of that Monday morning when I received the news about my mother. I didn't want to be in Cottonwood Creek an extra minute.

"Here Loring." Vick handed me a cup of coffee. "This morning I need to go over the district's proposal about your contract. After you left, the ash was too thick, so the forest was shut down. We have not received any rain since, and this spring is turning out to be exceptionally dry. Soil moisture is getting so low that we would like to negotiate the remainder of the contract. There's no use in planting dead trees."

"I can agree to that," I said as I happily nodded my head.

"We propose that you finish planting what you can this week, and we'll pay you for up to that point. The district is willing to terminate the contract without any penalty to you. Then you can start your other contract building that trail and fuel break with Bud. Can we agree on that?"

"That's fair, Vick. Everyone has been through a tough time. We'll be done Friday."

Later that evening, Don came to me and said he and Cherie were resigning on Friday. Then Chris gave me notice. Then Alicia. By the end of the day, I had resignations from all but Kevin. *Why is he staying?* I had only known him for a week, and he stayed loyal to me. I knew the volcano situation was tough, but no one could understand what I had been through.

The next morning Kevin knocked on my camper.

"I'm still with you, boss. You've been good to me and paid me well. I knew this was going to happen."

"Why did you know it was going to happen?"

"Well, it all started the last Sunday we worked before the volcano. Cherie told you in the middle of the morning that she didn't feel like working that day."

"I remember. And I told her if that was the case, I didn't feel like paying her that day. If she said that in fun, I answered in fun. If she was serious, then so was I."

"Exactly. I heard you say that. I thought it was all in fun. But all the downtime we had in Missoula, she wouldn't let go of it, and started telling everyone you were dogging it back in Pennsylvania, expecting the crew to make you lots of money. All that downtime made everyone squirrely. Don just let her rant."

"Me, make lots of money tending to my mother's funeral? Come back to Earth, my man."

"I know; I know. You gotta listen to my plan. Screw them. I knew they were going to bail whether this was their last week or not. I met this gal named Angie in Anaconda. She's a bartender at the Motherlode. Good looking, outdoorsy, but divorced with a four-year-old boy. I left Missoula and spent some time with her this month in Anaconda. We have something going."

"I'm so happy you're getting laid, Kevin, but the plan?"

A-ha Kevin. Now I know why you stayed.

"Dig this. This is the best part. Angie has two older brothers, Kyle and Jason, who were laid off from the smelter. The Anaconda Copper Company closed the Berkeley Pit in Butte. You can't close one of the world's largest open-pit copper mines and not have massive layoffs at the smelter. They have a couple friends who are laid off, too. Tough sons of bitches. You know Butte-Anaconda guys. They shake your hand with their right hand and are buying ya a beer with their left. They're really into hunting. Angie told me they'd jump at a chance to work in the woods 'til November when they would start chasing elk around."

I had always believed miracles occurred in the strangest of places.

"So, if I got this right, we have a new crew, woods savvy, just waiting for the word?"

"You got it, big guy."

I was back in Montana less than a week and experienced my company flame out and die, but like Phoenix in Greek mythology, GARP arose from the ashes of Mount Saint Helens and was born again. Before starting a new project with a new crew, I needed a mountain fix, and Kevin's news provided the opportunity.

"Hey Kev, you said Angie is into hiking and camping?"

"Oh, hell, yeah. Her dad always took the family camping."

"How about we take the work trailer that Don is still letting me use and set camp up at Southern Cross. We need to convert the augers and do some maintenance. Then I have to connect with Bud on contract specs. Ellie is still away helping her aunt, and I want my sister out here. I think a trip to the West Big Hole, maybe Upper Miner Lakes, would be good therapy. I'd feel better if you and Angie came, too. You know, another woman around may make it easier for my sister."

"Angie loves the Big Hole, and her mother can babysit her boy. She's off on weekends, so just say when."

If Kevin only knew how he had just made my day. I felt like giving him a giant bear hug.

"Okay, I'll call home and get my sister booked. I can meet Angie and her brothers this week. Let's plan next weekend. Get your cowboy hat out, stud. We're riding to the Big Hole."

Chapter 75

Kevin and I searched the tiny ghost town of Southern Cross. We claimed an empty cabin that had minimal restoration and no running water but a pump outside. There were three rooms, and a pair of rusted bedsprings sat in one of the rooms. It had rustic charm, but the two best things were that it was rent-free and less than two miles to our contract site. The two or three full-time residents never cared that we took up residence in Southern Cross.

At the Butte airport, I welcomed a still-numb Katie to Montana. She seemed lost in a lost world. There was little show of emotion except for the grief she wore for all to see.

"Sure, I miss Mom, Katie. There's no getting away from her loss, but I hope Montana can help ease your pain."

"It was all my fault."

"You can't own that feeling. Telling Mom to stay home that day because she didn't feel good was in no way connected to God's plan."

There was so much pain etched into her young, pretty face. She needed relief, some rest, and a way to find some peace. I was her big brother, but I didn't know her. I was always gone, and Katie was a girl who kept her feelings to herself. *Can this Montana trip help?*

"Anyway, how was your flight?" I asked her.

"Oh, okay."

I settled for two-word answers. My mother's death came at a formative time in Katie's teen years, with her high school graduation and starting college at Pitt. These were pivotal moments in her life, and dealing with my mother's loss had made them more difficult.

She had not adjusted to a world in which my mother was no longer there. I ached for her and prayed that the restorative power of mountain solitude could help her as they had helped me. I was at a loss for other alternatives.

"Get ready to explore some of the most beautiful lakes in Montana. The views are breathtaking, and you'll see why I love Montana so much. Monument Peak rises up behind Upper Miner Lake. Maybe we can climb it."

"Oh, okay."

I was concerned about pushing Katie too hard to where she was uncomfortable. Climbing a mountain is not only physical but requires constant attention to the terrain. A loose rock, a patch of pink snow, or poor visibility can imperil a day's adventure on the mountain. I knew Katie had ballet, competitive ice skating, and cheerleading in her past, so I knew she could be physical enough, but maybe we could have used a few cheers that day.

Angie was a relative stranger to me, but I felt that her being a Montana native with a warm disposition could be invaluable on our mountain sojourn to help Katie open up to the wonder that was Montana. I was ten years older than Katie, and at times I was tenderly aware I didn't know the first darn thing about my sister. What were her dreams, her favorite foods, or her favorite color? I only knew she loved cats. Lots of cats. Her green T-shirt told me that she liked Bob Seger and the Silver Bullet Band, and that was one thing we did have in common.

It was easy to see why Kevin and Angie were so smitten with each other. She was a dark-haired, lovely young woman with warm brown eyes. She smiled a lot. I had never changed about liking smiles on a woman. Angie seemed comfortable and secure in her own skin, unpretentious about her good looks, yet tough enough to handle a crowd of thirsty miners or guys from the smelter. I found she was a great listener, a skill she had probably developed by having to relate to so many different types of people from behind the bar. Kevin was a good-looking, swashbuckling Irish man with tousled hair the color of a used penny. He was a raconteur of the first order. His panache, fresh and invigorating in a mill town, captured

Angie's attention, and so did his tales of adventure commercial fishing the high seas of Alaska or hitchhiking through Mexico.

Angie greeted Katie with that big Montana smile, and I thought I saw just the smallest light in my sister's eyes.

"I'm happy to meet you, Katie, and have your brother take us to Upper Miner Lakes. I heard it's fantastic. Wait till you see the Big Hole. It's so awesome. Do you fish?"

"No."

"You just never had a chance to fish a high mountain lake in Montana, that's why. I'll fix that. I've fished since I was a little girl."

"Oh."

At the trailhead, the Big Hole mosquitoes had just came to lunch, and Katie was twitching, shaking, and hopping, beginning to look like a young woman with St. Vitus's dance. She swatted and swiped at the bloodsuckers as they circled and attacked her face while she tried to scratch her right calf with her left shoe. But she never complained.

"Let's get more bug dope on you right now," I said. "I've done this hike in two hours, Katie. The climb's not that bad, a little rocky in some places. But we'll take our time, and I'll show you the different trees, birds, and wildflowers along the trail. Not many huckleberries though."

"The pack feels okay, Lor. I'm ready."

Okay. She's getting in tune.

My eclectic, fearless foursome hit the trail before eleven o'clock with me leading the way, soaking up any sun that filtered through the trees and longing for the mountain wind to brush my face. The smell of ancient spruce trees filled the air. Once my feet hit the trail, I knew I was back home at last. *I'm alive again!*

There were two lakes that made up the Upper Miner Lakes. The higher of the two was at almost nine thousand feet. Both lakes were in a cirque below Monument Peak and Sacajawea Peak.

When we all came to Upper Miner Lake, the view of the headwall at the lake's edge was one of wonder and unparalleled beauty. Snow cornices still teetered on the top of Monument Peak, and the avalanche chutes on the headwall were still snow packed. Fine rock, soil, and other mountain debris had accumulated over thousands of years at the base of the headwall. It had been two years since I had been to Upper Miner, and I felt euphoric once more to live the mystic experience of being in the high country with its infinite views.

"What a scene this is," Angie shouted, waving her hands above her head in joy. "This should be on the cover of *National Geographic*."

"No way, Angie. *National Geographic* just had an article about building a fence around Montana," Kevin said, ribbing back.

"Far out," Katie cried with long-lost emotion.

Two word sentences are better than nothing. Breathe in the good air, Katie. Let it revive your spirit.

The next morning I scuttled our plan to scramble Monument Peak because of snow cornices that still lingered at the summit in the middle of the summer. Although we did not try for the summit, Katie and I climbed as high as we safely could. Through the years, I have savored looking at a photo of that Miner moment, Katie and I raising our hands in triumph at our highest point. Many years have passed, and the photo is losing its quality, but Katie's face is still exuberant as the day that it was taken.

The Cherokee believed in the healing power of mountains and so had I from my time in the Smokys. Was it the fresh air and the clear, rumbling water from melted ice of ancient times? Or maybe it was a sense of being closer to a higher power, or the feeling of how small and transient you were in relation to the power and permanence of the mountain… No, I thought. It was all of these, and these forces started to uplift Katie from despair and realize the beauty that surrounded her.

Back at camp, Angie worked with Katie on rigging up my Eagle Claw rod to fish, and Kevin took Sackett to play fetch on the other end of the lake. I had curled against a log at the lake's edge with a paperback book that I bought at the Pittsburgh airport. The novel was *Shibumi*, by Trevathian. The book drew me in after reading the back cover that described the main character trying to attain a rare kind of human excellence, the effortless state of living in shibumi. Shibumi was powerful silence, it was simplicity, and it had spiritual tranquility. Shibumi comes naturally to some people or does not come at all.

If shibumi had come my way, it would have been the frosting on my Montana Dream cake. Meeting Smoke, owning a home, and having a family were the parts of my Montana Dream that still needed to bake. I would have given Smoke the biggest piece of that cake.

"You have a fish on, Katie," Angie shrieked.

I had periodically glanced up to watch Katie's awkward handling of the fly rod, remembering my Mystic Lake experiences. Katie had slapped at the water with the rod and had fly line looped at her feet, but Angie stayed patient, and Katie was rewarded. Katie scored no style points while catching her first fish, and the trout made a run, peeling yards of floating fly line off the reel. Katie had hooked a bigger-than-average fish. Tough, long Montana winters did not let the fish grow to great size in high Alpine lakes, but occasionally a fourteen- to sixteen-inch trout made it through several winters. They were hard to catch, but Katie had hooked a dumb one.

"You have him hooked, Katie. Raise the rod tip up now," I yelled. My advice came from experience—I had plenty of experience with fish that got away. "Pull the slack in the line. I'm a comin'."

Jumping to my feet, I grabbed my net, and we managed to land the magnificent rainbow and took a picture before releasing it.

"That fish looks like a rainbow, with all those pretty colors."

"You're right Katie. That's why they are called rainbows," Angie said.

"Nice job, Katie. Are you hooked on Montana yet?" I asked, half-kidding.

When it came time for Katie to leave, I called Marke to let him know Katie's return time. "I think she's better after a few days in Montana," I told him, but we agreed that it most likely was a temporary geographical fix.

"Good, good. She needed to get away from here. Too many memories."

"How's Dad?"

"You know, he's trying to get it together and went back to work, but his buddies cover for him on his bad days. Those guys take care of one another, I tell ya. Oh, sorry. I got some bad news for you, too. Uncle Johnny passed away this week. There's no funeral. It's a wonder he lived this long, but he was sober for fifteen years."

"What about Gram?"

"She's doing okay. Johnny was her closest brother. You know how she is. She sings her Polish hymns and meditates at the kitchen window. Do you want to tell Katie, or wait till she comes home?"

"I can tell her. She has to live in the real world."

Later that evening, I told Katie about Uncle Johnny.

Her main concern was how Gram's staunch faith was holding up.

Katie's introduction to Miner Lake.

Chapter 76

A nd so we meet again, Loring."

"Yes, Bud, we meet again."

"I'm sorry to hear about your mother."

"Thanks. It's hard, but I have a new crew and a new contract. Ham Gulch seems like it happened years ago. I want to introduce my new crew. You remember Kevin. And the two brothers, Jason and Kyle, and their friend Ed."

"Well, good to meet all of you. Let's go over a few things, and I'll let you get to work. A large fire burned this area about seventy years ago, and now there is this beautiful mountainside of even-age lodgepole pine. The district has decided to establish a fuel break to facilitate fire management on parts of the mountain that didn't burn. In case of another fire, we want to reduce fire spread and the intensity of a fire moving to the younger, even-age stand of lodgepole. We must protect the aesthetic value for Georgetown Lake and Discovery Ski Area. What we need is a three-hundred-foot swath of fuel reduction. Feather the edges of the fuel break as realistic into the adjacent protected areas for aesthetic purposes. There are a limited number of large, dead, wildlife trees, which are painted with orange stripes, to leave standing. Any questions?"

"Yeah Bud, I got it. You want me to be an artist and not show my brushstrokes. How is the eastern boundary designated?"

This question set up a lengthy discourse by Bud, explaining that three vertical blue stripes were painted on trees designating the boundary line. He had made sure to tell me that it was freshly painted, while he winked at me.

"Stihl is how you spell chainsaw," Kyle remarked. "Thank God you don't have Homelites or those butt ugly, yellow McCullochs. We can kick ass with Stihls."

"You got that right," I answered.

Jason and Ed were just as happy to be working in the woods and not drawing unemployment.

"If I draw unemployment, I'm required to look for work, so I might as well do what I like," Kyle had told me. "Three months of work in the woods, how can I bitch about that?"

At first I thought I might be a man short, but I listened to Kyle.

"I've worked with Jason and Ed for years, and I guarantee you we'll get this done by November first. We don't mess around when there's work to be done. Then we can draw unemployment and hunt elk. Heh-heh-heh."

It was clear to me that Kyle, Jason, and Ed did not want to lose money by me hiring another man to take work away from them. I agreed, letting them use all the discretionary effort they wanted.

One week later...

"Hey Kev, we're making good progress. Ellie is finally coming back home today, and I think I'll head out tonight. Just record everyone's hours, and I'll be back Monday morning."

"You got it."

I had not seen Ellie in over six weeks, or was it seven? I had lost track of days and weeks and realized I never had a chance to share my feelings of grief with her. Dwelling deeper, I understood over time that while she was carrying a heavy box of rocks dealing with the loss of her family, she simultaneously had run out of any emotional surplus, keeping only a subsistence ration for herself. I had accepted that about her, but it did not help heal the hole in my heart from all my early losses or make my box of rocks any lighter. I saw our marriage like a plate of peanut brittle, a salty and sweet imperfection that consisted of clusters of flat, broken pieces, embedded with pain, loss, and sorrow. But there were rare times, as rare as the fish Katie caught, that there was just enough warmth, just enough magic, to melt the jagged edges and hold the pieces together.

"Boy, I'm glad to be home. Tell me about Uncle Jack. Is he going to pull through, Ellie?"

"The doctors found his cancer has spread throughout his body, and they told him to get his papers in order. He worked in that zinc mine for all those years and never saw the sunshine."

"Oh man, I could never work in a mine for one day, let alone thirty years."

"It's sad because they had no kids, but you would be amazed at what he did in his garden. He treated his apple trees like children, always babying them. I took him outside for his first walk, and he really perked up when he saw that his apple tree grafts took."

"He grafted his own apple trees? That's some serious horticulture. I know how it's done, but I'm not sure about how successful I would be."

"He wanted me to tell you that he doesn't have a forestry degree, either."

Uncle Jack had missed his calling.

Chapter 77

The chill of an early September morning on Cable Mountain left my fingers cold, but not numb, as I changed a spark plug and sharpened my saw, using the tailgate of my truck as a workbench. From farther up the hill, I heard the throaty roar of Stihl chainsaws. I didn't hear Bud's pickup grind to a halt behind me. Bud had left us to our work, and I wondered what brought him to the site that morning.

"Loring, I need to talk with you for a few minutes."

"Yeah, what you got?"

"I got a call this morning…"

Oh, no.

"Nine Mile Ranger District is trying to get hold of you."

"Nine Mile on the Lolo National Forest near Missoula? For what? I don't know anyone there."

"They told me that your name came up to fill a sales administration position for the rest of the year. Someone knew of your work in Wisdom and wondered if you were available."

"I don't know Bud. I did four years with the Forest Service in Wisdom, and I think my time with them is over. Besides, I have this contract, and even though this year was tough, my plan is to rebuild with two or three crews for next year, and be more in the management and planning of work."

"I've seen many contractors come and go, and I also have seen your work ethic. I'm sorry, but I think you should change your plan. You're wasting your talents out here," Bud asserted, pointing a shaking finger at my chest.

"Why Bud? Why change my plan? I plan on finishing what I started."

Bud shook his head.

"Look Loring, I'm ready to retire. The Forest Service needs young people like you. I'll tell you once more to make my point clear. I see how you work with your crew and conduct business. Don't compare Wisdom to Nine Mile. Wisdom is a forgotten outpost, far from the district and regional office. Nine Mile is a historic ranger station, built by the CCC in the thirties and a half hour from the Regional Office. There will be more opportunities. And remember, they called for you, you never called them."

Bud was like the grandfather I never had. Bonding with older men had always provided valuable insight for me, and I tried to think through Bud's reasoning. Owning my own business. Going back to the Forest Service. It was hard to balance this equation, but maybe Bud was right. The Nine Mile Ranger District had a rich history of being the central depot to supply pack stock and serve as a training base for packers to standardize packing practices in the forests. Experiments in fire control and new firefighting equipment were tested there. Nine Mile also had a more diverse forest ecosystem where Western Larch and Douglas fir thrived instead of the boring, colder lodgepole forests of Wisdom. But there was no West Big Hole Primitive Area or the Anaconda-Pintler Wilderness to play in.

"I still have this contract to finish, Bud," I replied, hoping that my commitment could eliminate me from making a tough choice.

"That's right, but we can take care of that with a pencil. You could transfer the contract to Kevin, and that would eliminate any conflict of interest. If he's willing that is. Nine Mile wants you on Monday at 0800. Can I tell them yes?"

Bud had earned my trust six months previously in dealing with the tree planting boundary conflict at Ham Gulch. Now he was telling me to change my plans. There was no hidden message. I accepted the Forest Service job offer later that afternoon, and I was hoping that I made a good choice. After six months of living like a gypsy, I now would have a home to come back to every day and sleep in my own hand-built poster bed made of mine timbers from Southern Cross. I thought of Sackett lying by the Blaze King wood stove, and a warm shower every day, and dinner with Ellie. It all sounded so normal.

"It'll work out great for me," Kevin told me. "I still have free rent at Southern Cross and can hang with Angie on weekends. Angie and I talked about taking her son and the three of us moving to Hawaii come winter where I can work construction. I think I should still give you some money for equipment rental."

"Forget it. You're a family man now. I'll keep one Stihl for myself and sell the augers, planting bags, and the other saws when you're done. At best, I should break even for the year, and maybe have enough left to fill up my truck. Aloha, Kev. It's been real."

I trusted Kevin to finish the contract. Angie's brothers would see to that.

Chapter 78

Nine Mile is what a ranger station should look like, I determined as I pulled into the parking lot. A new beginning. More opportunities. Maybe this call to Nine Mile would provide the chance to put the cherry on top of my Montana Dream Sundae and buy that home and start a family?

In the middle of beautiful pastures and mountain landscapes sat the Cape Cod architecture of the Nine Mile Remount Station. All the office buildings, barn, saw shop, and administrative housing were white clapboard with green trim and steep roofs. Two sorrel-colored mules were munching hay in a corral. I drove past a historic sign that read: *When the roll is called up yonder, don't be there by accident.* I immediately felt an abundance of rich, Forest Service history and sensed that my ambitious thinking had come true. Nine Mile would be where I could land my Montana Dream. I felt it in my bones.

Once again, my father's voice reminded me to walk in like I owned the joint, and I laughed to myself about how far removed Nine Mile was from a joint as I walked through the door of the administrative office.

A red-haired woman with a ponytail to her waist was mopping up her spilled cup of coffee that seemed headed for some important-looking documents on her desk. She was frantically trying to stop the spread of coffee by stretching the front of her shirt to dam the flow. Evidently these documents were very important. I waited for her to gain control.

"Good morning, Helen," I called, looking at the nameplate in front of her, sitting next to her green, stainless-steel Aladdin thermos. Though not issued by the Forest Service, it was an unwritten rule that all employees have one. "I'm new here and am reporting in."

"Oh, welcome to Nine Mile. You must be Loring. I have your paperwork right here somewhere to sign. Then just walk next door to the timber office. John and Rick should be in. Hope you enjoy Nine Mile."

"Thanks, Helen, I'm liking it already."

Rick, one of the foresters in timber management, gave me a warm welcome. A show-me trip of the compound was followed up with a quick review of protocol at Nine Mile. Rick elaborated on my duties.

"We have a sale up in Mill Creek that we need you to administer. There is a contractor piling logging slash with a D6 dozer. Forest Service contract specs do not allow a machine operator to work alone, so we need you on site."

"So, Rick, I'm supposed to sit and watch this guy pile logging slash all day?"

"That's it. He's working ten hour days, and so will you. I authorized your overtime. Here is a map, and I circled where the unit is."

I could not believe it. I had a forestry degree with four years of experience in reforestation, timber sale mapping, and administration, and I was now assigned to watch a bulldozer pile logging slash all day. Rick must have noticed my quizzical facial expression.

"Oh, don't sweat that. We have bigger plans for you after this slash piling contract ends," Rick said trying to buoy my emotions. "I have some timber sale administration duties lined out for you. And next year, we want you to supervise the district's tree planting."

Supervise tree planting? Rick had to be kidding, but he wasn't. I felt like calling Bud to tell him all about my new opportunities.

I had just finished my first month of watching logging debris being piled for later burning when sad news arrived once more. Uncle Jack's passing took Ellie away from home to assist her Aunt Phoebe.

"I may be gone for two weeks," Ellie said while packing her suitcase. "Aunt Phoebe needs me, but I just can't handle some days back there. I have so many bad memories, and even nightmares. And now, with Uncle Jack passing, there will be so much to do."

"Take whatever time you need to help Aunt Phoebe," I told her. "I just mailed Uncle Jack my college horticulture book last week, and now he's dead."

"But his apple trees are alive."

"And that's a beautiful legacy to leave behind for Aunt Phoebe."

This was one time that neither one of us pushed each other's hot button. I couldn't explain the amount of energy we wasted in driving one another away. *I want chicken. She wants fish. Please bring me a cup of coffee. You never bring me a cup of coffee.* Our marriage, if set to music, could have been called the Antipathy Concerto in F–flat major. We both tired of the daily parrying and trying to block each other's verbal thrusts. And then just like the wind, harsh words blew away and there would be periods of calm air and tranquility. Apart, we were different people. I had never fought with my parents, my friends, Gail, or my employers. *This is not who I am.* We brought out the absolute worst in each other.

Rick was true to his word, and I finally got involved with laying out a small timber sale. In the middle of a chilly November day, Rick found me blue-flagging a boundary line for the proposed small sale.

"Hey, I tried to raise you on the radio. The Lolo just received news that we have been mobilized for the California wildfires. All available hands have been ordered to go. The dry Santa Ana winds are being clocked at a hundred miles an hour, and there have been major losses of life and property. Go home and pack and be back at the smokejumper base at 1800. We're flying to San Bernardino."

The only exciting thing about a fire was traveling to it. Every minute after that could be utter exhaustion of hauling fire hose, digging fire lines, and eating lots of smoke during long shifts. Or, one could wait for hours to get an assignment while sitting in a bus playing hearts.

A charter jet took us to John Wayne Airport, and a bus ride to the Rose Bowl to mobilize gave me a glimpse of the fiery night sky. Orange glowed everywhere in the distant foothills. Not by choice, I had been on several wildfires, but nothing could have prepared me for the fire's intensity and for the searing black smoke from burned vegetation consisting chiefly of tangled shrubs and thorny bushes of manzanita and chaparral.

The Nine Milers were detailed to the Panorama Fire, where on the Monday morning of November 24, 243 homes were burned and four lives were lost in a fire that spread over 14,000 acres.

"Good God, look at that," I said to Charlie, a fellow crew member. "The wind lifted that home off its foundation and hurled it through space before it blew up into a thousand splinters."

Later we passed by Waterman Canyon where home after home was blackened, but the swimming pools were still blue and inviting.

That Thursday was Thanksgiving, and I was thankful for the life that I had as I watched the dreams of local people go up in smoke and their loved ones be burned alive. Locals rallied their support of the firefighters, and I felt like a liberator who helped battle back the front of the Panorama Fire. Years later, I found out that Bob and Brad were within shouting distance of where I stood. One woman came up to me and handed me a turkey drumstick. Other crew members got pieces of pie or dollar bills handed to them. I was one grimy, physically exhausted firefighter among thousands of others dressed in their Nomex flame-resistant green pants and yellow shirts with their fire shelter, or as we referred to them, "shake and bake bags," strapped to their waists. The only difference was that a news camera caught me with the drumstick, and Ellie saw me on national news that evening.

After mopping up for another week, I returned home on December 8, the day of John Lennon's assassination and a year to the day that I sat in my makeshift office and formed GARP.

Chapter 79

March 1982... Nine Mile District Ranger's Office.

Jerry, our district ranger, was easy to appreciate. He was a critical thinker and slightly more evolved than others I had known in the agency. Since I first started at Nine Mile, Jerry had looked out for me, entrusting me with special assignments and keeping me away from crew work. I had thirsty thoughts of another special assignment when I was called to his office.

"Loring, I want to talk to you about something special we're rolling out this year. There is a plan to hire some hard-core, unemployed people. Now, they all have a record of some kind, no felonies, just petty stuff but enough to be turned down for employment. Some are in alcohol- and drug-recovery programs. Senator Melcher's idea is to give ten people a chance to be part of a team and work on forest projects here at the district. I would like you to supervise this program."

"Really?"

I was stunned by this news and took a moment to respond. My two years at Nine Mile provided more personal growth in timber management, but I still was not full time, although I did get to work part time during winters in building and making snow for the tree cache.

"We'll make you proud, Jerry. I've always wanted back in supervision, and I think you just gave me an assignment to aspire to."

"We are committed to have our best man run the show. And you'll love this part. I got budget approval to buy ten new Stihl 045s for your crew. The fire crew will bitch about working with the older

Homelites, but I believe in giving these people every chance to succeed, and that starts with a good supervisor and good equipment."

"Gee, thanks Jerry. I'm fairly intimate with that model of saw. Did you know that Stihl is how you spell chainsaw?"

One month later...

I waited for my new team to be fingerprinted...

What a motley crew you guys are. I assembled them in the saw shop. There was, Pete, a long haired ex-biker who reported in a dirty white pair of high-topped Keds tennis shoes.

"Pete, canvas shoes won't work. I'll loan you an old pair of my leather boots 'til payday."

And Corey, who decided he was thirsty, had opened his Little Oscar cooler to sip a chilled Rainier pounder while I talked.

"Corey, save that chiller for after work and off the premises. No alcohol at work. Savvy?"

Jerry did not tell me that my crew also included Gunther, a young man with Asperger's Syndrome. Could I mold this group of men into a workforce where no one cut their leg off? *I will tell them that they are responsible for their own safety. I have a unique opportunity to inspire others. Will my enthusiasm in them help this group of men stand up to the challenges and be noticed for their achievements and not their transgressions? Can I do this? You're damn straight I can. I thrive in this type of arena, and I never like to fail.*

After a week of training, the men hit the ground running. The hinge point to their gusto was based on each guy having their own personal saw to care for. It was brilliant on Jerry's part to recognize this incentive, and I told him so.

"Watch how sharp my chain is boss," Stan said, asking me to witness on our test log.

"Nice, very nice Stan. Watch about too fine of a filing edge, though," I told him.

After returning from the field each day, the men washed their truck as needed and cared for their saws in a way that the storied Nine Mile fire crew stared at in disbelief. At the end of two months, these men had made a name for themselves by their hustle, camaraderie, and safe work. I had received kudos from lower district offices before, but now my work was praised by the district supervisor and the regional office. The recognition was appreciated, the piece of parchment with fancy calligraphy and the small $100.00 check that was attached, but I already had a folder full of recognition letters. Heartfelt for sure, but I wanted a career position.

There was a signboard posted in the center of the compound that listed upcoming events or programs of interest to the ranger station or Nine Mile valley residents. There was a notice of the community picnic, a list of road restrictions, and a Smokey the Bear sign pointing an arrow to the forest's fire danger. But that morning in May, I noticed a new poster had been pinned to the board announcing that a three-day workshop was going to be held starting on June 2. The workshop was to learn how to pack into the wilderness with horses and mules. The workshop was going to be taught by the legendary outfitter and guide, Smoke Elser.

Smoke Elser was coming to Nine Mile. Holy shit!

For years I had waited to make Smoke's acquaintance, but I never understood why I didn't pursue it more fervently... and then I knew why. The first five years in Montana, I was galactically high on crisp mountain air, challenging summits, and wilderness trails. But now, the desire to meet Smoke had ripened and matured because I had tales of my own adventures to offer. Never one to believe in coincidence, my meeting Smoke at the historic Nine Mile Remount Station seemed like a piece of well-orchestrated music. A local coffee shop wasn't the place to have such a meeting. He had punched my ticket to Montana at fourteen. He had given me reason to believe in my dream as I lay awake at nights at Presby. My internal compass had always pointed to Smoke.

My mind swirled with the news. It had been sixteen years since I cut the article, "Exploring a Mountain Wilderness", from my *Boys' Life* magazine, and the article was still preserved behind the glass of my baby picture. Smoke, the man who lit my fire. Smoke, the man who created the dream catcher that held all of my wildest dreams of wilderness adventure, was coming. It was like looking for a long-lost treasure, only to have the treasure find me.

Wednesday, June 2... noon. I had a very important date.

I left home that morning with the irreplaceable, single folded *Boys' Life* article in a manila folder. After sixteen years of having it pressed behind a glass pane, protected from sunlight, its re-entry into the world would be first shared with Smoke.

It was noon, and members of the workshop were eating lunch at a picnic table. I had never seen a picture of Smoke but noticed that none of those people at the picnic table was dressed like a modern cowboy. Smoke had to be inside the barn, hopefully alone.

As I walked slowly inside the barn, the rich smell of worn leather from eight Decker pack saddles hit my nose. These saddles that had been used for decades of packing into the Bob Marshall Wilderness were now being used for training others interested in wilderness packing.

On the floor there were large pieces of cream-colored canvas with a large metal cargo container alongside each. It appeared the class was to learn the art of "mantying," cowboy lingo for gift wrapping the cargo containers in the canvas with origami-type folds.

I looked up. The back of a man of medium height, wearing new blue jeans, a checkered shirt and a leather vest, stood alone. On his head sat at a well-worn western felt hat that he wore tipped halfway back on his head. He was working on the latigo, a piece of leather that tightened and secured the cinch on a Decker pack saddle.

I shook my head in disbelief, quietly staring. There he stood, alone, a man deep in the secrets of the wilderness, grizzly bears, and the Chinese Wall, a man who had slept over three thousand starry nights in the Bob, who now just seemed to be waiting for my introduction.

"Hey Smoke," I called out, my voice full of sixteen years of anticipation.

Turning slowly to his right, Smoke let out a "Yes-s-s," in a jolly voice and a smile wide as the Continental Divide.

Pulling the article from the manila folder, I unfolded it and held it for Smoke to see with his sparkling, blue eyes.

"Smoke, do you remember this trip?"

"Oh, golly yes. That was a trip to remember, heh-heh," Smoke chuckled while wiping his forehead with a red bandana that he pulled from his back pocket.

"I'm Loring Walawander, Smoke," I said, as I extended my right hand. I had the feeling that I had known Smoke forever. "I was a scout when this article appeared in *Boys' Life*. I want you to know that I had an epiphany that someday I would live in Missoula, Montana. I wanted my own wilderness adventure like the boys in Troop Seven."

"Well, how did that go?"

"Beyond my wildest dreams. Once I stepped foot in Montana, I knew that I could never go back to Pennsylvania. I owe my life to Pittsburgh. It's a great place, but it's not for me. I would love to tell you my story sometime."

"That's kind of funny in a way. I was an Eagle Scout and grew up in Cleveland. I left Cleveland a long time ago, and once in Montana I knew I could never go back either, and hey, I'm always up for a good story."

"I guess we're both Lucky in a way then."

"How so?"

"You know, it's Lucky when you live in the West."

Epilogue

Montana is more than the nation's fourth-largest state. Montana is more than towering snowcapped peaks that shatter the sky or unpolluted pristine rivers and creeks flowing in a serpentine path through prairies and forests. Montana is a remote hinterland with a feeling of independence coupled with its limitless vistas. After forty-one years of living in Montana, I have come to love the sense of freedom of living in a wild place where the seasonal changes can bring summer snow or the instant warmth of a Chinook wind upon the face in the winter. The bugle of a bull elk during the fall rut can send quivers up and down my spine. Ruby-throated humming birds sing a pleasing series of monotonous chips just at daybreak in the spring, their wings humming as they flit from flower to flower in search of nectar. This is my Montana... big and small, raucous and serene, pure and pristine, just like I imagined it when I first read about Troop 7's adventure into the Bob.

When I first viewed the Big Dipper from the wilderness, I saw it holding all of my Montana Dreams. It took time, but one of the last two dreams finally fell to Earth. In August, 1986, I was blessed with a son, a son that Father Ben promised would come my way, and I believed him. My son would be a bright light in my life, so I chose the name Luke, from the Greek, meaning "light giving." In the Bible he was known as "the beloved physician," and I was very familiar with physicians. We would share the same initials.

When I held him for the first time, he was swaddled and crying. I cuddled him close to my chest, near my heart, and the metallic clicking of my heart valve seemed to calm him. He fell asleep in

317

moments. On the Sunday morning he was born, he already had something I never would. He was a native Montanan and was born in Missoula, the city of my boyhood wonder.

I built him a tree house, we played tee ball nights on end, downhill skied, and we formed our own club, *The LW Club*, named after our shared initials. I had LW Club T-shirts made for our outdoor adventures. Sackett, old and frosted gray, was an honorary member. From when he was one year old, I read Martin Luther King's speech, "I Have a Dream," to him every year, even during his college years, hoping it would make a difference in one boy's life.

After Luke was born, I worked as a consultant forester in Colorado. While there, I received a call from the US Postal Service. It seems that my name had come up on the register after taking the postal exam, on a whim, several years earlier to see what I could score. I accepted the job and rose in the ranks to a professional, executive position. The Postal Service, was a quantum leap of faith, but it was the perfect fit for me in my pursuit of developing and inspiring people in the work force. In my heart, I would always be a forester, but now I only plant trees in my yard. My purest passion was people, helping them aspire to be better, and find the "discretionary effort," that dwelled in all of them. This, I found, was my true calling.

Ellie and I finally divorced, and I was free to once again become a new man, this time faced with an indescribable aloneness from watching my five-year-old son become a visitor in his home.

"Daddy, why don't you and Sackett live with me anymore?" was the hardest question I ever faced.

The last dream that fell was another miracle in my life, and happened, once again, in the strangest of places.

In December of 1995, I flew to Huntington, West Virginia, to watch the Montana Grizzlies play in the I-AA championship game at Marshall University. Montana won the championship, but I stumbled into grace, and found the love of my life, while standing in line at the airport in Huntington after the game.

"Could you please watch my bag while I use the restroom?" I asked her casually.

Our eyes locked, and when I returned, we started talking like we had known each other for a hundred years.

"Do you ski?" she later asked before boarding our long-delayed flight.

"Yes, I love it. It gets me into the mountains. Here, let me give you my phone number on the back of my boarding pass. Call me when you return from visiting your family during Christmas."

Her name was Jacque, and I found out that she was born in Great Falls and lived in Missoula. *A classy, beautiful, spirited Montana woman to complete my Montana Dream. Of course! Was that how it was meant to be?* I had never seen her before in my life, but when I looked at her, and she at me, we both knew we found what we were looking for. The last of my Montana Dream had become real, and we later consecrated a marriage where love and intimacy has no end. I discovered that my big Montana Dream took years to develop and parts came to me only when I was ready to receive such gifts. I never thought that my dream would not be actualized. I wished for big things to come into my life. I never wished that something should never have happened. There was nothing I could change about the past.

I could have lived a diminished state of happiness if I had let Tourette's syndrome take charge and define my life. From an early age, I saw it as an intrusion, awkward and embarrassing, that produced an invisible barrier between me and people who did not know me. I was excluded. I wanted to be included. As a younger man, I felt that I had to wear a name tag that said, "Hi, I'm Loring and I have Tourette's syndrome." But in time, I found it was better to show people who I was than what I looked or sounded like. Learning to use my differences as a strength, I was successful in hunting deer and elk while making grunting sounds of my own during the hunt. I learned the game of golf, finally able to shoot rounds in the low eighties while Tourette's would offer up a twitch or an eye blink at inopportune times during my swing or putt. These pursuits only made me tougher; I never backed down, and I refused to play on a tilted playing field because I wanted to play and live on a level field with everyone else. When I found out that the National Institute of Health in Washington D.C. was looking for patients to participate in a clinical trial for Tourette's syndrome studies, I quickly volunteered.

"No, I'm afraid there probably won't be a cure in your lifetime," Dr. Belushio told me. "But you are helping others, so we can find a cure."

I hope that sharing my life with Tourette's has helped one person with this socially embarrassing affliction. I hope that I helped one person who doesn't have it understand how to treat someone better who has it. I hope that I have reached out to afflicted people to help them believe that they can be loved without reservation, just as they are. I was a fortunate young man to meet Gail, who showed me this life lesson early. I was even more fortunate to find Jacque later in life, who reinforced that message. If sharing my story helps someone, then I will feel I have not wasted my time on this Earth. Tourette's syndrome is the unpredictable but beautiful part of my life.

In my office hangs the original *Boys Life* article, yellowed and under glass, autographed by Smoke. At arm's reach lays the well-worn, curled copy of *Shibumi* on my bookshelf. Shibumi. Miner Lake. Both are many summers in the past. I've climbed more mountains and caught bigger fish since that day, and some got away. I have witnessed surreal tequila sunrises and the hallelujah moment of a sinking, ember-colored sun slipping below the tallest peak in West Big Hole. The essence of Shibumi, best defined as achieving personal excellence and total clarity, eventually found its way to my heart as an older man, along with the spiritual tranquility that came from a life spawned from a boyhood dream and lived to its potential. Tranquility was a choice. It is not something that just happens, I've found.

During the winter months at Walden Pond, Thoreau amused himself by watching wildlife at work and play. Looking out my office window, I see the record January level of snowfall in my backyard. My backyard is a squirrel sanctuary, and I feel like Thoreau as my eyes catch a glimpse of Preston, the wild Columbian ground squirrel that inhabits my yard. I have watched Preston for over a year, burying seeds and nuts under trees and shrubs. He knows exactly where he has them stashed. Preston amazes me with how he claws his way head first with his tail up, down the Ponderosa pine tree and tries to dig through the snow to find the nuts he buried in the fall. Preston stays busy, but he can't dig deep enough to uncover his peanut cache. He then scurries to another spot, and another, and still has no luck digging for the buried peanuts. Preston has showed up several days in a row, and he just keeps trying, hoping for that one spot that will reward his efforts. He never gave up searching. But today, he remembered that one peanut he buried in the large flower planter on my covered deck. Success.

I see a lot of myself in Preston. If I had never ventured west to live my Montana Dream, I would wake up every day wondering, scratching my head, pondering what Montana was like, and asking myself questions that I would never know the answer to. I thought Gail and Dixie would be part of my Montana Dream, but they never had that choice. I wished for a career with the Forest Service, only to find my calling elsewhere. When I faced adversity, I found I always came to a crossroads. The left fork could lead to darkness and despair. The right fork could lead to hope and aspirations. But through all my disadvantages, including Tourette's syndrome, setbacks, illnesses, and losses, there remained two constants—to dream big and never stop believing.

Loring Walawander

Acknowledgements

I started writing *Montana Epiphany* on January 6, 2015. It was the day of Epiphany, but also would have been my parent's sixty-fourth wedding anniversary. After nearly fifty years of aging, I was ready to tell my story. I never had a formal writing class, and realized immediately that I needed help in organizing and structuring a lifetime of events that could form a narrative arc to tell my Montana Dream. I wish to thank the following people who believed in my story and supported me along the way.

First, I would like to thank my writing coach, Laura Munson of Whitefish, Montana, a kindred spirit and New York Times bestselling author, who helped me find my writing voice, even if it meant holding my heels to the fire.

Second, I would like to thank August Tarrier, adjunct professor of English at Villanova University for her work as a developmental editor in organizing Montana Epiphany and outlining the strengths and weaknesses of my narrative. August, it was your editorial comments that made me a stronger writer.

It is fitting that a book about Montana should have a true Montanan be involved in editing. I wish to thank Melanie Calahan, a fourth-generation Montanan from Missoula for her outstanding, meticulous work as copy and line editor. Melanie, thanks for believing in my words and story. You are fantastic.

I would also like to thank my good Missoula friend, physical therapist and mountaineer John Fiore, for his West Big Hole photo of Miner Lake, and keeping me in shape to keep climbing those Montana peaks.

Lastly, the completion of this book would not have been possible without my beautiful wife, Jacque, a true blessing in my life, who gave me the freedom, the support, and encouragement to write on.

Readers may write the author about Tourette's syndrome, or any parts of this book at: loringwalawander@gmail.com.

The dream lives on. Hiking Headquarters Pass in the Bob Marshall Wilderness in 2017.

Made in the USA
San Bernardino, CA
05 December 2018